Praise for A

"Louis Markos lives with the entire panorama of history in his mind. In *Atheism on Trial*, he ranges from ancient philosophers to contemporary scientists to show that the same fundamental objections to Christianity have been raised—and refuted—in every age. The so-called new atheists do not differ substantially from the old atheists, whose challenges have been met by competent Christian thinkers throughout history. It is time to avail ourselves of their wisdom, and this literate, colorfully written book is a good place to begin."

Nancy Pearcey, author of *Total Truth, Finding Truth,* and *Love Thy Body*

"I was thrilled to read this new book by Louis Markos. I work every day in the academic world of Christian apologetics and have never seen a book quite like this. He shows very effectively that the major arguments set forth in the modern world against God and the Christian worldview have been answered by thinkers from ancient times. His survey of 'chronological snobbery' is profound and beautifully written. And make no mistake, this book is for everybody—clear, accessible, and wonderfully encouraging."

Craig J. Hazen, PhD, founder and director,
MA Program in Christian Apologetics, Biola University
author of *Five Sacred Crossings*

"Louis Markos's timely book *Atheism on Trial* shows that the claims of the new atheists are anything *but* new. Because of our modern-day culture's disconnection from intellectual history, we often don't realize that these same atheist arguments were raised in the ancient, medieval, and early modern eras—and addressed by some of the greatest philosophers and theologians in history, from Plato to St. Thomas Aquinas. As a result, many people don't realize just how strong the arguments for Christianity really are. In this readable and engaging book, Markos sets out to rectify this situation. With enthusiasm that draws us into the story, he gives the reader a guided tour through the philosophical insights of pagan and Christian thinkers of centuries (and millennia) past to provide a firm foundation for the consideration of the biggest questions of life. *Atheism on Trial* thus serves both as a valuable apologetics resource and as a lively and interesting introduction to the study of philosophy."

Dr. Holly Ordway, author of *Apologetics and the Christian Imagination: An Integrated Approach to Defending the Faith*

"In this highly engaging book, Louis Markos takes the reader on an adventure through more than 2,500 years of ideas and arguments from the most influential thinkers in history. From Lucretius to Augustine, from Aquinas to Nietzsche, from C.S. Lewis to Stephen Hawking, journey with him through the thoughts of atheists, deists, and theists and judge for yourself whether it is reasonable to believe in the God of Christian faith. You will not be disappointed!"

Chad Meister, Professor of Philosophy and Theology, Bethel College

"Markos offers a clear, insightful, and revealing look at how all the 'modern' arguments against God have been around for centuries… and how they've *always* failed to sufficiently explain reality. Very approachable for those new to the subject, yet filled with remarkable depth for a book of this length, *Atheism on Trial* is a highly valuable read for anyone interested in evaluating common atheistic arguments. It will undoubtedly leave you convicted of how strong the case *for* God actually is."

Natasha Crain, author of *Keeping Your Kids on God's Side* and *Talking with Your Kids About God*

~~ATHEISM~~
ON
TRIAL

LOUIS
MARKOS

HARVEST HOUSE PUBLISHERS
EUGENE, OREGON

Atheism on Trial

Copyright © 2018 Louis Markos
Published by Harvest House Publishers
Eugene, Oregon 97408
www.harvesthousepublishers.com

ISBN 978-0-7369-7307-6 (pbk.)
ISBN 978-0-7369-7308-3 (eBook)

Printed in the United States of America

18 19 20 21 22 23 24 25 26 / BP-SK / 10 9 8 7 6 5 4 3 2 1

For Gilbert Farah—
for his friendship, his hospitality,
and his willingness to engage in discussion,
dialogue, and debate,
even, and especially, when we disagree.

CONTENTS

Nothing New Under the Sun

According to the wisest man who ever lived, there is nothing new under the sun. Though the truth of that statement may appear self-evident, the modern age has fashioned a competing story that has been accepted, mostly unconsciously, by the vast majority of Americans and Europeans. According to that story, or narrative, the history of human civilization can best be portrayed as a staircase or ladder that begins in darkness, ignorance, superstition, and barbarism and slowly ascends toward light, truth, science, and secular humanism.

The modern world, so the narrative goes, has decisively judged the past and found it sorely lacking. Nowhere is this more evident than in the area of religion. The court of empiricism, skepticism, and utilitarianism has put theism, particularly Christian theism, on trial, and the verdict of all logical, rational, objective jurors has fallen against belief and in favor of nonbelief. True, those who need God and religion as a crutch may be allowed to cherish their illusions, but they must understand that their faith is purely emotional and personal and that it has no standing in our enlightened Age of Reason.

It is a compelling narrative; in fact, it has become the controlling narrative of our age, the metanarrative which gives meaning and authority to all other narratives. But it has one serious flaw. It is not true.

Back in my high school days, I took a history class with the provocative title "From Barbarism to Humanism." After learning that the class would begin with the ancient Greeks and finish with the twentieth century, I respectfully suggested to the teacher that the class should be more accurately titled "From Humanism to Barbarism."

Okay, maybe I was being a bit snide, but when the teacher graciously agreed with me, it started me off on a lifelong quest to look—*really* look—at history in order to gauge how much we *really* had progressed as a species. That quest was strengthened during my college years when I first encountered, from C.S. Lewis's spiritual autobiography *Surprised by Joy*, the phrase "chronological snobbery." It seemed like everyone around me, both my fellow students and the adults of my parents' generation, had taken for granted that everything necessarily improves with time. Lewis opened my eyes to see that newer is not always better—that, while our technology was superior to that of the past, our ancestors often surpassed us in courage, wisdom, loyalty, joy, and in what I would call basic sanity.

He also taught me that no trial had ever been held in which atheism had defended its (non) beliefs and emerged victorious. Atheism had no more been proved than Christianity had been disproved. To the contrary, the more I studied the past, the more I discovered that a long line of theists and Christians had, again and again, successfully put atheism on trial and shown it to be sorely lacking in intellectual force and integrity.

No, atheism (then or now) had not won the debate against theism; it had merely convinced everyone that it had somehow *evolved* past theism. And it was that word, *evolved*, that, taken together with Lewis's "chronological snobbery," opened my eyes to how potent and wide-ranging the myth of Darwinian evolution is. So ingrained has the evolutionary mindset become in the Western world that little resistance is raised, either by believers or nonbelievers, when the past is dismissed, or at least patronized, as backward, unenlightened, and riddled with prejudice. Of course, that word *past* is a slippery one. It can be used to mean any number of things that the critic doesn't like (or understand): the Middle Ages, the Catholic Church, belief in miracles, wars of religion, pre-Copernican science, the epistles of St. Paul, traditional families, social and political hierarchy, original sin, absolute standards of goodness, truth, and beauty, feudalism, and so forth.

As a corollary to this evolutionary ladder, the modern world, deeply infected with chronological snobbery, has taken for granted that its scientific, philosophical, theological, sociological, and aesthetic "advances" have superseded what was believed and practiced in the past. Those people who lived back then thought "x," but we know better today. If only they could have had access to all the things we now know to be true, they would have been able to step out of their ignorance and blindness. But Europe just had to wait for the coming of Marx, Darwin, Freud, and Nietzsche to find out how the world really works.

It's a lovely myth with the power to make one feel wise and privileged, but it is no truer than the metanarrative to which it has attached itself. In matter of fact, there has been no clean-cut progression from creation to evolution, absolute truth to relativism, supernaturalism to naturalism, revelation to empiricism, authority to experience, faith to cynicism. To the contrary, these pairs have always existed side by side, struggling and competing with one another. And when anything like a trial was held to determine which member of the pair came closer to the truth about God, man, or the universe, it was more often than not the former that won the debate.

Pre-Socratic philosophers like Thales and Greek sophists like Gorgias advocated strict empiricism and moral relativism more than 2,500 years ago. The Epicurean Lucretius was a full-blown evolutionist 2,000 years before Darwin. The Stoic Marcus Aurelius, who ruled the Roman Empire in the second century AD, believed firmly that men could be good without God. In the early church, Marcion dismissed the God of the Old Testament as a moral monster and distinguished him from the New Testament God of love. In the Middle Ages, nominalism reduced words to mere names, thus dethroning Goodness, Truth, and Beauty as real absolutes. In the seventeenth century, Spinoza denied the authority of the Bible and reduced God to the laws of nature; in the eighteenth, Hume was quite sure that he had disproved miracles once and for all and that the problem of evil had rendered null and void the Christian view of God.

All of the above ultimately denied the immortality of the soul, the resurrection of the body, or both. Indeed, the idea that, at death, we join an amorphous One Soul—an idea that most associate with the East—has had advocates in the West from the Pre-Socratic Pythagoras and Parmenides, to the Gnostics of the early and medieval church, to the American Ralph Waldo Emerson.

What, then, I asked myself, had prevented these ideas from gaining the kind of ascendancy they have attempted to achieve over the past two centuries? The none-too-subtle answer I received from my graduate professors and from the textbooks they assigned was that these "enlightened" ideas had been held back by ignorance, superstition, and religious hierarchy. Needless to say, I was not satisfied with that answer. So I tossed the textbooks aside and began to read the actual words of the great thinkers of the Western tradition.

It was only then that I realized that materialism, empiricism, skepticism, nominalism, and a dozen other *isms* had not been held at bay by credulous people and corrupt priests, but by such spiritual and intellectual giants as Plato and Aristotle, John and Paul, Irenaeus and Tertullian, Augustine and Aquinas, Luther and Calvin, Jonathan Edwards and Blaise Pascal. Long before the days when Christopher Hitchens, Richard Dawkins, Sam Harris, and Daniel Dennett helped make atheism a household word, these great philosophers, theologians, and apologists had put atheism on trial and uncovered its faulty logic, its inconsistencies, its special pleadings, and its decidedly mixed motives.

Of course, that is not to deny that ignorance, superstition, and religious (and secular-scientific) authority have exerted a negative force on society. Such things have been and ever will be with us, but they do not follow the nice, neat contour lines of the modern metanarrative of evolution, progress, and secularization.

Perhaps the best way to sum up the strength of the modern metanarrative is to note how many secular academics really think that the only reason the early Christians believed in the virgin birth was that they were ignorant of the science of human reproduction. That sounds like a compelling argument until one realizes that, though Joseph did not know about the meeting of sperm and egg, he *did* know that a woman does not give birth unless she has sex with a man. That's why he was preparing to divorce her when the angel appeared to assure him that Mary was still a virgin.

Far from springing out of ignorance of the laws of nature, miracles are only *recognized* as miracles because those who witness them know that nature does not normally work in such a manner. If the inhabitants of first-century Palestine did not know that people do not come back from the dead, they would not have recognized the raising of Lazarus as a miracle or Jesus as a miracle worker.

My own intellectual and spiritual growth has been marked by such flashes of insight—flashes that have allowed me, for a brief searing moment, to see through the modernist metanarrative to the deeper truths that are so often obscured by its all-encompassing shadow. It is my hope that through this book I will offer my readers a series of such flashes—not as an end in itself, but as a method for allowing them to re-see, from a new angle, religious and philosophical debates that have been with us for more than 2,500 years.

Let us together step outside of the modernist bubble to take a second look at the history we think we already know. Let us put atheism on trial in such a way that we will discover, when we are done, that the trial has already been held...and won.

•   •   •   •   •   •   •   •   •   •

As for organization, I will focus on ten arguments (grouped into four broad categories) that have been leveled against the orthodox Judeo-Christian worldview with increasing intensity: arguments that, though they have been championed by the four new atheists mentioned above, have actually been with us for well over a thousand years.

Under category one, the nature of the universe, I will consider the longstanding arguments

- that everything we see can be explained by natural, physical causes
- that nature is a closed system
- that miracles are scientifically impossible

Under category two, the nature of knowledge, I will explore age-old arguments

- that we can only know things through our senses
- that there are no moral or philosophical absolutes

Under category three, the nature of God, I will engage with a long line of thinkers who have denied

- God's goodness—on account of the events recorded in the Old Testament
- God's power—on account of the problem of pain and evil
- God's providential involvement in history—by making him either fully transcendent (deism) or fully immanent (pantheism)

Finally, under category four, the nature of man, I will present two perennial perspectives that, though they promise to ennoble man, end up robbing him of his innate dignity, purpose, and joy:

- man is a product of his environment
- man is by nature good and can perfect himself apart from God

In surveying each of these ten arguments, I will adopt a narrative rather than academic approach, writing throughout in layman terms and striving to use as little jargon as possible. As such, I will dispense with notes, providing instead an annotated bibliography for each of the chapters.

My goal is not to write a cold scholarly tome, but to engage the reader in the ongoing dialogue between two contrasting worldviews: one that believes in a powerful but loving, just but compassionate God who created the universe and is actively involved in it; another that regards the universe as a machine and we ourselves as products of impersonal forces. The first ascribes to absolute standards conveyed by God to man through revelation; the second trusts only knowledge that is gained through experience and the use of our five senses. The former considers all things under the auspices of eternity; the latter keeps its gaze firmly fixed below.

These worldviews, or paradigms, are not chronological, with the first giving way to the second, but are ever contemporaneous with each other. They have waged war off and on for two-and-a-half millennia, with neither defeating totally the other—though the former held sway for much of the Middle Ages and Renaissance, while the latter has slowly gained the upper hand since the Enlightenment.

Join me, then, as we enter into the dual court of public opinion and universal truth. Watch with me as these mighty combatants strive to overthrow the arguments, cases, and worldviews of their opponents, and, by so doing, secure the right to define the way society views God, man, and the universe and answers those central questions of life: Who am I? Why am I here? What is my purpose?

The trial is about to begin. The judge has entered, and we must all take our place in the jury box.

PART ONE:

The Nature
of the Universe

CHAPTER ONE

In the Beginning

Being the descendant of four grandparents who were born in Greece and immigrated to America around 1930, it was perhaps natural that I would become a lifelong lover of Greek mythology. The stories of Zeus and Athena, Daedalus and Icarus, Apollo and Daphne, Theseus and the Minotaur, Perseus and Medusa: these were the stories that shaped my dreams and, in many ways, my sense of myself. Over time, my love for the Greek myths expanded to take in Roman mythology as well; however, many years would pass before I felt the desire to move outside the Greco-Roman world to seriously explore the myths of other nations.

When I finally did, I must admit, I was a bit horrified. I didn't have to read too far into Norse mythology before I learned, to my dismay, that the first man and woman had dropped out of the armpits of a frost giant; or, in a different version, had been licked out of the salt ice by a great cow. Egyptian mythology was even worse, with its primal deity rising spontaneously out of a mound of earth and masturbating the other primal deities into existence. Indian mythology proved even stranger and more disturbing, with goddesses of death dancing on human skulls and an inexorable cycle of creation and destruction from which there was no escape.

No loving gods here, no higher purpose, no special creation.

It wasn't much better than the Darwinian myth I had absorbed growing up in secular schools, with single-cell organisms arising, somehow or other, out of the slime and evolving, randomly and purposelessly, into human creatures bereft of any special status. I would stick with my beloved Greek myths, thank you very much.

That is, until I looked more closely at them and found that, for all their sense of fun and adventure, they were marked by the same uncaring deities, the same lack of a greater purpose or plan, the same horrible deeds perpetrated by those who were supposed to be our divine standard bearers: Kronos, the father of Zeus, for example, castrated his own father, Ouranos, to seize control of the heavens! Worse yet, it turned out that Greek mythology agreed with the other myths *and* with the Darwinists that the supernatural did not create the natural, but that impersonal nature had, somehow or other, given birth, not just to man, but to the gods as well.

But now I'm moving too fast and getting ahead of myself. Let me slow down and trace the story step by step.

Out of Chaos or Out of Nothing?

The Bible alone of all ancient books makes the remarkable claim that "in the beginning, God." Every other book holds that in the beginning there was matter. Contrary to popular opinion, the primal myths of Greece and Rome, Egypt and Babylon, India and Scandinavia do not begin with an eternal God or gods who have always existed and who created the world out of nothing. That vision arose, not from the empirical observations and experiences of primitive man, but from the revealed words of Genesis.

The ancient myths of our forefathers do not teach creationism; to the contrary, they teach evolution. The divine and human drama invariably begins with chaos: that is to say, undifferentiated matter. Out of that purely physical matter all other things, including the gods, are born. Once they have come into being, those gods often take part in the shaping of the chaos, but they are themselves products *of* that chaos. The gods, though they often have no ending, have a definite beginning. If they are immortal, they are, like biblical angels, immortal in only one direction.

Now, once the gods exist and are established in power, they will, in one way or another, manipulate the natural world and give birth to the human world. And primitive man will use those divine tales to explain why things are the way they are: why, for example, there are thunder and lightning, sunrise and sunset, wolves and dolphins. The gods will be seen as taking an active part, often a meddling part, in the affairs of men, and a high premium will therefore be put on appeasing those gods.

Still, let me emphasize again the too-often overlooked fact that the Bible is unique in its insistence that matter has not always existed but was brought into being, *out of nothing* (*ex nihilo* in Latin), by an eternal Creator. It took several thousand years for science to catch up to this revelation and discover the shocking reality of the Big Bang: namely, that space and time—matter and minutes—*began* at a specific moment some fourteen billion years ago.

I will have much more to say about the Big Bang; for now, let it suffice to point out that the Bible and the Nicene Creed—which affirms that God is "the maker of heaven and earth, and of all things visible and invisible"—far from mirroring mythology, lines up with modern scientific discoveries in physics and cosmology.

> In sharp contrast to the myths of the ancient world and the theory of evolution, the Bible teaches that the universe was created *ex nihilo* ("out of nothing"). In this longstanding debate, the modern scientific discovery of the Big Bang supports the Bible.

The Natural and the Supernatural

I can still recall the moment that I realized, in a flash of insight, that mythology lined up not with the Bible, but with Darwinism in its foundational belief that the ultimate origin of all things is physical rather than spiritual. That realization stunned me for a while, and threatened to rob myth of its awe and wonder. But only for a short time. I soon realized that mythology, despite its beginnings in chaos, nevertheless presented an enchanted world shot through with divine interference. Reality existed and worked on two levels: the physical and the metaphysical, the natural and the supernatural, the mortal and the immortal, the human and the divine. Within that two-story system, appeals are made to the gods to explain everything from droughts to earthquakes, hurricanes to plagues. Religion dominates society, often leading, it is true, to ignorance, superstition, and paranoia, but more often inspiring obedience, piety, and gratitude.

Although the endlessly repackaged charge that religion is an outgrowth of superstition and that the two represent nothing more than the two sides of the same coin does not square with history, I will here concede that the two *can* and often *have* gone hand in hand, and that, as such, secular critics of the religious world-view have been partly justified in their critiques. Religious people, whether pagan pantheists or Christian monotheists, can easily fall into the fallacy of ascribing every single natural event to a direct supernatural cause. And when they go to that extreme, it should not be surprising that their immoderate, excessive action often provokes an equal and opposite reaction.

Such a reaction occurred in the sixth and fifth centuries BC along the coasts of Asia Minor (modern-day Turkey), Greece, and Italy. In such bustling port cities as Ephesus and Miletus (Asia Minor), Elea and Crotona (Italy), and Akagras (Sicily), the free flow of fresh, culturally diverse ideas from across the Mediterranean inspired a group of scientists and philosophers—the words were used identically at this stage—to fashion a new, naturalistic view of the world that contrasted sharply with the more established supernaturalism of the priests, soothsayers, poets, and common people. In the works of Thales, Anaximander, and Anaximenes, Xenophanes, Heraclitus, Parmenides, and Zeno, Pythagoras, Empedocles, and Anaxagoras, and Leucippus and Democritus—a group collectively referred to as the Pre-Socratics—man's gaze is turned away from the heavens and focused back on the earth. Answers are to be found not in the realm of the spiritual, but in the realm of the physical.

Perhaps the best and fullest embodiment of the supernatural view against which the Pre-Socratics reacted can be found in the two mini-epics of Hesiod, a late eighth-century Greek poet-farmer who was likely a contemporary of Homer: *Theogeny* and *Works and Days*. Like Homer, who lived in Asia Minor, Hesiod looked to the actions of the Olympian gods of the Greek pantheon (Zeus, Poseidon, Hades, Hera, Aphrodite, Apollo, etc.) as a way of explaining events on earth.

Unlike Homer's *Iliad* and *Odyssey*, however, where the gods play a dramatic role in furthering the plot and in assisting (or setting up obstacles in the way of) the mortal heroes, Hesiod's *Theogeny* presents the gods as more removed forces that initiate, guide, and direct. The *Theogeny* (Greek for "birth of the gods") is an etiological poem, one that seeks to trace the origins and causes of things. It is in *Theogeny* and *Works and Days* (a sort of poetic farmer's almanac) that Hesiod explains how Hades's kidnapping of Persephone, daughter of Demeter ("mother earth"), led to the seasonal cycle, how human creativity was born when Prometheus stole the fire from the gods and gave it to man, and how all the evils of the world were set loose when Pandora opened a box. On a more subtle level, Hesiod shows as well how strife and reconciliation in the heavens manifest themselves on the earth. As in Homer, our earthly existence is played out in the midst of a two-story universe.

> The ancient pre-Christian religious worldview is best
> summed up by Hesiod and Homer's vision of a
> two-storied universe, where the divine, the immortal,
> and the supernatural affect and interact with the
> human, the mortal, and the natural.

The First Evolutionists

In reaction to this two-tiered worldview, the Pre-Socratics, like their evolutionary heirs, set about to fashion a new scientific-philosophical method for exploring the nature of reality that did not rely on, or even take into account, the actions and intrigues of the divine pantheon. Though the complex visions of Pythagoras and Parmenides retained a strongly spiritual flavor, the other Pre-Socratics looked to material explanations for why things are the way they are. This was particularly true of Thales, Anaximander, and Anaximenes, a group known collectively as the Milesians, since they lived in the cosmopolitan city of Miletus.

Thales (c. 624–c. 546 BC), universally hailed as the father of science in the West, initiated this new worldview by asking a simple question: What is the *arche* (Greek for "origin" or "first principle") of all things? Although, as I explained above, mythology begins with chaos (matter) rather than gods (spirit) and is ignorant of the biblical creation *ex nihilo*, a religious writer like Hesiod would nevertheless have chosen one or more of the gods as his explanatory *arche*. Ultimate questions could not be answered by referring only to physical matter; divine intention and intervention needed to be factored in.

Not so Thales. He insisted that the *arche* was material and then argued that that material *arche* was water. Out of water came the other three "elements" that make up the building blocks of life: earth, air, and fire. Nothing outside these four elements—and the endless combinations and permutations formed by their joinings and disjoinings—was needed to account for the world and life as we know it.

Whereas religious writers like Hesiod wanted to know the *who* and *why* of things, Thales limited himself, and all those thinkers who followed in his wake, to the more impersonal, mechanistic questions of *what* and *how*. Though Thales did not espouse atheism, he was not interested in the plans or desires or motivations of a supernatural designer (or designers); he was interested only in the physical, mechanical processes by which things were formed and broken.

In this, Thales was followed by his pupil Anaximander (c. 611–c. 547 BC), who, coming somewhat closer to modern nontheistic thinkers like Carl Sagan, posited that the *arche* was an amorphous mass that he called the unlimited (or boundless) and that he believed predated the four elements. The third Milesian scientist-philosopher, Anaximenes (sixth-century BC), backed away from Anaximander's cosmic soup to posit air, rather than water, as the *arche*. More importantly, Anaximenes worked out a more detailed system for exactly how the four elements performed their changes from one form to the other.

Anaximenes lined up the four elements from the coldest and heaviest at the bottom to the hottest and lightest at the top: earth, water, air, fire. Through a process he called rarefaction, earth gave way to water which gave way to air which gave way to fire. By an opposite process he called condensation (or compression), the elements shifted downward from fire to air to water to earth. Thus, airy clouds gather (compress) together to produce rain which waters the earth, while ice (solid) melts into water (liquid) which itself, at the right temperature, transforms into steam (gas). This dual process proceeded impersonally and mechanically, unplanned and unguided by any kind of divine hand or supernatural will. Like Thales before him, Anaximenes did not declare himself an atheist; he simply made God (or the gods) irrelevant to the creation and transformation of life.

The reductive theories of the Milesians—reductive because they reduced the vast mysteries of life to the random motions and changes of four material building blocks—were reduced even further by the atomists Leucippus (fl. 535 BC) and Democritus (c. 460–c. 370 BC). Rather than speak of a single *arche*, they argued that only two things exist in the universe: atoms and the void. By atom (*a-tom*, a Greek word that means "cannot be cut") they meant a tiny piece of matter that could not be subdivided any further. These bits of "stuff," these cosmic pebbles moved—or, to be more precise, fell—ceaselessly through empty space: that is, through the void. As the atoms moved, they collided with one another to form all things.

Though Leucippus and Democritus worked diligently to refine their atomic view of the universe, it would be left to the first-century BC Roman poet Lucretius (c. 98–55) to take their atomic theories—as passed down through the Epicureans—and rework them into a grand sweeping vision. In his epic poem *De Rerum Natura* (*On the Nature of Things*), written in the same meter as Homer's *Iliad* and *Odyssey* and Virgil's *Aeneid*, Lucretius conjures for his readers a cosmic dance that, while being rigidly materialistic, shocks and enthralls the reader into a kind of metaphysical awe.

> Like modern evolutionists, the Pre-Socratics narrowed
> and reduced science to questions of what and how,
> rather than who and why, and insisted that all
> phenomena be ascribed to physical, material causes.

From Atoms and the Void to Ones and Zeroes

Let me pause here and admit that I am very much a fan of Lucretius, even if I disagree sharply with his worldview. He was a skilled poet who magically transformed ideas and images best suited to a dull science textbook into the matter of a great epic; in fact, so skilled was he that he almost singlehandedly made Latin poetry as respectable and pure as Greek poetry, thus paving the way for one of the four or five greatest poems ever written, Virgil's *Aeneid*. Still, for all my love of Lucretius the poet, I must, for the sake of seeking after the truth about us and our world, critique him as I would Darwin or Carl Sagan, Stephen Jay Gould or Richard Dawkins.

Although Lucretius, in the now-familiar mode of the modern new atheist, is both censorious and dismissive of religious thinkers who would look to the gods for answers and explanations, he is also highly critical of Thales, Anaximander, and Anaximenes. Thus, while championing their materialism and their search for a physical *arche*, he sharply criticizes their attempts to identify that arche with one of the four elements. In a passage dripping with irony and condescension, he takes the Pre-Socratic Heraclitus (fl. 500 BC) to task for asserting that that *arche* was fire. He even ridicules the Pre-Socratic Empedocles (c. 484–424 BC) for his attempts to refine the condensation/rarefaction processes of Anaximenes into an elaborate system of attraction and repulsion.

According to Lucretius, all these early pioneers missed out on two important scientific truths: (1) that the true building block of life (the indivisible atom) is far smaller than any of the four elements, and (2) that there exists a universal void through which these atoms move. Because the four elements are in constant change, they must themselves be composed of something else that does not change. For Lucretius, all of this is obvious to anyone who has eyes to see and ears to hear. No, we cannot see the atoms—they are, as we would say today, microscopic. But we can see and experience their effects, as we do with wind or the fragrance of a flower. Some things grow while others decay; we do not see that growth or decay, but we can infer by the result that atoms have been added or taken away.

Lucretius takes obvious pleasure in refuting the Pre-Socratics and exposing the gaps in their logic. Still, he clearly prefers their naturalistic attempts to describe the workings of the world, error-ridden though they be, to what he considered the metaphysical ravings of prophets and oracles. Indeed, he treats Empedocles as a saintly man with a godlike mind. Like his heirs among the new atheists, Lucretius looks to scientists, rather than priests, as the true seekers after truth, and therefore as the ones who should guide society forward.

I will return many times to Lucretius's epic in the chapters that follow, but I hope that this brief overview will make clear that materialism is by no means a discovery of the twentieth century or even of the Enlightenment. From the sixth-century Thales, to Epicurus, the founder of Epicureanism who flourished around 300 BC, to the first-century Lucretius, who based his poem closely on the teachings of Epicurus (c. 341–271 BC), the desire to explain all things in terms of physical, material, natural processes was strong, carefully nuanced, and uncompromising. And it did not refrain from heaping scorn on religious thinkers who insisted that neither our world nor we ourselves could be accounted for apart from the supernatural and/or the divine.

Whether the vehicle of generation be the interplay of the four elements, the movement of atoms through the void, or the accumulation of small incremental changes selected for survival, the materialist desire has remained the same for over two-and-a-half millennia: to construct a purely natural system that can proceed apart from any supernatural design, guidance, or purpose. How is that possible? For Empedocles it was the impersonal forces of love and strife that drew the elements together or drove them apart; for Lucretius, it was the arbitrary swerve of the atom as it fell through the void that caused it to collide with other atoms and form various compounds; for Darwin it was the blind process of natural selection that "decided" which random changes would be passed down to the next generation; for the modern evolutionist, it is the chance mutations each time the DNA replicates itself that provide the vehicle for micro- and macroevolution.

If I may be somewhat playful, I would compare the materialist systems of Empedocles, Lucretius, Darwin, and Steven Jay Gould et al. to the transporter in Star Trek. Even a child understands immediately and intuitively the concept behind the transporter: (1) a man's body is broken down into a million atoms; (2) those atoms are projected through space; (3) they are collected back together and reassembled. Now, even a minute of impartial and commonsensical thought will reveal that neither the complexity of the human brain nor the insubstantiality of the human soul could be successfully broken down and reassembled. Yet we accept the possibility—not because it is physically possible, but because we can *imagine* it happening. We can make a mental picture of it in our brain, and we can verbalize the process in words.

Today our ability to imagine the possibility of atomism (or the transporter) has been strengthened by the invention of binary technology. Amazingly, all the information contained in a symphony or an epic film can be reduced to a series of ones and zeros and imprinted on a CD or DVD. Our knowledge that such things can be makes it far easier to give credence to the atomism of Lucretius, since atoms and the void appear to line up nicely with the ones and zeros that provide us with such stunningly lifelike sounds and images. But then we must not forget that binary codes were invented and put into use by intelligent purposeful agents, not blind, random chance. Furthermore, binary code works with nonliving inorganic material, not with trees or ants or sheep, and certainly not with living, breathing men and women.

No, it is no more possible to transport a human being with all his physical and nonphysical complexity by reducing him to binary atoms than it is for blind, unguided forces to produce something as intricate as the human eye or the DNA code through the random collision of elements, atoms, or mutations. Indeed, even the most intelligent breeder of animals cannot so manipulate the genes of a cat as to transform it into a dog or a horse or an ape. It simply doesn't work, but, again, we can *imagine* it working. The appeal may seem to be to our brain and our reason, but it is ultimately to our imagination: as if the fact that the Dutch artist M.C. Escher can sketch fish turning into birds with his magical inks and pens proves that such a transfiguration could actually take place in the real world given sufficient time and chance.

> Lucretius is but one of many thinkers who have
> tried to construct a system in which everything can
> be explained by the random interactions of a few
> key material building blocks.

Avoiding Accountability

The materialist theories—or better, visions—of Thales, Lucretius, and Darwin make a strong and vivid appeal to our imagination, but their real strength lies in the appeal they make to our human capacity for wishful thinking. If only we can convince ourselves that random collisions can create all that we see and know, then we can free ourselves from any kind of accountability to a supernatural designer. On this score, Lucretius, unlike many (though not all) of the new atheists, is refreshingly open and honest. Through his system, he promises to free both himself and his readers from the icy grip of religious teachings and leaders.

Four times in *On the Nature of Things*, near the openings of Books I, II, III, and VI, Lucretius repeats this revealing refrain:

> This fright, this night of the mind must be dispelled
> not by the rays of the sun, nor day's bright spears,
> but by the face of nature and her laws.**

The fright to which Lucretius refers is the fear of punishment in the afterlife, a fear propagated by power-hungry priests and cruel, retributive deities. Lucretius promises to free us from such things not by seeking fuller divine revelation or reforming religious rituals, but by subjecting all things to a logical, reasoned analysis of the laws of nature.

Moderns associate the concept of the clockwork universe with Galileo and Newton, but the desire to systematize and codify the movements of the heavens is an ancient one. However, whereas the Christian Galileo and the at-least strong theist Newton saw the hand of God in the workings of the world—"nature and nature's

---

** For full bibliographical information, including the page number, for this quote, as well as for all other quotes in this book, please consult the annotated bibliography, which begins on page 267.

God," to quote the Declaration of Independence—Lucretius and his heirs have sought to construct a cosmology that works apart from divine initiation, impulse, and intention. The magi of the Nativity studied the stars to discern the will of the gods; philosophers and scientists like Thales and Lucretius studied the stars to liberate themselves from any and all reliance on supernatural forces. The former looks to science—that is, to reasoned observation of nature—as an aid to understanding and drawing closer to the will of the divine; the latter looks to science as a way of evading the claims and demands of religion.

There is nothing inherent within science or religion that should set them at odds. Indeed, until the Enlightenment, most scientists in the West had no problem embracing a worldview that included the supernatural. Still, there have always been some in the scientific camp who have insisted on excluding anything outside or beyond the physical, just as there have always been some in the religious camp who have demanded that all natural phenomena, from earthquakes to diseases to floods, be traced back to a specific supernatural cause. The latter encounters severe mental illness and says it *must* be a case of demonic possession; the former sees the same case and refuses even to consider that it might have a spiritual dimension.

My point here is not to ridicule either of these two extremes, but to make clear that *both* extremes have always existed. The science *versus* religion worldview is not a new one; it has merely been the minority viewpoint until quite recently. The possibility of setting up science as a defense from, if not a substitute for, religion has been there as an option at least as far back as Thales. There wasn't some clearing of the eyes that happened 250 years ago; if anything, our eyes have become increasingly dimmed so that they can only see the natural, the physical, and the material.

> Materialistic systems that try to explain all things
> apart from the supernatural are not always neutral
> and objective; more often than not, they are
> constructed as a means for avoiding accountability to
> a divine creator.

Christian Cross-Examination #1: The Cosmological Argument

Such has been the ongoing case for atheism for the past 2,600 years, a case that was no more proved in the time of the Pre-Socratics than it has been in the time of the new atheists. Do Christians have a response? Do they possess arguments strong enough to turn the tables and put the atheists themselves on trial? They do! Indeed, they always have. The side of God has never lacked skilled attorneys to cross-examine the usually baseless claims of materialists, skeptics, and secular humanists.

Ironically, one of the strongest arguments against materialism is to be found in Book I of *On the Nature of Things*. Following in the footsteps of Epicurus, Lucretius begins from the premise that nothing comes from nothing. Lucretius cites this foundational principle of Epicureanism as a way of refuting any notion of gods miraculously bringing things into existence out of nothing. If such things could happen, Lucretius asserts, then all would be chaos, and madness would reign in the natural world. No, he asserts, the material laws of nature work their processes on atoms (bits of matter) that have always existed and always will exist. Each species has its own unique, essential atoms and propagates after its own kind.

So Lucretius insists, but, in the very act of insisting, he makes necessary what Aristotle called an Unmoved Mover. Granted the swerve of the atom might cause collisions that might make new compounds apart from external guidance or purpose. But what set the atoms in motion in the first place? True, we might be able to construct a material chain of causation for each collision that reaches back and back to the dawn of time, but if we don't have a Prime Mover to start the motion and the swerve, then we are left with infinite regress.

This argument, known in philosophy as the cosmological argument, is most often associated with the great medieval Christian philosopher-theologian Thomas Aquinas (1225–1274). But Aquinas's arguments can be traced back directly to the fourth-century BC pagan philosopher Aristotle (384–322 BC). A generation before Epicurus and three centuries before Lucretius, Aristotle had already shown that, since nothing comes from nothing, there must be a beginning to motion, just as there must be a beginning/cause for existence itself.

We are what philosophers call contingent beings: that is to say, beings that do not contain life within themselves. Just as a time will come when our life will end, so there must have been a time when we did not possess life. We are, and continue to be, reliant upon something outside of ourselves for our life and our existence. As contingent beings, Aristotle (and Aquinas after him) taught, we could not have created ourselves; nor could we simply have been. There must have been a First Cause that does not itself have a cause—a Being whose existence and essence are the same, who has Life in himself.

And just as we are contingent, so is our universe. Aquinas understood this as did many medieval Arabic philosophers—for they all drank from the same Aristotelian well. In the Muslim world, the cosmological apologetic for the existence of God—of a Cause who was not himself caused, a Mover who is himself unmoved—was known as the Kalam argument, a simple but profound argument that has been resuscitated in the West by the American apologist William Lane Craig.

The argument is constructed in the form of a syllogism. The major premise, the self-evident principle that does not need to be proven, states that anything that begins to exist must have a cause. Essentially, this premise is identical with Epicurus's assertion that nothing comes from nothing. The minor premise states that our universe came into being, which it must have done, for it, like us, is contingent. On the basis of these two premises, we are compelled to conclude that there must be a cause for the universe. But if that is so, then that cause cannot be a part of the universe it caused: it must be a transcendent cause, both supernatural and metaphysical.

> The cosmological argument of Aristotle and Aquinas states that if there is no First Mover to initiate movement, then we are left with infinite regress. Both we and our universe are contingent—that is, we rely on an outside cause to give us being and motion.

Christian Cross-Examination #2: The Big Bang Demands a Big Banger

Logic then pushes us backward to God—to an Unmoved Mover/Uncaused Causer who has Life within himself and in whom existence and essence are one and the same. And yet, wonderfully, serendipitously, modern physics has done an about-face since the days of Thales, Epicurus, and Lucretius and backed up the logic of Aristotle and Aquinas. The discovery that our universe had a beginning, perhaps the greatest scientific discovery of the twentieth century, has given flesh and blood to the cosmological argument.

Or has it? Desperate to shake off the theistic implications of the

Big Bang, Stephen Hawking, one of the architects and populariz-
ers of Big Bang cosmology, has tried to make an end run around
the singularity that brought our universe into fiery existence. Perhaps, he theorizes, channeling and even exceeding the imaginative
power of Lucretius, our universe is but one of multiple universes
(or multiverses). Given billions of these potential universes springing into existence one after the other, surely one would arise that
could support our planet and the organic life it contains.

Just like Thales, Epicurus, and Lucretius before him, Hawking
insists that our world did not require the intervention of a divine,
supernatural Mover to get it started. But if that is so, then what
was there before the Big Bang that had the power and ability to
initiate all these failed multiverses? It's as if Hawking and his fellow
materialists, finding themselves unable to explain the existence of
a single universe, thought to cover their tracks by positing the
existence of millions of them.

But Hawking is not to be defeated so easily. He *does* have an
answer to the question of origins, one that lines up nicely with the
vision of Lucretius. It is the material, impersonal, mechanistic laws
of nature, specifically the law of gravity, which drives the multiverse
machine. Hawking makes this argument in *The Grand Design*
(2010), which he co-wrote with Leonard Mlodinow—an argument
that was answered one year later by Oxford mathematician John
Lennox in his brief but penetrating book *God and Stephen Hawking:
Whose Design Is It Anyway?*

As Lennox shows, there is a world of difference between
physical laws and the kind of personal agency it takes to create
something and bring it into being. The law of gravity is an effective
formula-tool for defining the interaction between material bodies
in space, but it cannot cause that material to come into existence.
Besides, Hawking's faith in the creative capacity of the law of

gravity is unfounded, a species of scientific wishful thinking. First, to say that the law of gravity helped initiate the Big Bang is to say that the law of gravity existed before it existed—since the Big Bang brought everything, including the law of gravity, into existence. Second, it makes no sense to say the law of gravity initiated the Big Bang because the law of gravity can have neither existence nor meaning until there is physical matter for it to move—and that physical matter did not arise until after the Big Bang.

The tools of science may have advanced, but the materialist dream of being able to explain all things by the movement and interaction of matter has not changed in the more than 2,000 years that separate Lucretius from Stephen Hawking. The latter remains just as adamant as the former in his belief that the fixed laws of nature working on the physical building blocks of life can account for every aspect of the universe—both external and internal—that we perceive with our senses.

And yet, ironically, in pressing that dream to its extreme, Hawking posits the very thing that Lucretius most feared. If multiverse theory is true, then we live in a truly chaotic, haphazard universe where anything can spring into being at any time, and then just as quickly cease to exist. In Hawking's multiverse world, nothing is stable.

Incidentally, Hawking is not the only modern materialist who, while being fully aware that there was nothing before the Big Bang, chose to ignore completely the theistic implications of that scientific truth. Any American who was born before the mid-1960s will likely remember the late Carl Sagan's pathbreaking TV series *Cosmos* (1980). In that unforgettable series, Sagan took an awestruck audience on a tour through the depth and breadth of our vast and complex universe.

Although the general public was not yet fully aware that the

Big Bang had already been proven beyond the shadow of scientific doubt—a full fifteen years earlier, Arno Penzias and Robert Wilson had discovered the "smoking gun" of the Big Bang—Sagan *was* aware that matter is not eternal but came into existence at a specific moment. And yet, despite this knowledge, Sagan did not hesitate from beginning his series with an assertion that scientists, most of them secular, had already shown to be false. The cosmos, Sagan declared, boldly co-opting the language of the praise of God in Revelation 4:8, is all there is, all there has ever been, and all there will ever be.

How did Sagan manage, in the face of Big Bang cosmology, to convince the public that our universe is eternal? The same way Lucretius was able to convince many of his readers that time + chance + the swerve of the atom was enough to "create" all the complexity we see around us: by the overwhelming power of his rhetoric and the desire of his audience to avoid accountability before a divine and personal Creator who might just expect something from the creatures he had made. Even for left-brained scientists, subjective imagination often proves a stronger force than objective reason and logic.

> There was nothing before the Big Bang: no atoms, no void, no physical laws of nature; neither Carl Sagan nor Stephen Hawking can get around the theistic implications of the Big Bang.

Postscript

I recently watched *The Theory of Everything*, a well-made biographical picture of the tragic but triumphant life, loves, and career of Stephen Hawking. Skillfully directed by James Marsh and featuring the chameleon Eddie Redmayne in the lead role, the film stays quite close to the truth; it even, surprisingly, succeeds in being fair to the Christian faith of Hawking's first wife, Jane. And yet, for all its attempts to honor Jane's religious beliefs, the filmmakers made a biblical error that would be funny if it weren't so revealing about the ingrained materialism of our modern age.

In the film, the atheist Stephen and the Christian Jane have some entertaining sparring contests over their opposing world-views. At one point, Jane seems to win over, temporarily, her skeptical partner. As the lovers stare together at a numinous sky twinkling with stars, Jane quotes the opening verse of Genesis, provoking a look of wonder in Stephen's eyes. But she misquotes the verse! Instead of saying, "In the beginning God created the heaven and the earth. And the earth was without form and void: and darkness was upon the face of the deep," she says "In the beginning was the heaven and the earth. And the earth was without form and void: and darkness was upon the face of the deep."

There you have it. Even when the modern secular mind tries to be true to the Bible, it finds itself unable to conceive of a cosmos created *ex nihilo* by a self-existent, noncontingent God who dwells outside time and space. Whether the scientist be Thales or Lucretius, Sagan or Hawking, the imaginative and emotional power of materialism is just too strong to leave a space in the universe for the Light of the One whose name is I Am that I Am to shine through and illuminate the darkness of the void.

CHAPTER TWO

The Laws of Nature

There are three things that I never get tired of repeating again and again: reading The Chronicles of Narnia; watching The Lord of the Rings film trilogy, preferably in one twelve-hour sitting; and attending, in costume, the Renaissance Festival held annually in north Houston. It took me quite some time to discover what those three things had in common, but when I discovered what it was, it opened my eyes to something which our modern world is sadly lacking.

Narnia, Middle-earth, and the Ren Fest are all, at their core, medieval places: lands where there is a more human, personal connection between rulers and subjects, landlords and serfs, and clergy and laity, between members of families, members of churches, and members of guilds, and between man and God, man and nature, and man and the universe. Everything then seemed to be in sympathy with everything else and to be saturated with meaning and purpose. If I had to choose one word to describe what it felt like to step into that medieval world, it would be *connection*.

What I had felt in my oft-repeated journeys through the medieval landscapes of Lewis and Tolkien and the spacious fields and booths of the Renaissance Festival was later confirmed when I read

C.S. Lewis's brilliant overview and analysis of the medieval cosmo-logical model, *The Discarded Image*. In that somewhat technical but still highly accessible book, Lewis contrasted the view of the universe held by the great thinkers of the Middle Ages with that held by nearly all people since Newton and the Enlightenment. For Dante and Aquinas, the heavenly bodies move out of love for God even as they shed their influence down upon the earth and upon man. For moderns, all things move in accordance with the imper-sonal, mechanistic laws of nature.

Although Lewis did not advocate a simple return to the medi-eval model, he did teach me that both models *are* models, founded upon metaphorical language and strongly influenced by our cul-tural desires. The medievals loved pageantry and hierarchy, and when they looked up to the heavens, that is what they saw; we are a society that venerates both technology and the legal system, and so it should come as no surprise that what we see when we gaze upward are the laws of planetary motion.

And yet, Lewis helped me to understand those laws are no more "real" than the angelic beings that the medievals believed moved the planetary spheres. The laws of nature are not "things" as stones or rivers or tigers or people are things, but mathematical constructs that help us understand the way the universe works. Not so for ancient, medieval, or modern materialists. For them, I soon came to realize, the laws of nature mean a great deal more. They are not just descriptors; they are causative agents—as if the Pythagorean Theorem could create right triangles, or the law of conservation of energy could have brought the initial energy into existence.

Living in a Closed Universe

As I tried to show at the end of the previous chapter, Stephen Hawking, one of the true geniuses of his generation, is so enamored of the laws of nature that he is willing to risk absurdity to push those laws back to before the Big Bang. And yet, despite Hawking's attempts, the fact remains that the laws of nature don't do anything: They define, measure, explain, but they do not act. In that sense, they are like chance. Chance has no existence in and of itself and can neither cause nor guide anything; yet, Darwinists speak as if chance were a living thing, as if it possessed creative properties that could propel forward the evolution of species. But they must do so, for all materialists, from Thales and Anaximander, to Epicurus and Lucretius, to Marx and Freud, to Sagan and Hawking, hold unswervingly to a belief that our universe is a closed system, that there is nothing outside the material world.

Here is how Lucretius explains the closed nature of our universe in Book II of *On the Nature of Things*:

> Nor can any power alter the Sum of Things,
> for there's no place where matter of any kind
> could escape outside the All, nor any source
> from which new force might break into the All
> to change nature and rearrange her patterns.

And here is how his master, Epicurus, explains it in his "Letter to Herodotus":

> Truly this universe has always been such as it now is,
> and so it shall always be; for there is nothing into which
> it can change, and there is nothing outside the uni-
> verse that can enter into it and bring about a change.

For Epicurus, Lucretius, and their heirs, nature is all there is; there is no getting beyond her. She is, as Lucretius makes clear, the Sum of Things, the All. We are part of that nature, and there is nothing within us that transcends, or can transcend nature. There is no spirit separate from body, no mind separate from brain; there is only matter.

For those who know something about Epicureanism, that last statement is sure to sound false. Lucretius, after all, speaks both of souls and of gods in his epic poem, and, in doing so, he is faithful to the teachings of Epicurus. But do not be fooled by his language. For Lucretius (and Epicurus), both the gods and the human soul are purely material, composed of atoms just like everything else. The difference between soul and body, gods and nature is that the former two are made of extremely fine, small, and delicate atoms that give them greater cohesion and integrity. Still, Lucretius makes it clear, when the body dies, the soul dies as well, its fine atoms dissolving and dissipating to join once again the perpetual fall of atoms through the void. The gods too are subject to dissolution and exert no influence whatsoever on the natural or human world.

Though the soul can exert some guidance upon the body, there is nothing that controls or directs the dance of atoms—nothing, that is, except the finally deterministic laws of nature. There must be laws; otherwise, there would be chaos. But those laws must be impersonal and mechanical; else, they will become gods themselves.

It was a lot to take in, this at once expansive and closed universe, but once I bent my mind around it, I realized that it was nothing more than a very large, mostly dark prison from which escape was impossible. One could go mad in such a prison, but one could hardly grow and mature. For in a universe so constructed and conceived, there was no higher perfection which one could grow toward or mature into. There were laws, sure enough, but they were just as much a part of the closed system as we were; they offered no promise of release or of transcendence.

> The universe of the materialist Lucretius is a closed
> universe: neither the human soul nor the immortal
> gods can escape from it, for there is no place outside
> the material world to which they can make their
> escape.

Having One's Cake and Eating It Too

Once I understood what Lucretius's vision of the universe really meant, I saw that it did not differ significantly from the vision of the new atheists—especially from that of one of the chief architects of modern materialism and atheism, Karl Marx (1818–1883). Marx believed all of history was moving unstoppably toward pure Communism. But how could he believe that when he did not believe that anything outside of nature existed that could move his historical timeframe forward? He could believe it, because, in place of spiritual direction and divine intervention, Marx, like the Soviets and Maoists he inspired, posited history as a force in and of itself with the ability to propel things forward. Like the laws of nature, the force of history is somehow both blind and purposive, descriptive and causative, impersonal and yet capable of something suspiciously like agency.

In common parlance, this is known as having your cake and eating it too: desiring a system, a framework to give shape, stability, and purpose to life, but equally desiring that that system make no actual, enforceable moral demands upon us. This dual desire not only animates Epicureanism, but plays a central role in Stoicism, pantheism, deism, Unitarianism, and transcendentalism. How wonderful it is, when all is well, to be able to celebrate order and meaning in the universe. But how convenient it is, when one wants to break the rules, to know that the universe is finally an uncaring, impersonal place.

In seeking to fulfill this dual desire, the ancient Epicurean is no different than the modern new atheist. The innate human yearning to find order and pleasure in life is just as strong as the yearning to be left alone, to be set free from those three intolerable burdens: obedience, gratitude, and accountability. One of the most effective ways of accomplishing this is to bar the gates against all outside interference by transforming our God-haunted cosmos into a closed system. There can be no fear of meddling deities or eternal postmortem punishments as long as the borders of the universe are protected on all sides from illegal aliens who might disrupt the sacred laws of nature.

Of all the thinkers who have helped to build this protective wall against active and involved divinity, the one I respect the most, but whom I am troubled by the most, is Baruch (or Benedict de or Benedictus de) Spinoza (1632–1677). It was, in fact, my close reading of Spinoza's *Ethics* that convinced me of the need to write this book. Though he wrote in the middle of the 1600s, a full century before the Enlightenment, Spinoza's work not only sums up the materialism and antitheism of the Pre-Socratics, Epicureans, and Stoics, but prefigures most of the arguments made by the new atheists and by theological liberals who deny the divinity of Christ, defang his teachings, and deconstruct the authority of the Bible. And he does so while writing about the nature of God and advocating, for himself and others, a highly ethical lifestyle.

> Materialists and atheists have their cake and eat it too by building systems that offer the promise of order, purpose, and stability without the burden of obedience to a personal, supernatural Creator of order, purpose, and stability.

The Forgotten Founding Father

Spinoza was born into a two-century-old identity crisis in the Sephardic Jewish community. Throughout the fifteenth and six-teenth centuries, Jews living in Spain and Portugal were either forcibly converted to Christianity or given the choice of conver-sion or expulsion. Though there were certainly some *conversos*, as they were called, whose embrace of Catholicism was sincere, many, if not most, continued to practice Judaism in secret (these were known as *marranos*). As the weight of the Spanish Inquisition bore down more and more heavily on the marranos, many fled to coun-tries where they could practice their Judaism in peace and safety.

In the early seventeenth century, large numbers of Portuguese marranos, Spinoza's parents among them, immigrated to the Neth-erlands, which boasted the most extensive religious freedom in Europe. Although the Portuguese Jews in the Netherlands were forbidden to proselytize or marry Protestants and were expected to keep quietly to themselves, they were allowed much leeway to grow and flourish. Many, like Spinoza, were afforded the opportu-nity of studying biblical Hebrew and the history of Jewish thought alongside medieval scholastic philosophy, a breadth of study that facilitated and encouraged free thinking but that also fomented a backlash amongst traditional Jews.

Spinoza, who boldly questioned every aspect of Jewish life, thought, and belief, fell foul of that backlash—so much so that in the year 1656, he was excommunicated from the synagogue of Amsterdam. Oddly, this excommunication converted the sec-ular Jewish Spinoza into something of a Christ figure. Just as the high priest Caiaphas was able to turn the Sanhedrin against Jesus by claiming that his teachings would stir up rebellions that would cause the Romans to bear down heavily on the Jews (see John

11:45-53), so the religious leaders of the Sephardic community in Amsterdam successfully branded Spinoza as a troublemaker, a threat to the relative autonomy that the Dutch had granted to the Jews. If Spinoza were allowed to divide the synagogue through his heretical teachings, he would incite civil unrest and precipitate persecution, or at least interference, by the Dutch Christian community.

Just as Jesus provoked enmity from Jewish and Gentile leaders alike, so Spinoza has the honor, or infamy, of having had his books censored by both the Christian church and the Jewish synagogue. Speaking for myself, I cannot help but feel great sympathy and respect for someone who stood alone against resistance on all sides. Certainly Spinoza must rank as one of the great defenders of the freedom of inquiry and of speech.

Still, there is little doubt, in my mind at least, that his teachings are not only heretical from both a Christian and a Jewish point of view, but are as destructive of true religion as the theories of the Epicureans. For despite the fact that Spinoza speaks incessantly about God and the soul, and despite the fact that he is generally labeled a pantheist, his vision is, in the end, just as crudely and stubbornly materialistic as that of Lucretius's. Indeed, despite the fact that he is little read today, Spinoza deserves to be hailed, or blamed, as the forgotten founding father of the new atheists.

Spinoza's major work, *Ethics*, is not an easy book to read. It is not written in the dialogue form of Plato or the narrative form of Augustine or even the odd, question-objection-argument format of Aquinas's *Summa*, but in the form of geometrical logic. After laying down his definitions, postulates, and axioms, he works his way through a series of propositions, backing up each with various proofs, corollaries, and scholiums. The form is as cold as it is unwieldy, lacking the warmth of Descartes, the forcefulness of Hobbes, the clarity of Locke, and the wit of Rousseau. What it embodies instead is the almost dehumanized voice of Kant, a kind of voice that provides the illusion of objectivity.

I say illusion because Spinoza, for all his seemingly objective logic, loads the deck from the beginning. He does not prove, but simply takes for granted that *both* God *and* nature are eternal. Now, it is true that Aristotle posited both an eternal God and an eternal nature, but how different he is from Spinoza! Spinoza had access, through the Old and New Testaments, to the doctrine of creation *ex nihilo*, a doctrine of which Aristotle was ignorant. Neverthe-less, Spinoza chose to reject that doctrine and act is if it were clear and incontestable that matter has always existed. Though I cannot prove it, I am convinced that if Spinoza were alive today, he would, like Sagan and Hawking, have continued to advocate a materialis-tic view of the universe in the face of the Big Bang.

> Though a man of courage who spoke freely at great risk to himself, Spinoza propounded theories that are destructive of religion in general and Judaism and Christianity in particular.

God = Nature

It may sound strange to say it, but Aristotle's vision of God comes far closer to that of the Old Testament than does the vision of God that emerges from Spinoza's *Ethics*. Though the two think-ers shared a belief in an eternal universe, Spinoza's God is far more removed and mechanistic than Aristotle's Unmoved Mover. He (or, to be more precise, it) is also far less personal than the philoso-pher God of Descartes, who seems to have nothing to do but exist. Or the watchmaker God of deism, who, once he sets up the laws of nature, absents himself and lets them run on their own. Indeed, not only does Spinoza merge completely his eternal God and his eternal nature; he makes God equivalent to and ultimately bound by the laws of nature.

All begins well, with Spinoza seeming to affirm the monotheistic Yahweh (whose name means "I Am that I Am") of the Torah:

> By God I mean an absolutely infinite being; that is, substance consisting of infinite attributes, each of which expresses eternal and infinite essence (Part I, Definition 6).

Here, and in the definitions leading up to it, Spinoza makes clear that God is a self-caused being whose existence and essence are the same. So far, this is consistent with Jewish and Christian orthodoxy. But then, without batting an eye and without offering any kind of scientific or logical (inductive) proof, he asserts that nature shares in the unique divine life of God:

> Substance cannot be produced by anything else and is therefore self-caused; that is, its essence necessarily involves existence; that is, existence belongs to its nature (Part I, proof following Proposition 7).

Spinoza here affirms the foundational tenet of Epicureanism that nothing comes of nothing, but in a much more radical sense. Refusing even to entertain the possibility that his self-caused God might have brought all of nature into being, Spinoza spins a new creation myth: one in which divine life and material life are finally indistinguishable from one another.

While conceding that we are contingent beings who do not have life in ourselves but rely on something outside of ourselves for life, Spinoza insists that both God and nature are noncontingent. Inasmuch as he believes in one eternal, indivisible God, Spinoza is a monotheist, but inasmuch as he believes that nature is also one, eternal, and indivisible, he is a pantheist—that is, he believes that God is dispersed throughout, and finally contained by, nature.

In chapter 8, I will return to Spinoza's pantheism—at which time I will argue that his pantheism is really a form of monism. At this point, however, I simply wish to suggest that Spinoza's "pantheism" is, functionally speaking, no different than the materialism of Lucretius. According to Paul, after the second coming and the resurrection of the dead, God will be all in all (1 Corinthians 15:28). According to Spinoza, nature is already all in all. Or, to be more precise, in Spinoza's philosophical system, to say that God is all in all and that nature is all in all is to say the same thing. True, such an equivalency *could* yield an enchanted world where all of nature is filled with the grandeur of God. In Spinoza, it yields the exact opposite: a world run not by the loving will of a personal God, but by the impersonal, indifferent laws of nature.

In many ways, I would argue, Spinoza plays a trick on his readers. He begins by affirming that God is wholly other, that his ways and thoughts are so far above ours that there is no equivalency whatsoever between the two. He makes this particularly clear in a lengthy scholium following his seventeenth proposition (Part I). Spinoza will have nothing to do with the biblical teaching that man was made in God's image; for him that is a human invention, a kind of anthropomorphism that makes God too much like us. To put it in theological terms, Spinoza presents God as absolutely and utterly transcendent:

> For the intellect and will that would constitute the
> essence of God would have to be vastly different from

human intellect and will, and could have no point of
agreement except the name.

This taken alone would seem to lead Spinoza to an extreme
form of Judaism or Islam, where God's radical otherness renders
impossible God becoming a man (the incarnation).

Instead, Spinoza follows this passage with an eighteenth proposition that turns it on its head, making God not a fully transcendent deity separate from the universe, and the humans, that he
created, but a fully immanent deity who is identical with nature:
"God is the immanent, not the transitive, cause of all things." Spinoza's God, like the Epicurean gods of Lucretius, neither wills nor
controls nor guides anything. All forms of causation come through
the laws of nature.

> For Spinoza, God and nature are not only equally
> eternal; they are identical. Spinoza's God does not
> exist apart from nature, but is one with it.

A God Who Neither Loves nor Chooses

Let's pause here, as I myself paused the first time I read these
passages in Spinoza. To my great surprise, what I was meeting in
Spinoza was the same unsettling paradox I had encountered when
I had first tried to read the writings of the radical Christian mystic
Meister Eckhart (1260–1328). As with the Sufis of the Islamic tradition and the Cabbalists of the Jewish, Eckhart began by treating
God as wholly and absolutely other, a Being about whom nothing positive could be said. So far so good; the eternal God certainly
transcends all human categories. But this admission on the part of
Eckhart led him not to a fuller sense of himself as a creature made
in God's image yet fallen, but to the collapsing of all distinctions

between himself and God: not to the perfecting of his identity as a child of God but to the loss of all identity whatsoever.

In chapter 8, I will return to the dangers of making God either fully transcendent or fully immanent. For now, I merely wish to make clear the unsettling—and, I would suggest, ultimately dishonest—paradox at the center of Spinoza: that the more he seems to exalt God, the more he makes him utterly irrelevant. Spinoza may ascribe fancy philosophical titles to his God, but his God is inert. Causation does not proceed from Spinoza's God but from and through the laws of nature.

"Things could not have been produced by God," Spinoza goes on to assert in proposition 33, "in any other way or in any other order than is the case." He then elaborates this point in the proof to proposition 33:

> Therefore if things could have been of a different nature or been determined to act in a different way so that the order of Nature would have been different, then God's nature, too, could have been other than it now is, and therefore this different nature, too, would have had to exist, and consequently there would have been two or more Gods, which is absurd.

At the risk of belaboring the point, I must emphasize again that Spinoza's "God" has no existence apart from nature and no will apart from the laws of nature.

I mentioned earlier that Spinoza was born into a two-century-old Jewish identity crisis. As part of that crisis, Spinoza was deeply troubled by the central biblical teaching that God set aside the Jews as the chosen people. Spinoza came to reject utterly the chosenness of the Jews, a rejection that so spiraled outward that Spinoza came to believe, as a matter of faith rather than of logical proof, that God does not choose anyone or anything. Spinoza's God possesses neither will nor passion nor desire. He does not make plans and execute them; he does not love some and hate others; he does not make promises that he later fulfills. He is perfection, but he is an inert perfection that cannot be loved or worshiped or even obeyed as the moral authority of the universe.

In some senses, Spinoza is less like the atomists than he is like another Pre-Socratic philosopher, Anaxagoras (b. 500 BC), who posited that the universe was composed not of atoms and the void, but of eternal bits of matter (seeds) ordered by an eternal, universal mind (*nous* in Greek). Although Anaxagoras's *nous* seems to be somewhat purposive, it is finally impersonal: the soul of the universe, perhaps, but not a soul possessing any kind of separate, transcendent existence. Like Spinoza's God, Anaxagoras's universal mind is spiritual (well, noncorporeal), but it is not a divine Being who wills some things and not other things.

Still, the God of Spinoza lacks even the slight, nonpersonal agency of the *nous* of Anaxagoras; God's hand, invisibly or otherwise, does not move or guide or even set parameters for the world that he neither fashioned nor desired. Anaxagoras was expelled from the polis of Athens just as Spinoza was excommunicated from the Jewish community of Amsterdam—in part, because their teachings were seen as impious and thus conducive to impiety. In chapter 10, I will focus on the moral and ethical dimensions of Christianity and its critics. For now, my concern is with the scientific tenability of Spinoza and Anaxagoras's view of the universe. Are the laws of nature enough on their own to "create" the world we see? Can there be order in the cosmos without a mind, a purpose, an essence that is deeper and higher than mere physical matter?

> In sharp contrast to the God of the Bible, Spinoza's
> God does not act or guide or choose a people for
> himself; he is merely the impersonal, inert mind of
> the universe.

Final Causes and Purposeful Ends

In the previous chapter, I mentioned Carl Sagan's breathtaking but decidedly materialistic television series *Cosmos*. Whether or not Sagan was aware of it, the title he chose for his series is highly ironic. The Greek word *cosmos* is not simply a synonym for nature or the universe or the world we see with our eyes. The etymological root for *cosmos* is the same root for the seemingly unrelated word *cosmetics*. What could those two words possibly have in common? The answer is unclear until we realize that *cosm*, in Greek, means "order" or "ornament." Just as a woman uses cosmetics to adorn her face, so the cosmos is the ornament of God; it shows forth his beauty, harmony, and design.

There is precious little of that design in Anaxagoras, and none at all in Spinoza or Sagan. To see why that is a problem, we need not consult modern Christian apologists or even look to Augustine or Aquinas. We need not even consult the Bible. A century after Anaxagoras, Aristotle (384–322 BC) had already addressed the issue. Simple laws of nature, even laws kicked off by an Unmoved Mover, are not enough to account for the order and purpose we find in the cosmos.

Too often modern readers try to drive a sharp wedge between Plato and Aristotle, making the first a "religious" thinker and the second a "secular" thinker. Plato had his head in supernatural, metaphysical clouds, we say, while Aristotle brought philosophy back to earth. Well, there is some truth to that, but only a little. Aristotle may have moved away from Plato's theory of the Forms, that the Original Essences of all the things we see and know on the earth exist in the heavens in a state of transcendent perfection. But he did not thereby reject the need for originals and for essences. What Aristotle did is move the Forms from "up there" to "inside here."

For Aristotle, every stone, every plant, every animal, every person has a *telos* (Greek for "purposeful end") that has been written within it. It is that *telos* that makes a tree a tree, a dog a dog, and a man a man. Yes, we can often identify simple, natural, "scientific" causes (Aristotle calls them efficient causes) for why a plant, an animal, or a human being does something. But that does not eliminate the need for a higher, more ultimate cause (what Aristotle calls a final cause) that flows from the essence that has been inscribed in the agent who performs the action.

Epicurus, and, after him, Lucretius, thought they had solved the problem of causation by saying that the atoms that made up the various species of plants, animals, and men were different and distinctive, but that does not answer the question of what instructed the various atoms to form themselves into the different species. Modern Darwinists, who live in the firm faith that all things can be explained solely by natural, physical, material processes, run into serious problems when they face such molecular machines as proteins, cells, and DNA.

> Four centuries before Christ, Aristotle demonstrated that there is a higher end and purpose behind the mysteries of nature that cannot be accounted for by a simple chain of material causes and effects.

Christian Cross-Examination #1: Irreducible Complexity

Although the pre-Christian Aristotle helped lay the groundwork for identifying God's signature in the design and purpose

that run rampant throughout nature, it has been the last generation of Christian apologists who have perfected that argument by
referencing recent scientific breakthroughs in cellular-molecular
biology. Darwin simply could not have conceived the level of complexity that exists in each cell and in each strand of DNA. And yet,
sadly, his evolutionary heirs, though fully aware of that complexity, persist in arguing that it can be accounted for by undirected
time and chance.

They continue to point to the laws of nature to help them measure the intricate microscopic workings of proteins, cells, and DNA
while refusing to concede that those laws, like Spinoza's God, are
incapable of programming proteins, cells, and DNA with the
(frontloaded) information needed for them to run in the first place.
Impersonal, unconscious, nonpurpose nature cannot do this, and,
if God is equivalent with nature, then Spinoza's God cannot do it
either. Nor, for that matter, can the Epicurean gods of Lucretius or
the amorphous *nous* of Anaxagoras.

As Michael Behe has shown in *Darwin's Black Box*, the biological "machines" that maintain our cells are "irreducibly complex"—
that is to say, they do not perform a helpful function for the cell
until all their many parts have been assembled and are in proper
working order. What that means from a scientific point of view is
that they could not have evolved through slow, gradual, unguided
changes, for nature would have had no reason to select the inter-
mediate stages leading up to the final design.

Meanwhile, Stephen Meyer, in his monumental *The Signature in the Cell*, has gathered all-but-incontestable evidence that
the DNA, and its system of replication, demands an intelligent
Designer. True, Meyer shows, the way DNA replicates itself, with
each copy allowing for chance mutations, can facilitate some
adaptation within species (microevolution). What could not have

evolved, however, is the DNA itself. Even more than the biological "machines" that maintain our cells, DNA is too irreducibly complex to have been assembled by the types of mechanisms that drive natural selection. The DNA could not have been assembled by blind evolutionary forces, for it contains within itself—and, as far as we can tell, has always contained within itself—the detailed blueprint in accordance with which all the various parts of our proteins and cells have been assembled.

Rather than summarize here the lengthy arguments made by Behe and Meyer, let me offer instead an analogy for the kind of complexity we are dealing with when we speak of DNA and the miniature assembly lines that run continually in each of our cells. Imagine, if you will, a world filled with hourglasses. Every sixty minutes, finely grained sand moves from the top of the glasses to the bottom. When all the sand has run through, a mechanical arm turns the glasses, allowing the sand to run again. And so on without ceasing. Imagine further that this world of hourglasses has no rational creatures on it—only minerals, plants, and animals to whom time is meaningless. Then a new creature arrives who is conscious and has the capacity for reasoned analysis and speech. After much study, these new creatures come to understand time and the exact way in which the hourglasses measure that time.

Will these creatures think that they invented time? In a moment of pride, perhaps, but one would hope that a little bit of rational—and humble—thought would convince them that they had merely discovered something that "someone" higher than them had created. Further thought would reveal that the same "someone" who made the hourglasses also made them; how else could they possess the ability to recognize (not invent) the measuring power of the hourglasses? And if they kept using their reason, they might also realize that the hourglasses don't themselves create time, but only measure it. Leading to the final conclusion that the "someone" who created the hourglasses and their own rational ability to read and understand them also created time itself.

In the same way, Einstein did not invent $E=MC^2$; he discovered it. The formula, the relationship, was already there, inscribed into our cosmos, and, I would argue, into our rational capacities. Einstein simply put that relationship into a mathematical equation. He no more invented the law/principle that he discovered than the law/principle created the relationship between matter and energy. "Someone" above Einstein and the laws of nature created the matter/energy relationship, the law defining it, and Einstein's ability to discover and formulate that law. And that "someone" cannot itself be the laws of nature or the random motion of particles of matter. It must be conscious and purposive.

> Modern science has shown that our cells, proteins, and DNA are irreducibly complex; they could not have been assembled by slow gradual changes driven by blind, purposeless time and chance.

Christian Cross-Examination #2: Specified Complexity

Some who read the last few paragraphs will argue that I am merely resuscitating the old tired design argument of William Paley (1743–1805). In *Natural Theology* (1802), Paley famously argues that if we come upon a rock, we can ascribe its unique shape to natural patterns of weathering and erosion. But if we come upon a watch, with all of its intricate working parts, we must theorize a watchmaker.

William Dembski, taking this argument to the next level, has provided, in *The Design Inference*, a helpful filter for determining whether a given structure or phenomenon is random or designed.

Mere complexity, Dembski explains, is not enough to gain it the label of "design"; it must possess "specified complexity." Paley's watch meets the criteria for specified complexity for its intricate cogs and gears have been fashioned *and* assembled to perform a specific function that transcends the physical watch itself. Just so, writes Dembski, if we come upon a mountain in South Dakota bearing the rough shape of a human eye and nose, we can write it off to the natural processes of weathering. But if we pass a second mountain that bears the impression of four faces that are not only distinctly human but that match up with the faces of four Presidents we have encountered in history textbooks, then we conclude that its specified complexity demands an intelligent designer.

Now, whether or not Paley and Dembski's design argument is old or recent, tired or energetic is irrelevant to its truthfulness or falsehood. The fact of the matter is both the argument itself and the various criticisms *of* the argument have existed side by side for more than 2,000 years and continue to do so today. That a growing number of PhDs have ceased to believe in the argument does not, in and of itself, disprove the argument.

As evidence of the persistence of the design argument, I would like to close this chapter by referencing a work that was written not by a twenty-first century Christian apologists, but by a pagan Roman statesman and rhetorician named Cicero (106–43 BC) in the middle of the first century BC: *The Nature of the Gods.* In this delightful—if flawed—work, Cicero mounts a dialogue between three people, each representing a different philosophical-theological school: Velleius the Epicurean, Balbus the Stoic, and Cotta the Academic (a school which preferred, like Socrates, to debate various sides of an issue rather than come up with a single answer). Though Cicero himself gravitated toward Cotta's position, he affords a great deal of respect to Balbus, giving him many of the best arguments.

While mostly dismissing the Epicureanism of the pompous Velleius, Cicero's rhetoric clearly champions the design arguments of Balbus. In this passage from Book II, Balbus uses the same watch analogy that Paley would use more than 1800 years later:

> When we see some example of a mechanism, such as a globe or clock or some such device, do we doubt that it is the creation of a conscious intelligence? So when we see the movement of the heavenly bodies, the speed of their revolution, and the way in which they regularly run their annual course, so that all that depends upon them is preserved and prospers, how can we doubt that these too are not only the works of reason but of a reason which is perfect and divine? So let us put aside all casuistry of argument and simply let our eyes confess the splendour of the world, this world which we affirm to be the creation of the providence of God.

No modern scientific discovery has disproved this argument. If anything, our modern knowledge of how precisely fine tuned our universe needs to be to accommodate human life (macrocosm) and how unfathomably complex our DNA and its system of replication is (microcosm) has only strengthened the design argument.

Chance collisions alone cannot create such specified complexity. Nor can materialists and antitheists get around that problem by saying that the laws of nature oversaw and guided those collisions. In the absence of a transcendent, eternal God who is not simply a part of the natural world, random collisions cannot "create" laws of nature. The laws define a complexity and order that already exists.

Swerving atoms simply cannot make all that we see. "If any-
body thinks that this is possible," Balbus argues,

> I do not see why he should not think that if an infi-
> nite number of examples of the twenty-one letters of
> the [Latin] alphabet, made of gold or what you will,
> were shaken together and poured out on the ground
> it would be possible for them to fall so as to spell out,
> say, the whole text of the *Annals* of Ennius. In fact I
> doubt whether chance would permit them to spell out
> a single verse!
>
> So how can these people [the Epicureans] bring
> themselves to assert that the universe has been created
> by the blind and accidental collisions of inanimate
> particles devoid of colour or any other quality?

Or, to put this in modern parlance: A million monkeys typing
away at a million laptops for a million years will not, by chance,
type out Shakespeare's *Hamlet*. They could not even come close to
typing out the "To be or not to be" soliloquy from Act III.

> Our world is filled with structures that possess
> specified complexity—that is, a recognizable design or
> pattern that has meaning apart from the physical
> structure itself and thus could not have been evolved
> by blind, random forces.

Postscript

> I believe in Spinoza's God who reveals himself in the
> orderly harmony of what exists, not in a God who con-
> cerns himself with fates and actions of human beings.

It seems to me that the idea of a personal God is an anthropological concept which I cannot take seriously. I feel also not able to imagine some will or goal outside the human sphere. My views are near those of Spinoza: admiration for the beauty of and belief in the logical simplicity of the order which we can grasp humbly and only imperfectly.

The author of these two quotes is none other than Albert Einstein. The first dates from 1921; the second from 1947. Taken together they reveal that Einstein, like Spinoza, believed in a God who was ultimately equivalent to the laws of nature.

Of course, one can only believe in Spinoza's God if one believes, as did Spinoza, that both God and nature are eternal. I suggested earlier that if Spinoza had lived after the discovery of the Big Bang, he would nevertheless have persisted in his belief that nature is eternal. I feel quite assured in making that prediction because of an embarrassing little fact about Einstein that is often overlooked. Even when it was becoming clear in the world of physics and cosmology that the universe had a beginning, Einstein resisted the trend, even inventing a fudge factor (the cosmological constant) to account for the growing evidence that the universe was expanding from a single point. (Einstein later dubbed this the biggest blunder of his life.) For all his so-called scientific objectivity, Einstein did not want the universe to have a beginning, did not want it to be contingent upon a power or force or reality outside of itself. He knew quite well the theistic implications of a universe that came into being out of nothing, and he preferred to insulate himself and the scientific community from that uncomfortable knowledge.

In the end, he conceded to the Big Bang, but, as far as I can gather, he never repudiated Spinoza's God. He continued, it seems, to believe that the universe was God and that the laws of nature, rather than some invasive supernatural deity, were calling the shots and defining the *telos* of our world and its rational inhabitants. Traditional-minded Christians, it turns out, are not the only people prone to wishful thinking.

CHAPTER THREE

Miracles

Although I'm embarrassed to admit it, there was a period in my life when I was tempted, on several occasions, to hurl my Bible across the room. I was attending a secular college at the time, and the religion professor had assigned us the Oxford Annotated Bible as our main textbook. Now, it wasn't the Bible itself that tempted me to set the book in flight, but the notes on the various miracles recorded in the Old Testament.

I'm sure some of you will know what I mean. Those scholarly, oh-so-rational notes that set themselves the task of dismissing, disproving, and demystifying the verses to which they are appended. With bravura feats of academic contortion that would make Houdini blush, the writers of my textbook provided "scientific" explanations for every miracle performed in the book of Exodus: The entire Egyptian army, as it turns out, was drowned in a couple of feet of water; the turning of the Nile to blood was a natural phenomenon; and the children of Israel lived for forty years on "the honey-dew excretion of two scale-insects which feed on the twigs of the tamarisk tree." Ugh! Maybe they were right to yearn for the flesh pots of Egypt. No "logical" explanation, I might add, was offered for the killing of the firstborn of Egypt, it being the contention of the scholars, I surmise, that people do, after all, die.

As I read through the notes, I seemed to hear the voice of the annotators crying out in prayer: "Why, O Lord, could Thou not have found a way to get those Jews through the wilderness without messing with the natural order of things? And that Red Sea business! The less said the better."

Now that I've indulged my adolescent urge to scoff, let's get to business and see to what extent biblical miracles do or do not mess with the natural order of things.

Pagan Tales vs. Biblical Miracles

The life of the Roman comic poet Ovid (43 BC–AD 17) overlaps with that of Christ. As such, a period of roughly fifty years separates the writing of the Gospel of Mark from Ovid's great epic, *Metamorphoses* (c. AD 8). Both works are generously sprinkled with miracles of various kinds, and yet, how vastly different are the terrifying transformations in Ovid from the joyous healings, exorcisms, and triumphs over nature that occur in Mark's eyewitness-based account of the life, ministry, death, and resurrection of Christ.

Those who dismiss the miracles in Mark, or the other three Gospels, as pagan literature have clearly not read *Metamorphoses* and pondered the distinctions between the supernatural events recorded in Ovid's mythological compendium and those in Mark's sober biography. To put the difference in the simplest of terms: whereas Ovid's miracles (men and women turning into trees, rocks, birds, insects, and bears at the whim of callous deities) provoke fear, horror, and disgust, the miracles in Mark inspire hope, wonder, and thanksgiving. If Ovid's miracles are true, then we live in an uncaring, arbitrary universe where nothing is stable and life (and identity) has no fixed or final meaning. If the miracles performed by Christ are true, then the God who created nature and ourselves has come among us and begun the redemption of a broken world and a broken humanity. That's why no reader could enjoy *Metamorphoses* if he even vaguely suspected it might be true, but why those who read Mark from the perspective of belief rejoice and are glad.

The great Greco-Roman poets, from Homer and Hesiod to Virgil and Ovid, knew that the law of history was entropy rather than evolution. They all shared a belief that man had devolved from a happy Golden Age of innocence into successive ages of Silver, Bronze, and Iron. And yet, though they knew this, they lacked the two-part biblical revelation that (1) we and our world were fashioned by the loving hands of a single, transcendent God who declared both us and nature to be good, but that (2) we sinned and fell, causing both us and nature to be subjected to futility by the one who made them (see Genesis 1 and 3:17-19 and Romans 8:18-23).

What that means is that, from Christianity's point of view, Aristotle only got it partly right. Aristotle understood well enough that God had written a *telos* into every part of his creation. What he did not know, what he could not have known apart from the special revelation of the Scriptures, is (1) that though the *telos* remains, it has been broken and frustrated; and (2) that the Creator who imbued his creation with purpose has the power and the will to restore that *telos*—in part now, and perfectly in the future.

Unless one knows and understands these two cardinal points, he will not be able to accept, or even grasp, the nature and purpose of miracles. He may cower in fear before whimsical gods—or whimsical priests and medicine men—who threaten him with their magic, but he will not be able either to comprehend or appreciate what miracles really mean.

Ironically, it was not until I read Ovid closely that I was able to understand fully the message conveyed by the miracles I encountered in the Bible. The miracles performed by Moses, Elijah, Elisha, Christ, Peter, and Paul were not an ancient form of entertainment meant to pass the time, or a kind of witchcraft meant to provoke fear (though they did have that temporary effect on the enemies of God); they were a natural outgrowth of God's character and of the broken nature of ourselves and our world.

> Whereas the supernatural stories told in pagan literature provoke fear, horror, and disgust, the miracles recorded in the Bible inspire hope, wonder, and thanksgiving.

The True Nature of Miracles

But don't try to tell that to modern materialists or to the editors of the Oxford Annotated Bible. Such people, whose worship of the laws of nature seems at times to exceed that of pagans for their pantheon of nature gods, are decidedly uncomfortable with the very idea of miracles. They view them as an aberration, an obstruction, rather like a blackout in a major industrialized city; at best an embarrassment, like that bothersome anatomy professor who insists on telling unfunny jokes about the workings of the human body. For such people, miracles are like glitches in a computer program or missing notes in an elaborate symphony. Just when they thought they had it all figured out—just when they thought they had categorized, systematized, methodized everything to the tiniest detail—along comes a miracle to tear down the whole elaborate house of cards.

It's really not fair of God to pull the rug out from under them like that. Here they are in the twenty-first century, monarchs of science, technology, and progress, and all it takes is one little flick of the finger of God to tear down all their conceptions of the proper and natural ordering of the universe—their grand vision of a closed universe run by impersonal laws in which nature is the Sum of Things, the All. Like some Dickensian character who has memorized the railway timetable and lives his life by and in and through its fine web-like intricacies, they have hitched their psyche to a rationalized view of the universe that has emptied the cosmos of all the wonder and mystery that their ancestors once saw in it.

Why, I have asked myself again and again, do so many people in our modern world reject and even mock miracles and those who profess faith in them? Well, why does anyone mock anything? Is it not to hide some deeper wound, to put yet another layer of protection around those old desires and passions that would be better left asleep? Prick beneath the surface of a cynical matron whose acidic tongue is ever quick to burst romantic bubbles, and you will find a shy and sensitive girl jilted one too many times by those she'd set her heart on. Or the worldly wise politician who scorns the young idealist. Was he not once that very same idealist—that is, before he compromised? Facile pop-psychology? Perhaps. But as psychological specimens we are remarkably self-protective.

Slap away our hands a couple of times, and soon we'll stop reaching out. Label us as gullible, and we'll soon stop trusting. Convince us that romance in marriage must eventually die, and we'll kill it ourselves rather than let it happen. With age comes a stiffening: hardening of the arteries, swelling of the joints, wrinkling of the skin. And something far worse: a contraction of the soul, a shriveling of the spirit, a tearing scar in the elasticity of the imagination. Being realistic, we call it growing up, learning to accept the world as it is. I call it a failure of will, an abandonment of wonder, a loss of that third, oft-forgotten virtue: hope.

And what of miracles. What old wound do they reopen, what long-forgotten dreams do they recall to life? Not any wound or dream, but *the* wound, *the* dream. That child-like dream that this world is a garden filled with life and joy and growth; that painful wound when we learn that the world is none of those things. At some point in our lives, we reconcile ourselves to the harsh realities of our world. With painful steps we fall in line with the grinding rhythms of time, death, and decay. We close, often unwillingly, the fantastic box of youthful dreams, and once we do, we would rather it not be opened again.

How impertinent of God to work a miracle that will force us to rethink those practical verities we strove so painfully to achieve. Why teach us to hope all over again when we know what it all will lead to in the end? Just leave us alone; don't tease us with something we can't really have. We don't want to hear that someone has escaped the Cerberean mouth of the devourer—for that someone has only eluded it, not escaped it. And that someone, after all, is not us. For that matter, what good is a miracle? It doesn't really fix anything. If it's not inherent in the fabric of this world, then it must be doomed to fail. It's really just a nuisance, an obstruction, an aberration.

And there, precisely, is where the modern world has got it dead wrong. It is not the miracle that is the aberration but our fallen world with all its death and decay and disease that is the aberration, the mote in the eye of the sun. A miracle is *not* a violation of the laws of nature, but a sublime act during which the Creator, for a brief, glorious moment, restores the truly natural (that is, original) order of his creation.

> A miracle is not a violation of the laws of nature, but a sublime act during which the Creator temporarily restores the original order of his creation.

Why Miracles Must Be Proscribed

That definition of miracles came to me in a flash some two decades ago, and I have not felt any need to revise it. If only the modern materialist could wrap his mind around that definition, he might be willing to reassess his prejudice against miracles. Alas, that prejudice, my reading has taught me, is deeply ingrained in the Western consciousness. Not 300 but 2,300 years ago, Epicurus had already rejected both the possibility and the desirability of divine intervention in the world. His gods lived in a state of sublime blessedness, utterly unconcerned with the troubles or triumphs, sorrows or joys of mortal men. To gain happiness and pleasure—the chief ends of life for Epicurus—one had to achieve complete serenity and peace of mind. But one could not do that if he feared that divine beings might be meddling in the world and in his life.

If we would gain peace of mind as we gaze up into the heavens, writes Epicurus in his "Letter to Pythocles," then we must learn to see only the impersonal, mechanical laws of motion:

> The gods must not be drawn into the discussion in any way, but must be left free from duties and in perfect blessedness. If this warning is neglected, all our explanations of celestial phenomena will be wasted, just as has been true for some who have not held to the method of the possible but have been carried away to what is vain; that is, to the belief that each phenomenon has a single cause. Casting aside all the other possible causes, they are swept into an area where reason

does not apply and are unable to take into account the
things that are seen, from which we ought to receive
suggestions about other things.

It's not just particular miracles that are out of bounds for Epicurus; any mention of the gods in relationship to the physical
workings of the universe is to be proscribed. Reason demands that
all explanations be purely natural; even gods who are themselves
made of matter are to be left out of the conversation.

This must be done, Epicurus asserts, for the sake of his rational,
scientific method of exploration. But it is also, for Epicurus, an
emotional necessity, a way of protecting his coveted peace of mind
from anything that he cannot control and put into a formula. Epicurus is up front about this emotional dimension to his method-
ological naturalism in Chapter XII of his "Principal Doctrines":

It is not possible for one to rid himself of his fears
about the most important things if he does not understand the nature of the universe but dreads some of
the things he has learned in the myths. Therefore it is
not possible to gain unmixed happiness without natural science.

If only modern materialists were as honest as Epicurus about
the role the natural sciences often play in insulating us from the
unpredictability of, and our accountability to, the divine. Just
the word *science* is often enough to scare away the shadows of the
supernatural, the vestiges of the divine that haunt our world and
our dreams.

Epicurus, like his epic successor Lucretius, makes it clear that
the fear of punishment after death is the chief thing that their materialist teachings protect their disciples from. But Epicurus, in his

"Letter to Menoeceus," adds to the fear of death and judgment the popular belief that "the gods send great evils to the wicked, great blessings to the righteous, for they, being always well disposed to their own virtues, approve those who are like themselves, regarding as foreign all that is different."

If even this just distribution of divine favor/disfavor were true, it would blot out Epicurus's peace of mind and leave him prey to incertitude. No, the world must be purged of all supernatural intervention, whether it come in the form of fairies casting spells, lustful gods changing into bulls and swans to seduce mortal women, or the incarnate Son of God giving sight to the blind, walking on water to rescue his terrified disciples, feeding 5,000 hungry men with a few meager loaves and fish, and setting free poor captives who had been bound for years by the lies and the malice of the devil.

No, say the Epicureans of the past and present, we must close the door on all of that intrusive metaphysical claptrap; let none of it slip by. To allow even one miracle into the laboratory is to jeopardize the method, the system, the protective wall. Let one miracle in and anything—anything!—is possible. Why, a man might even rise from the dead.

> By purging the world of miracles, Epicureans and modern materialists alike protect themselves from the fear of exposure that accompanies supernatural intrusion.

Efficient Causes in Disguise

Please do not be fooled. No one from Epicurus's day to our own has disproved miracles; our scientific, educational, and political leaders have simply stopped believing in them. And, because they have, they have rewritten the rules so that no one else, not even readers of scholarly Bibles, can believe in them either.

Enlightenment thinker David Hume, as I'll show in a moment, played one of the central roles in this rewriting. However, nearly all his arguments were anticipated a century earlier by Spinoza. In the preface to Part IV of his *Ethics*, Spinoza clearly rejects not only the biblical teaching that nature has been subjected to futility, but the Aristotelian teaching that nature has a *telos*. For Spinoza, it is not God but we ourselves who impose a *telos* on nature. The laws of nature simply exist, and have done so for all time. They were not created or designed; like God and nature, they simply are.

Behind Spinoza's rejection of nature's purposiveness and brokenness lies his deeper and more foundational rejection of all final causes. There are only efficient causes in Spinoza's universe. One material action causes another material action; there is no higher, ultimate purpose behind any of the actions. Indeed, every time we think we have found a bona fide final cause, it merely turns out to be another efficient cause. Nothing can be traced back to the "will of God" or to some hidden divine plan. Remember that Spinoza's God has no passions or desires and does not choose or promise or redeem.

The point here is so vital that it merits a lengthy quotation:

> ...we see that men are in the habit of calling natural phenomena perfect or imperfect from their own preconceptions rather than from true knowledge... Nature does not act with an end in view...the eternal and infinite being, whom we call God, or Nature, acts by the same necessity whereby it exists...Therefore, just as he does not exist for an end, so he does not act for an end; just as there is no beginning or

end to his existing, so there is no beginning or end to his acting. What is termed a "final cause" is nothing but human appetite in so far as it is considered as the starting-point or primary cause of some thing. For example, when we say that being a place of habitation was the final cause of this or that house, we surely mean no more than this, that a man, from thinking of the advantages of domestic life, had an urge to build a house. Therefore, the need for a habitation in so far as it is considered as a final cause is nothing but this particular urge, which is in reality an efficient cause, and is considered as the prime cause because men are commonly ignorant of the causes of their own urges; for, as I have repeatedly said, they are conscious of their action and appetites but unaware of the causes by which they are determined to seek something. As to the common saying that Nature sometimes fails or blunders and produces imperfect things, I count this among the fictions...(preface to Part IV).

Were the author of this passage to be presented with incontrovertible proof of a miracle, it would make no difference. There is no need for miracles in his natural world, for his natural world is not fallen or broken—it simply is as it has always been. Nor would his God be able or willing to initiate a miracle, for he is identical with that unfallen nature.

Our desire for miracles, our yearning that this world and our bodies would be what we know they should be, what the *telos* inside us tells us they should be, does not, for Spinoza, point to God, creation, and the fall. The desire is no more than an animal urge, a passion whose origin is purely natural. We may fool ourselves into believing that our desire for the restoration and renewal of ourselves and our world is the result of a final, spiritual cause, but that does not take away from the brute "fact" that the cause is efficient and material.

Spinoza makes a similar argument in the preface to Part III, but there he does so with reference to our emotions. Those who claim that their emotions are affected by something outside of nature, Spinoza writes, are woefully mistaken, for nothing exists outside of nature.

> Most of those who have written about the emotions and human conduct seem to be dealing not with natural phenomena that follow the common ways of Nature but with phenomena outside Nature. They appear to go so far as to conceive man in Nature as a kingdom within a kingdom. They believe that he disturbs rather than follows Nature's order, and has absolute power over his actions, and is determined by no other source than himself. Again, they assign the cause of human weakness and frailty not to the power of Nature in general, but to some defect in human nature, which they therefore bemoan, ridicule, despise, or, as is most frequently the case, abuse.

Spinoza knows very well that from a Judeo-Christian point of view, we are precisely a kingdom within a kingdom. Yes, in terms of our physical body, we are part of the animal kingdom, but, on account of the divine soul God breathed into us at creation, there is a part of us that transcends nature. That part of us, like nature itself, is fallen, weak, defective, and frail, but we can and will be redeemed. In the end, body and soul together will be restored and resurrected and will dwell on a renewed and perfected earth.

But not for Spinoza. The struggle within our emotions and our will is not linked to the competing influences of God's creative purpose and the ill effects of the fall. As with our perceptions of natural phenomena, we wrongfully convince ourselves that we are responding to a higher final cause, when, in reality, we only think this way because we are ignorant of the efficient causes behind our emotions.

> For Spinoza, what Aristotle or Aquinas would call a final cause is just an efficient cause in disguise, an animal urge that we don't recognize as such.

Tracing Out Chains of Causation

Once I understood what Spinoza was trying to say, once I realized that he had truly convinced himself that there was no higher purpose behind our actions, no divine plan that required eyes of faith to see, it helped me to further grasp the modern refusal to accept miracles. But there was one more step to go before it all came clear. Spinoza's method for simultaneously canceling out miracles and final causes went beyond labeling everything an efficient cause. It meant nothing less than constructing a material *chain* of efficient causes that leads back and back to…well, back to something or other.

Spinoza never solves, or even addresses, the problem of infinite regress as it is described by Aristotle and Aquinas. I suppose he thinks he solved it by positing the existence of God, but that does not solve the problem; for, as we saw in the previous chapter, Spinoza's God is fully immanent in nature and does not cause anything.

Spinoza can cast miracles out of his system, for he believed he could explain everything by means of a material chain of causation: not only physical occurrences, but emotional, mental (cognitive), and imaginative ones as well. Again, Spinoza, like Epicurus before him, does *not* disprove miracles; he simply will not allow them into his materialistic system. All things *must* have a "scientific" explanation, via a known or unknown materialistic chain of causes. No amount of evidence can or could make Spinoza budge from that assumption. Of course, if Spinoza is right and God is equivalent to nature—if, that is, there is no separate supernatural Person who transcends time and space—then miracles (as well as prophecy) become impossibilities.

Materialists from Epicurus to Richard Dawkins have, in one form or another, accused religious believers of clinging to a "God of the gaps" theology. If we don't understand something, we ascribe it to the workings of God (or the gods). There is, admittedly, much truth to this claim. But then those who level this criticism are almost always guilty themselves of what might be called a "science of the gaps" antitheology. Just give us more time, they promise, and we will discover how an unguided, material chain of causation managed to fine-tune our universe for human life, assemble the DNA, and create human consciousness—or, to return to the focus of this chapter, rescue the Jews from Egypt and empower the miraculous birth, ministry, and resurrection of Jesus.

Two centuries after Spinoza, another denier of miracles and of the possibility of miracles got so carried away with his rhetoric that he all but admitted his "science of the gaps" faith. I speak of T.H. Huxley (1825–1895), better known as Darwin's bulldog for his success at popularizing and defending evolution. After ridiculing older scientists for seeking a spiritual force or designer or director behind the unique and life-giving properties of water, Huxley makes the following prophecy:

> ...we live in the hope and in the faith that, by the

advance of molecular physics, we shall by and by be
able to see our way as clearly from the constituents of
water to the properties of water, as we are now able to
deduce the operations of a watch from the form of its
parts and the manner in which they are put together.

Like the Pre-Socratics before him, Huxley (and the same is true
for Spinoza) is concerned only with questions of *what* and *how*; all
why and *who* questions are irrelevant. As long as we can identify all
the material parts and their operations, then we need not bother
ourselves with anything so "unscientific" as final causes.

Please note that Huxley clarifies his point by making an analogy
to the operations of a watch. The choice of analogy is by no means
random; it is meant by Huxley as a refutation of Paley's argument
that the complex design of a watch points backward to a designer.
Not so for Huxley. Like Spinoza, he feels assured that if he can
understand all the parts and how they work together—the material chain of causation—then he can simply substitute the need for
a final cause (who designed the watch and why) with a series of efficient causes (this is how each separate gear affects the gear next to
it and what happens when all the gears work together).

> For Spinoza and Huxley, what we call a miracle is just
> an event whose material chain of causation we have
> not yet discovered; given enough time, science will
> learn to identify and trace that chain.

The Great Miracle-Basher

The past 2,500 years have given birth to scores of thinkers who
have not only rejected specific miracles but denied the very possibility of their occurring. Among them was one of our Founding
Fathers, Thomas Jefferson, who, though a believer in God, refused

to believe that the Supreme Being would monkey around with the laws of nature. So sure was he of this that he put together his own version of the Gospels in which he crossed out all the miracles, including the resurrection, leaving only Jesus's teachings. At least the editors of the Oxford Annotated Bible left in the miracles that they worked so hard to explain away in the notes!

The agenda of those editors was by no means the same as that of Jefferson, nor was either of their agendas similar to that of Spinoza. And yet behind all three lies the Epicurean faith that if we will only agree to confine all inquiry to efficient causes, then we can comfort ourselves with the belief that we live in a closed universe, one in which nature, or some impersonal God-nature fusion, is the Sum of All. But if we dare to allow even one final cause into our investigations, then we risk breaking open that closed universe to outside interference. And once we do that, miracles become not only possible but expected—especially if that open universe is run by an all-powerful, all-loving God who is actively involved in his creation and who has promised to heal its brokenness and transform its futility into fruition.

Many philosophers have played their part in barricading the doors of the universe against miracles. However, of all the barricaders, the one who has had the most influence is the Scottish philosopher David Hume (1711–1776). Hume devotes a full chapter to the subject of miracles in his *An Enquiry Concerning Human Understanding* (1748), a chapter that begins with his bold claim that he, David Hume, will, in the space of twenty pages, settle once and for all the pesky problem of miracles:

> I flatter myself, that I have discovered an argument
> of a like nature, which, if just, will, with the wise
> and learned, be an everlasting check to all kinds of

superstitious delusions, and consequently, will be use-
ful as long as the world endures. For so long, I presume,
will the accounts of miracles and prodigies be found in
all history, sacred and profane.

Like Spinoza, and so many before and after him, Hume makes
no distinction between the sober miracles recorded in the Gospels
and "superstitious delusions." Indeed, he takes for granted that
only the "wise and learned" will heed his arguments; the ignorant
masses will go on believing in miracles no matter what he says.

Hume fancies his argument will be fully objective, based solely
on reason, logic, and probability, but he loads the deck by defining the word *miracle* as "a transgression of a law of nature by a
particular volition of the Deity, or by the interposition of some
invisible agent." Like Spinoza, Hume worshiped at the shrine of
the Laws of Nature, and, as such, dedicated himself to preserving
them from all blasphemers who would dare to question their fixed
purity and supremacy. If a miracle dared to violate that purity and
supremacy, it would have to be banished from Hume's tight, well-
lit closed system.

> According to Hume, miracles violate the laws of
> nature and thus cannot be admitted into his closed
> universe.

Christian Cross-Examination #1: Miracles Suspend, Not Break, the Laws of Nature

So runs Hume's argument, an argument whose simplicity and
directness has frightened away many educated people from even
considering the possibility that miracles can happen. But Hume's
argument is based on a false definition. As C.S. Lewis effectively
argues in *Miracles* (1947), a book that deserves a much wider

reading than it has received, miracles do not, in fact, violate or transgress the laws of nature. Rather than break the laws that God himself established, miracles suspend them for a time. If I catch a falling vase and thus prevent it from smashing on the ground, I have not broken the law of gravity; I have merely suspended it by adding in an unexpected outside factor. If I let go of the vase, gravity will take over again, and the vase will fall and shatter.

The laws of physics determine what will happen to the billiard balls on a table if I hit one of them at a certain angle and with a certain amount of force. But if, while the ball is in motion, a hand reaches out and shakes the table, that pattern will be altered—not because the laws of physics have been broken, but because new information has been added in. When a miracle occurs, God's hand reaches into our world and catches the vase or shakes the table. But when he withdraws it, the laws of nature resume their normal course. That is why everyone whom Jesus healed in Palestine eventually died.

God's presence in nature in the incarnate Christ, Lewis argues, does not destroy nature but shows forth its hidden glory. Every day, water turns into wine and a few fish become many fish, but the process is slow and mostly invisible to the human eye. But when Christ, the one who created the mystery of fruitfulness, fermentation, and procreation, causes it to happen quickly and in a specific spot, we see the miracle that was always there and realize that the God of nature is in our midst.

Now, Lewis says, not all miracles are like that. A few of them—walking on water and the resurrection, in particular—offer a glimpse of what nature will be in her restored state of perfection, when the bounds of time and space have been overcome and the dwelling of God is with men (Revelation 21:3). Still, whatever the

exact kind or type, all the miracles in the Bible attest to God's
sovereign power over nature, health, and life itself. They are not
random, capricious, and terrifying, as they are in Ovid's *Metamorphoses*, nor do they smack of what Hume calls "the miraculous accounts of travellers" with "their descriptions of sea and land
monsters, their relations of wonderful adventures, strange men,
and uncouth manners."

Hume's protestations aside, there is nothing intrinsically ludicrous, barbarous, or fanciful about the miracles that crowd themselves around the Exodus of the Jews from Egypt, the prophetic
careers of Elijah and Elisha, the ministry of Jesus, and the spread of
the early church. Far from presenting us with a chaotic, arbitrary
world out of whack, they display a broken world being guided
back into wholeness by its Creator. The plagues on Egypt followed
by the parting of the Red Sea are not extravagant old wives' tales
but pointed, even calculated methods used by God to display his
sovereignty over the false gods of Egypt and to free his people
from bondage. As for the miracles performed by Jesus, it must be
remembered that none of Jesus's enemies denied his miraculous
powers; they simply ascribed his power to the devil (Mark 3:22).

Still, Hume insists, the testimonies that have come down to us
to substantiate the miracles of Jesus are too old and too incapable of
back-checking for us to weigh that over against what Hume never
relents from considering to be the impossibility of miracles: impossible because they break the laws of nature, and that, in Hume's
Spinozan vision of the universe, cannot be done. For more than
two centuries, Hume and his heirs have intimidated Christians,
especially those in academia, from mounting a rational defense of
miracles, convincing them instead to withdraw into the precincts
of the church and share their testimonies in private.

> Christ's miracles do not destroy nature but show forth
> its hidden glory; they are a sign to the world that the
> God who made nature is in our midst.

Christian Cross-Examination #2: The Resurrection Can Withstand Scrutiny

Thankfully, though, Humean hegemony in the area of miracles has broken down over the past few decades as Christians have boldly defended the historical claims on which their faith is based. The year 2011 even gave us a monumental, 1,200-page, two-volume, extensively researched and annotated work by Craig Keener, *Miracles: The Credibility of the New Testament Accounts*, which not only uses modern research methods and textual criticism to substantiate the authenticity of the miracles recorded in the Gospels and Acts, but documents the millions of people all over the world who have witnessed miracles of every variety—most of which cannot be explained away by "scientific" explanations.

However, the single most important development in the Christian defense of miracles is the large and ever-growing number of books on the resurrection of Jesus. As Paul makes clear in 1 Corinthians 15, the truth of the Christian faith rests squarely on the bodily resurrection of Christ. If Christ did not rise, Paul concedes, then our faith is useless and Christians are to be pitied rather than admired (verses 12-19). Belief in the literal, historical miracle of the resurrection is not optional for Christians; it is the foundation of their faith and their hope.

Hume claims that his disproof of miracles rests on probability and the weighing of evidence; he even refers several times to how an impartial judge might respond to the testimonies of people who claim to have witnessed a miracle. On that point, modern

Christian apologists wholeheartedly agree. Just how *would* a judge rule on the resurrection if he were presented with the evidence presented in the four Gospels?

Modern skeptics think they can dismiss the historical reliability of the resurrection because the various testimonies recorded in the four Gospels show slight discrepancies. In making this argument, the skeptics show that they know little of how a trial works. Were the testimonies in the Gospels carbon copies of one another, an impartial judge would count that evidence for collusion and throw out the testimony. If, on the other hand, the testimonies varied widely on important points, he would dismiss them as unreliable. What an experienced and discerning judge looks for are testimonies that complement, rather than copy, one another, agreeing on the major points, but showing the kinds of variations one would expect from witnesses who have different personalities, memories, and points of view. And that is exactly what we find in the Gospels.

But what of the news to which the witnesses bore testimony? Well, it is a simple fact of history that Jesus's tomb was empty on that first Easter morning. What happened to the body? Is there a natural, rational, "scientific" explanation for what happened to the body? If so, then we can give the benefit of the doubt to Hume. If not, then, whatever our materialistic presuppositions about miracles might be, we have to at least concede the possibility that Jesus rose from the dead, especially given the fact that this event miraculously changed his disciples from cowering defeated followers of a dead religious leader to bold witnesses to a faith for which they gladly gave their lives.

Let us eliminate, then, the chief naturalistic explanation for the empty tomb:

- Perhaps the Pharisees or the Romans stole the body…but if they did, they would have produced it and thus ended Christianity at its very birth.

- Perhaps thieves stole the body…but if they did, they would not have taken the body but the expensive burial cloths.

- Perhaps the disciples stole the body…but this is logically and psychologically unsound. History presents us with people who have been willing to die for something they believed (often falsely) to be true, but if the disciples stole the body, then they died painful martyr deaths for something they *knew was a hoax*.

- Perhaps the disciples only imagined or hallucinated that they saw the risen body of Christ…but the eyewitness evidence does not bear this theory out. Jesus was seen not only by individuals but by groups of varying sizes, and at different locales and times of day. Furthermore, the eyewitnesses claimed not only to have seen Jesus but to have touched him and even watched him eat (Luke 24:37-43; John 20:27; 21:15).

- Perhaps Jesus was still alive when he was put in the tomb…but based on what we now know about Roman crucifixion techniques, that is untenable. Besides, even if Jesus could have survived and pushed aside the stone blocking his tomb, his near-dead state would have convinced no one he had triumphed over death.

- Perhaps the women, being in an agitated state,

entered the wrong tomb on Easter Sunday and
jumped to the false conclusion that Jesus had
risen…but if that were the case, there would still
have been a body for the Pharisees to find and
produce.

As difficult as it may be for the Humean mind to accept, the
apostles' historical claim that Jesus rose bodily from the dead offers
the only logical solution to the disappearance of Jesus's body.

And please note that this inductive, rather than deductive, argument for the resurrection does not rest on a belief that the Gospels were directly inspired by God. It merely makes the historically
sound claim that the Gospels—whose textual reliability far exceeds
that of any other document from the ancient world—preserve a
reliable record of the eyewitness testimony. And I would claim,
along with a growing number of scholars, that that evidence would
be sufficient to convince an impartial judge—one who did not
take for granted that miracles violate the laws of nature and are thus
impossible—of the historical truth of the resurrection.

> A modern impartial judge would most likely accept as
> authentic the collective, complementary testimonies
> of those who witnessed the resurrection.

Postscript

A friend of mine who teaches history once suggested to me that
the strongest argument for the existence of God was the Jewish
people. How else can one explain the persistence, cultural homo-
geneity, and continued influence of the Jews through millennia of
unending persecution, including numerous attempted holocausts,
than that they were, as the Bible records, chosen by God? I end
with this rather creative argument not only because it constitutes

proof of God's miraculous intervention in human history, but because it uncovers one of the deeper, more emotional reasons that thinkers like Hume and Spinoza have been so categorical in their rejection of miracles.

In the second-to-last paragraph of his chapter on miracles, Hume lists, in order to ridicule and reject, the "miracles" recorded in the Five Books of Moses. I was not surprised to see on that list the Garden of Eden and the fall, the lengthy lifespans of the early patriarchs, the Flood, and the exodus from Egypt. But I was taken aback that Hume felt the need to add the following to his list of falsehoods that no serious person could accept: "Of the arbitrary choice of one people, as the favourites of heaven; and that people the countrymen of the author." We might be able to dismiss this comment as an instance of British anti-Semitism, until we remember that the Jewish Spinoza also denied, quite vehemently, the chosenness of the Jewish people.

This discomfort with, if not outright anger against, the clear biblical teaching that the Jews are the chosen people is felt strongly today by many educated Jews and Gentiles in the West. Though I can't prove it by scientific experimentation, I would argue that much of the modern rejection of the elect status of the Jews and of miracles comes from the same source: a deep-seated offense against, and envy of, the "unfair" notion that some people should be chosen and others not, some healed and some left to suffer pain.

PART TWO:

The Nature of Knowledge

CHAPTER FOUR

Seeing Is Believing

Several years ago, I was asked by a friend of mine to speak with an elderly radio evangelist who had been dissuading his listeners from reading C.S. Lewis. As I guessed, the man did not actually own any of Lewis's books; he had only read a misleading article on the Internet that had accused Lewis of holding views that did not square with a narrow definition of evangelical Christianity.

As I said, that did not surprise me. What *did* surprise me was the answer the man gave me when I asked him if he had read The Chronicles of Narnia. "Ever since I became a Christian forty years ago," he replied, "I have not read a single work of fiction." Now, if you were to ask that man why he did not read fiction, he would say it was because he was a Christian. But the *real* reason, I would argue, the reason that he himself was unaware of, was that he was a modernist and did not know it.

Though the man was a strong orthodox believer who had led many people to faith in Christ, he had bought in, subconsciously, to that part of the modernist worldview that privileges nonfiction over fiction, reason over imagination, the logical over the intuitive, the head over the heart. He believed that every word in the Bible, including the miracles, was true; yet he was, in his everyday life, suspicious of anything that wasn't clear, factual, and verifiable by logic.

Could that man, and others like him, have debated Hume, he would have done his best to defend the historical reliability of the Bible and the rational consistency of Christian doctrine. But, in the process, he would have unwillingly and unknowingly conceded too much to his opponent. Don't get me wrong, believers should and must muster all their reasoning skill in defense of Christianity. But they must be careful that, in doing so, they don't drive too sharp a wedge between faith and reason.

The Facts/Values Split

Near the end of his dismissive chapter on miracles in *An Enquiry Concerning Human Understanding*, Hume reveals a foundational prejudice of the Enlightenment that, though it has always been with us, has gained increasing ascendancy over the last two-and-a-half centuries. It is a prejudice that has seriously undermined, and continues to seriously undermine, the authenticity of Christianity. Yet Hume presents it, with amazing audacity, as a defense of the Christian religion.

Summing up his chapter, Hume asserts one final time that we should be quicker to reject, as violations of the truth, all eyewitness testimonies to a miracle than to accept the truth of the miracle, which itself constitutes a violation of the laws of nature—especially when those testimonies are tied to religion. He then quotes a corroborating passage from Francis Bacon in which Bacon counsels his readers to treat with "severe scrutiny" anything that smacks of magic and with healthy suspicion anything "which in any degree depends upon religion." Hume then comments:

> I am the better pleased with the method of reasoning here delivered, as I think it may serve to confound those dangerous friends or disguised enemies to the *Christian Religion*, who have undertaken to defend it

by the principles of human reason. Our most holy religion is founded on *Faith*, not on reason; and it is a sure method of exposing it to put it to such a trial as it is, by no means, fitted to endure.

There you have it, that cornerstone of Enlightenment thinking that most writers today refer to as the facts/values split. Christianity is to be tolerated, perhaps even cautiously celebrated, but only if it confines itself to issues of faith and emotion and leaves reason and logic to the scientists. Its followers may enjoy their faith and, if they aren't too rude, share it with others, but they must under no circumstance try to defend it with rational, logical, scientific arguments. If they try to do that, they will only succeed in looking and sounding ridiculous.

To prove something in our post-Enlightenment world means to appeal solely to experience and experimentation, to observations made by the five senses. Christians are a-rational, a-logical people who believe things not *because of* evidence, but *in the face of* evidence. Thus, Hume concludes his chapter on miracles by asserting that

> the *Christian Religion* not only was at first attended with miracles [under which category Hume includes prophecies], but even at this day cannot be believed by any reasonable person without one. Mere reason is insufficient to convince us of its veracity: And whoever is moved by *Faith* to assent to it, is conscious of a continued miracle in his own person, which subverts all the principles of his understanding, and gives him a determination to believe what is most contrary to custom and experience.

That is what is known in the trade as a backhanded compliment.

Hume makes it quite clear that the only "miracle" he believes in is the miraculous ability some people have of believing in things that violate logic, common sense, and the established laws of nature. Indeed, Hume comes very close here to defining faith as "the power to believe in things we know aren't true."

Now, the radio evangelist I mentioned above would, of course, have disagreed sharply with Hume's contention that Christianity is nonrational. And yet by insisting himself that facts should always be given priority over fiction, he inadvertently supports and furthers Hume's program of championing facts over values, stories, and faith.

> For Hume, religion is solely a matter of faith and values; to attempt to defend it rationally, through appeals to logic and facts, is to render it ridiculous.

Hume on Religion

It was only after I came to realize the central role that Hume had played in reducing Christianity from a rational worldview to an emotional faith that I learned, to my great surprise, that he had authored a book on religion that he modeled closely on Cicero's *The Nature of the Gods* (see chapter 2). Just as Cicero invites us to sit in on a debate between a Stoic, an Epicurean, and an academic, so Hume, in his highly readable *Dialogues Concerning Natural Religion* (1779), mounts a debate between Cleanthes, who bases his arguments on experience (particularly the argument by design), Demea, who takes a more mystical approach that treats God as wholly other (his focus is the ontological argument of Anselm), and Philo, who takes a middle position and seems to be Hume's mouthpiece.

Like Cicero's *Nature of the Gods*, Hume's *Dialogues* begins by taking for granted the existence of God, then attempts, through logical debate, to arrive at his character and his attributes. Although both inductive and deductive arguments are made, none of the speakers appeals to the Bible or to any other form of divine revelation. Indeed, nothing specifically Christian is ever mentioned in the *Dialogues*. Hume keeps things firmly in the precincts of deism, making no reference at all to the Trinity, the incarnation, the atonement, the resurrection, miracles, or even the Ten Commandments and the Sermon on the Mount.

If truth be told, nobody in the *Dialogues* comes within a mile of Christian orthodoxy. Only in the second-to-last-paragraph does Hume surprise us by having Philo, his supposed mouthpiece, contemplate how limited our reason is in understanding the true nature and ways of God. Exasperated by those limits, Philo exclaims,

> ...the most natural sentiment, which a well-disposed mind will feel on this occasion, is a longing desire and expectation, that heaven would be pleased to dissipate, at least alleviate this profound ignorance, by affording some more particular revelation to mankind, and making discoveries of the nature, attributes, and operations of the divine object of our faith. A person, seasoned with a just sense of the imperfections of natural reason, will fly to revealed truth with the greatest avidity: While the haughty dogmatist, persuaded that he can erect a complete system of theology by the mere help of philosophy, disdains any farther aid, and rejects this adventitious instructor. To be a philosophical sceptic is, in a man of letters, the first and most essential step towards being a sound, believing *Christian*.

This passage marks the one and only time in the *Dialogues* that Hume mentions the word *Christian* or invokes the Christian concept of revelation. But does he agree with Philo?

At first, the answer seems to be a resounding no. Hume's other works make it clear that he had no belief himself in the doctrines of the faith or gave any credence to what Christians claim to be the special revelation of the Bible. And yet, on second thought, it appears that Hume *does* agree with Philo—at least in a backhanded sort of way. By having Philo embrace Christianity and revelation only at the moment that he abandons reason, Hume subtly perpetuates the Enlightenment split of facts and values.

What Hume actually advocates at the close of the *Dialogues* is a kind of fideism that allows faith to take the place of logical, reasoned analysis. There is no middle ground for Hume; anyone who wishes to be an orthodox believer must abandon his intellect at the church door and move forward on blind faith and feeling alone. And so, ironically, at the very moment Hume seems to be conceding defeat, he is really declaring the triumph of reason and logic over emotion and intuition. If a Christian must give up his mind to believe, then Christianity hardly seems an honorable option for a man of learning and refinement.

And that takes us back to *An Enquiry Concerning Human Understanding*, where Hume, in his third-to-last paragraph, has this to say about the "science" of religion:

> Divinity or Theology, as it proves the existence of a Deity, and the immortality of souls, is composed partly of reasonings concerning particular, partly concerning general facts. It has a foundation in *reason*, so far as it is supported by experience. But its best and most solid foundation is *faith* and divine revelation.

There can, it seems, be reason in religion, but if and only if the element of reason is directly and securely linked to experience. Once anything like faith or revelation steps in, we move outside of reason and experience into the world of the abstract and the a-logical.

In many ways, Hume anticipates the work of the American pragmatist William James (1842–1910), who, in *The Varieties of Religious Experience* (1902), reduces religion to its emotional content and its factors of personal desire and need. In our post-Humean world, religion loses its ability to make rational truth claims; all it can do is observe the way subjective beliefs and feelings impact our objective behavior.

> Hume would have us believe that the true Christian must leave his intellect behind every time he enters a church.

Nonoverlapping Magisteria

All I have presented thus far in this chapter I have said to prepare the ground for one of the most persistent attacks on religion in general and Christianity in particular: an attack that is all the more pernicious because it comes in the guise of a flattering, seemingly win-win compromise. The compromise itself dates back at least as far as the Pre-Socratics, but it was given its clearest expression at the turn of the twenty-first century by the late evolutionist Stephen Jay Gould.

Men of science and men of faith, Gould argued, would do well to accept what he called "non-overlapping magisteria" (or NOMA). According to NOMA, the religious community must agree to yield to the scientific community the prerogative for studying and speaking with authority about the physical, material world—the world we perceive through our senses—while the scientific community must reciprocate by leaving issues of morality and ultimate meaning to be determined by the churches and seminaries. As compromises go, it sounds wonderfully sweet and appealing—but only if you are on the science end of the bargain. For any true person of faith, accepting NOMA amounts to nothing less than a deal with the devil.

For NOMA, whether it is offered by an ancient, medieval, or post-Enlightenment skeptic, brings with it two consequences. The first, which I will take up in the next chapter, is that followers of God lose the ability to make any absolute truth statements not only in the realm of science, but in the realms of morality (the Good), philosophy (the True), and aesthetics (the Beautiful) as well. The second, to which I will devote this chapter, is that once the deal is made, things can only count as true, important, and binding if they come to us via our five senses or experience. In a word, embracing NOMA means embracing the unquestioned dominion of empiricism.

But what exactly is empiricism, and what are its implications for Christianity and the more general religious worldview? It was not until I found answers to these questions that I was able to understand why the secular humanists who dominate the academy and the media find it so easy to dismiss those central religious issues that, for most of human history, have occupied, if not consumed, the thoughts and dreams, hopes and fears of the majority of people.

> According to Gould's concept of NOMA, matters of fact should be left to the scientists, while values and morality should be left to the priests.

A Brief History of Empiricism

"If I can't see it, smell it, taste it, touch it, or hear it, it don't exist."

That's empiricism in a nutshell. Or, to put it in an even smaller nut-shell: Seeing is believing. In one sense, the desire to limit the scope of reality to what we can perceive through our senses is as old as the Pre-Socratics, though Parmenides went to the other extreme, treating our senses as wholly unreliable. Plato set philosophy off on a stable path by arguing that the unseen things are far more real and eternal than the things we perceive with our eyes and ears, while yet avoiding Parmenides's total distrust of the senses. Plato did this by making a seminal distinction between our mortal, imperfect earth, the World of Becoming, where things are ever in a state of flux, and the immortal realm of the heavenly Forms, the World of Being, where things exist in unchanging perfection. We perceive the former with our physical eye, but the latter with our mind's eye.

The power of Plato's philosophical vision, mingled with the revelation of the New Testament and the writings of Augustine, held at bay, for almost two millennia, any kind of aggressive empiricism that would seek to overthrow the greater reality of the unseen world. With the Renaissance, however, there came a renewed focus on this world and a slow groping after a new kind of science that would be more practical and give us more control over nature. As the father of the scientific method, Francis Bacon (1561–1626) moved Europe away from deductive logic, which begins with general, usually unproven statements and works its way down to particulars (often bypassing the need for actual experiments), toward inductive logic that begins with careful observation and the accumulation of physical data and then works its way up toward a maxim or principle.

By doing so, Bacon set in motion the slow ascendancy of the senses, and yet it is really not fair to lay empiricism, especially in its extreme form, at his feet. Bacon ever sought to find a middle way between empiricism, with its concern only for facts, and the opposite extreme of rationalism, with its concern only for abstract reason and logic. Bacon, in *The New Organon* (1620), expresses this desire in a wonderful metaphor that later empiricists such as Locke, Hume, Bentham, James Mill, and John Stuart Mill would have done well to adopt. The true philosopher-scientist (or natural philosopher), Bacon writes, should not be like the empirical ant, who collects things it finds outside of itself, nor like the rationalist spider, who spins its web out of itself and its own self-centered ruminations, but like the bee, who gathers pollen and then transforms it within itself.

As we move from Bacon to Hobbes (1588–1679), the bee loses its wings and begins to settle down into ant-dom. Thus, Hobbes begins his *Leviathan* (1651) by boldly stating that "there is no conception in a man's mind which hath not at first, totally or by parts, been begotten upon the organs of sense. The rest are derived from that original." Together with this narrowed focus on the senses, Hobbes furthered Bacon's shift from deduction to induction by insisting that all conclusions be reached not by an appeal to authority—whether that authority be Aristotle, Cicero, or Aquinas—but by direct experience of the real world. As part of this dual program, Hobbes sought to purge and purify language of its metaphorical "imprecision," a program that, when carried out, ever marks the death of religious-spiritual-metaphysical terminology. Indeed, it would do just that in the later work of Hume, T.H. Huxley, and John Stuart Mill.

Still, empiricism does not stand at the center of *Leviathan*. Hobbes is far more concerned with political and social issues, a concern that leads him, in spite of his empirical presuppositions, to appeal frequently to the revelation of Scripture. The full flowering of empiricism would have to await the theories of John Locke (1632–1704), especially as they are set forth in *An Essay Concerning Human Understanding* (1689).

> Empiricism, the belief that information gained
> through the senses is the only reliable source of
> knowledge, privileges induction over deduction,
> experience over authority, and scientific terminology
> over metaphysical and metaphorical language.

Empiricism with a Vengeance

Like Hobbes before him, Locke was greatly influenced by the British Civil War. He was still a teenager when the Puritan revolutionaries, led by Oliver Cromwell, executed the Anglican King Charles I (1649) and set up a radical democracy that was also a low Protestant theocracy; and he lived, as did Hobbes, to see the monarchy restored in 1660 under the Anglo-Catholic Charles II. Unlike Hobbes, however, Locke went on to watch as England almost returned to Catholicism under James II, a fear that got Locke embroiled in the failed Shaftesbury-Monmouth plot to overthrow James II, which got him exiled to the Netherlands for five years until the Glorious Revolution (1688) allowed him to return to a securely Protestant England in 1689.

These experiences, together with the more general wars of religion between Catholics and Protestants that raged across Europe over the course of the seventeenth century, helped to convince Locke, as it had Hobbes, that he and his fellow Englishmen should henceforth only focus on things about which they could be certain and not disagree or fight over issues (like religion!) that lacked certitude. This desire for certitude also caused Locke, in the manner of Hobbes, to privilege experience over authority, to steer away from spiritual and metaphysical terminology, and to champion empiricism.

Indeed, Locke is an empiricist with a vengeance. He begins his *Essay* by utterly and categorically rejecting the belief that our soul is born with any kind of innate or intuitive knowledge. To the contrary, Locke asserts in Book II, Chapter 1, Paragraph 2 that each of us comes into the world as a white paper (or blank slate—*tabula rasa* in Latin) onto which experience-based sensations are written. "Our observation employed either about *external sensible objects; or about the internal operations of our minds, perceived and reflected on by ourselves, is that, which supplies our understandings with all the materials of thinking.* These two are the fountains of knowledge, from whence all the ideas we have, or can naturally have, do spring" (emphasis in original).

For Locke, *all* our knowledge and understanding—which rational faculties set us apart from the beasts—comes from a two-step process: (1) *sensation*, when we experience the world through our five senses; and (2) *reflection*, when our mind perceives and reflects on the information that comes through the senses. Without the first step, there is no raw material for our mind to work on; without the second, we do not fully experience the sensation. To prove the latter point, which may at first seem nonsensical, Locke reminds us that if we are hit by a flying stone, but our mind is distracted at the moment of impact, we will not feel physical pain.

Ironically, by insisting on this two-step process, Locke simultaneously limits reality to the physical, material world and makes our subjective perceptions of nature the final standard of reality. It might seem that we have returned to Bacon's bee, who both gathers and transforms, but Locke's bee can neither soar nor stand fixed on solid ground. Locke, anticipating Kant, was one of the major Enlightenment thinkers who helped push European philosophy away from ontology (the study of being) toward epistemology (the study of knowing). Increasingly after Locke, both God and the world lose their integrity, their concreteness, their "thingness"; instead, our perceptions of God and the world move to center stage. Things are not what they are, but what we perceive them to be.

> According to Lockean empiricism, all our knowledge comes via a two-step process of sensation and reflection; we can only be sure of the physical world and our perceptions of it.

Trapped in Plato's Cave

The first time I grasped this aspect of Locke, I thought, along with many of our Founding Fathers, that his philosophical viewpoint exalted man and his perceptions of the world. Certainly the secular humanists of the last 200 years have adopted that point of view. Only after I took a more searching look into the matter did I come to realize that the real upshot of Lockean empiricism is not to fix man's status as the crown of creation but to set him adrift in a world without standards or signposts.

Empiricism does not draw us closer to truth; to the contrary, it cuts off our access to that higher, permanent wisdom that transcends our physical, space-time-bound world. It may seem to empower us by granting us the freedom to perceive and reflect on—that is, interpret—sense experience as we see fit, but that freedom is illusory, since our ability to interpret must itself rest exclusively on our sense experience of the world. We may, unlike the beasts, be rational beings with the ability to know and to understand, but that ability is locked up in a tight, cramped prison from which we cannot escape. There is only the world and our perceptions of it.

Please do not misunderstand me here. Locke *does* affirm the existence of God and of the soul, but if our soul is a blank slate, with nothing transcendent written into it, and if God is unable to communicate directly with that soul—since empiricism does not allow for revelation that does not come via sense experience—then our soul ceases to be a conduit to a higher reality and becomes instead just one more pipe in the sewage system of our natural, material world. Plato understood this 2,500 years ago—that if all we have is our changing, decaying World of Becoming, if we have no access to the perfect and unchanging World of Being, then we are prisoners in a cave, unaware that what we consider to be reality is only the reflection of a reflection of the real reality that shimmers outside the cave.

Of course, the upshot of Plato's allegory of the cave—which I will consider in much greater detail in the next chapter—is that there *is* a real world outside of the cave and that we can access that reality not with our physical eye but with our mind's eye. And something more. Readers of Plato often miss the deeper reason why the Socratic method of question and answer helps us to reach for those absolute truths that get lost in our ever-shifting World of Becoming. For Plato, our soul pre-existed our body and thus brings with it, in nascent form, memories of those transcendent truths that exist in the heavenly World of Being. Through the Socratic dialectic, teachers help their students to access those memories—or, to put it in Lockean terms, their innate knowledge of Truth. That is why the Latin root of our word *education* does not mean "to teach," or "to observe," or even "to reflect," but "to draw out" (as in the English word *educe*).

Locke's insistence that we are born as blank slates stands as a challenge not only to Christian metaphysics, but to Platonic metaphysics as well. But which view of the world, I asked myself: the Platonic-Christian or the Lockean-empiricist, better accounts for the concrete evidence of our lived lives? Putting questions of metaphysics and revelation aside for the moment, does our experience of the world and of our own minds tell us, with Locke, that we are blank slates, or with Solomon, that God has written eternity on our hearts (see Ecclesiastes 3:11)?

> If our souls are blank slates, bereft of innate knowledge and incapable of accessing divine revelation, then we cannot rise above our earthly prison to perceive transcendent, eternal truths.

Intimations of Immortality

Romantic poet William Wordsworth (1770–1850), the subject of my doctoral dissertation, was, in many ways, a disciple of Locke. In his poetic autobiography *The Prelude* (subtitled *Growth of a Poet's Mind*), which, though published after he died, was composed between 1799 and 1805, Wordsworth details how his mind was formed by that very two-step process that Locke lays out in his *Essay*—with nature first impressing itself upon his senses and then the growing poet reflecting on those impressions and finding that his mind is lord over nature. And yet Wordsworth came to realize that there was something missing in Locke's radically empiricist view of the world, something that could not be accounted for solely by sensation and reflection.

In 1802, Wordsworth began a poem that would come to bear the lengthy title of "Ode: Intimations of Immortality from Recollections of Early Childhood." In the opening four stanzas, he shares with his readers a mental-emotional-spiritual crisis to which he has fallen prey, a crisis that is, at its core, perceptual. When he was younger, the poet explains, the world seemed baptized in light; a glory and a radiance hung over everything, filling him with a sense of awe, wonder, and gratitude. But when that glory faded, the world became empty and dry. Something was missing, something that once radiated from every tree and field and stream— something that transcended, that could not be contained by, either nature or his perceptions of nature. A third thing missing from the full equation of his humanity.

Unable to identify that third thing, and thus powerless to resolve his crisis and re-enchant the world, Wordsworth put down his poem for two years. In 1804, he took it up again, fortified by Plato's intriguing notion of the pre-existence of the soul.

> Our birth is but a sleep and a forgetting:
> The Soul that rises with us, our life's Star,
>   Hath had elsewhere its setting,
>   And cometh from afar:
>   Not in entire forgetfulness,
>   And not in utter nakedness,
> But trailing clouds of glory do we come
>   From God, who is our home (lines 58-65).

No, Wordsworth insists, we do not come into this world naked, an empty *tabula rasa*. Rather, we bear with us memories, traces, intimations of our divine, immortal origin. We perceive, and yearn for, a greater glory and splendor in nature because that greatness is inscribed deep in our soul.

Locke was wrong to dismiss innate or prior knowledge; yet it is understandable why he did so. The power of the physical world and of our sensations of—and reflections on—it does generally result in a decaying of those supernatural intimations.

> Heaven lies about us in our infancy!
> Shades of the prison-house begin to close
>   Upon the growing Boy,
> But He beholds the light, and whence it flows,
>   He sees it in his joy;
> The Youth, who daily farther from the east

Must travel, still is Nature's Priest,
And by the vision splendid
Is on his way attended;
At length the Man perceives it die away,
And fade into the light of common day (lines 66-76).

When Christ instructs his disciples that if they are to enter the kingdom of God they must become like little children (Matthew 18:3), he may have been referring in part to the child's openness to the divine, an openness that too often becomes dulled as we age and accept the narrow empirical limits of our world and the equally narrow perceptual limits of our mind.

In the end, Wordsworth realizes in a moment of poetic insight that it is not the strange extraordinariness of the world but its common ordinariness that blinds us to the direct, intuitive, unmediated insight that we brought with us at our birth. The vision fades not because it is illusory, but because we become so much a part of the world that we lose sight of its initial brightness and clarity. This gradual dimming of our innate knowledge leads to a sad irony that Wordsworth wrestles with in stanza eight: the irony that while children have access to transcendent wisdom but lack the fully developed rational capacity to share that wisdom with others, adults who have developed that capacity have mostly lost their connection to the supernatural.

Still, Wordsworth celebrates the innate knowledge he carried with him at birth—not merely because of the freshness that it brought to his youth or the potential for restoration it brought to his adulthood (via his recollection of his earlier intimations of immortality), but because of a different, more philosophical and epistemological role that it played both in his life and in the lives of all people. The deeper reason for which Wordsworth raises a "song

of thanks and praise" for his memory of those early days when the
glory that issued from his soul was more real and vibrant than the
physical, natural, material world is

> …for those obstinate questionings
>   Of sense and outward things,
>   Fallings from us, vanishings;
>   Blank misgivings of a Creature
>   Moving about in worlds not realised,
>   High instincts before which our mortal Nature
>   Did tremble like a guilty Thing surprised:
>   But for those first affections,
>   Those shadowy recollections,
>   Which, be they what they may,
>   Are yet the fountain-light of all our day,
>   Are yet a master light of all our seeing;
>   Uphold us, cherish, and have power to make
>   Our noisy years seem moments in the being
>   Of the eternal Silence: truths that wake,
>   To perish never (lines 141-56).

The innate knowledge inscribed in our soul is not so much a
shining light that we see as it is a guiding light that allows us to see
everything else.

When the poet was young, that guiding light allowed him to
see and to experience the transitory nature of our world and to
realize that there was something immortal and indomitable both
behind nature and within himself that transcended physical matter.
Now that he is a man, it continues to illuminate his way, empow-
ering his perceptions and highlighting that within (and beyond)
that is calm, all-embracing, and indestructible. Apart from that
guiding light, we are but so many prisoners in a self-imposed cave

of sensations and reflections that have no reference point outside of ourselves. Or, to put it another way, we are trapped in a rigidly finite world with no intimations of infinity to allow us to soar above and beyond our temporal limits.

> According to Wordsworth's Platonic vision, our souls are not blank slates but come into the world with a faint memory of the greater, metaphysical reality of heaven.

Descartes on Infinity

Descartes (1596–1650) understood well the philosophical-theological-epistemological need for there to be an actual infinity of which we possessed intimations. Aside from the real existence of that infinity and our access to it, we could never ourselves have come up with the notion of infinity. "It is true," writes Descartes in the third of his *Meditations on First Philosophy* (1641), "that I have the idea of substance in me in virtue of the fact that I am a substance; but this would not account for my having the idea of an infinite substance, when I am finite, unless this idea proceeded from some substance which really was infinite." Just as water does not rise above its source, so effects must have causes that are both prior and greater.

True, Descartes goes on to explain, we might be able to imagine rest and darkness apart from any innate knowledge of God, for they represent the opposites of things for which we possess physical, sensual experience: namely, movement and light. But the relationship between finitude and infinity is not like that:

> I clearly understand that there is more reality in an infinite substance than in a finite one, and hence that my perception of the infinite, that is God, is in some way

prior to my perception of the finite, that is myself. For how could I understand that I doubted or desired— that is, lacked something—and that I was not wholly perfect, unless there were in me some idea of a more perfect being which enabled me to recognize my own defects by comparison?

The lesser cannot create the greater. The fact that I am finite yet possess within me a prior idea of infinity for which the physical world offers no counterpart proves that there is something infinite in the universe (God) that is the origin of that idea. I might infer rest from the experience of movement, but I can't infer the infinite from my experience of the finite, for that experience does not carry with it any sense that there is a more perfect thing than finitude that I should desire to know and to possess.

Locke, writing a half century later, rejected Descartes's argument and its implicit critique of rigid empiricism. Though, as I stated above, Locke believed both in God and the soul, he saw no need either for God or for innate knowledge to account for our perception of infinity. We all perceive, Locke writes in Book II, Chapter XVII, Paragraph 3 of his *Essay* that when it comes to numbers, we can keep adding and adding without ever coming to an end. It is on the basis of this reflection on sense experience, and not the possession of innate knowledge, that we extrapolate our idea of infinity.

True, he continues in Paragraph 6, our perceptions of qualities like sweetness or the color white do not create in the mind an idea of infinity, but unaided sensation-reflection has no problem doing so when it comes to numbers: "space, duration, and number, being capable of increase by repetition, leave in the mind an idea of endless room for more; nor can we conceive anywhere a stop to a further addition or progression, and so those ideas alone lead our minds towards the thought of infinity." This may sound like an airtight argument, but it fails to take into account that, even when speaking of numbers rather than qualities, the difference between finitude and infinity is not quantitative but qualitative. The progression from the first to the second is not merely one of greater extension; it marks a leap from one kind of reality to another.

Just so the difference between the brain of the most intelligent monkey and the brain of the least educated human being is one of kind rather than degree. Add as much mass and as many folds and neurons to a monkey's brain as you like; it will not thereby yield the conscious, rational, aesthetically sensitive, morally-ethically-capacitated mind of a man. Consciousness is not an epiphenomenon that accompanies a certain quantity of brain mass; it is a wholly other thing than the mere mechanical firing of neurons.

> Whereas Descartes argues that our innate sense of
> infinity demands an actual infinity for its source,
> Locke counters that we could have inferred infinity
> from our experience of adding number to number and
> never reaching a limit.

Christian Cross-Examination #1: Qualitative Leaps Demand Innate Knowledge

There are many in our post-Darwinian world who would point to the so-called cave man as a quantitative bridge between the higher primates and primitive man, but the wise, witty, and widely read British man of letters G.K. Chesterton (1874–1936) gave the lie to that train of reasoning nearly a century ago in *The Everlasting Man* (1925). I cannot express how relieved and empowered I was when I first read that book and, through its bold refutation of the cave man, discovered that I had the freedom to question Darwinian orthodoxies that had been presented to me for years as irrevocable facts. Why had no one before spoken with such clarity and charm about something that had more in common with science fiction than real science?

Modern anthropology, Chesterton taught me in part 1, chapter 2, had too quickly leapt to the conclusion that the drawings of animals in the caves of France offered incontestable proof of the legendary cave man. If anything, they proved the opposite. The people who drew those animals were full human beings, not half-men or superapes; the art itself is an example not of "primitive" art but of art made with primitive tools. "Art," he explains,

> belongs to man and to nothing else except man; [it marks] a difference of kind and not a difference of degree. A monkey does not draw clumsily and a man cleverly; a monkey does not begin the art of representation and a man carry it to perfection. A monkey does not do it at all; he does not begin to do it at all; he does not begin to begin to do it at all. A line of some kind is crossed before the first faint line can begin.

Like the progression from finitude to infinity, the movement from the scratch marks of a monkey to the cave drawings of a man is not quantitative but qualitative. It marks, to borrow one of Chesterton's witty turns of phrase, not an evolution but a revolution.

Chesterton was a great critic of the limits and the inconsistencies of materialism and empiricism, but he was surpassed in this role by another British man of letters who has earned the well-deserved reputation of being the foremost Christian apologist of the twentieth century. An English professor by trade and author of some of the most beloved fantasy novels of all time, The Chronicles of Narnia, C.S. Lewis (1898–1963) was also a widely read, well-trained philosopher with a thorough grounding in all aspects of that Great Conversation that I have been trying to revive in this book. Lewis spent much time pondering the divide between Plato-Augustine-Descartes's insistence that a knowledge of and a desire for infinity has been written in our hearts, and Hobbes-Locke-Hume's insistence that all that we know and desire comes from our senses.

In fact, at the center of much of Lewis's apologetics lies his singular gift for putting his finger on those things that we could not have learned through sense-based experience and reflection alone: or, to put it another way, that could not have evolved solely by way of natural, physical material processes. Chief among those things, Lewis argues in Book 1 of *Mere Christianity* (1952), is our inbuilt sense of morality. We have an innate understanding of right and wrong inscribed in our conscience that does not change radically from age to age or culture to culture. That understanding is not something that we make up; rather, like the mathematical tables, it is something that we discover and recognize as binding on ourselves and our fellow human beings. That is why, when a person or a nation breaks that code, we get angry and hold them accountable; we certainly don't let them get away with arguing that their moral code is a result of their own personal/national sensation-reflection and so cannot be judged by a higher standard. (Locke, despite his empiricism, actually makes a similar link between math and morality in Book IV, Chapter III, Paragraph 18 of his *Essay!*)

> For Chesterton and Lewis, art and morality are not the material products of sensation and reflection but transcendent ideas inscribed in our souls from birth.

Christian Cross-Examination #2: Two Things that Could Not Have Evolved

In the next chapter, I will return and expand on this key Lewisian apologetic. For now, I will end this chapter by considering two other things that Lewis highlights as common human phenomena that cannot be explained by Lockean empiricism or Darwinian sociology-anthropology.

As surprising as it might sound, one of those things is religion itself. In the first chapter ("Introductory") of *The Problem of Pain* (1940), Lewis surveys the argument for the origin of religion that was common in his day: namely, that primitive man's fear of wild animals evolved into a fear of the unknown that itself gave way to a fear of the spiritual realm and a desire to appease it through spells, ceremonies, and sacrifices. Like Locke's argument that our knowledge of infinity was extrapolated from our experience of adding and multiplying numbers again and again, this argument sounds rational and conclusive at first glance. And yet, like Locke's argument, it falsely replaces a qualitative leap with a quantitative progression.

We may, Lewis explains, use the same word *fear* to describe our sense of panic when we face a wild animal and our sense of terror in the face of the unknown, but those two fears differ not in degree but in kind.

> Suppose you were told there was a tiger in the next room: you would know that you were in danger and would probably feel fear. But if you were told "There is a ghost in the next room", and believed it, you would feel, indeed, what is often called fear, but of a different kind. It would not be based on the knowledge of danger, for no one is primarily afraid of what a ghost may

to do him, but of the mere fact that it is a ghost. It is "uncanny" rather than dangerous, and the special kind of fear it excites may be called Dread.

The first kind of fear does not evolve into the second; there is a leap between the two that cannot be brought about by the mere counting up of fearsome encounters with lions and tigers and bears. Our sense of Dread, of what Lewis calls, after Rudolf Otto, the numinous, is the source of our religious sense, but that sense of Dread is wholly unique to human beings and could not simply have evolved.

In part 1, chapter 2 of *The Everlasting Man*, Chesterton offers a similar critique of materialist-empiricists such as H.G. Wells, who fancy that religion evolved out of primitive man's reverence for the chief and for sacrificial harvest ceremonies.

> To me it seems obvious that nothing but a spiritual sentiment already active could have clothed these separate and diverse things with sanctity. To say that religion came from reverencing a chief or sacrificing at a harvest is to put a highly elaborate cart before a really primitive horse. It is like saying that the impulse to draw pictures came from the contemplation of the pictures of reindeers in the cave. In other words, it is explaining painting by saying that it arose out of the work of painters; or accounting for art by saying that it arose out of art.

Once again, the desire of empiricists and evolutionists to insist on a physical, material source for all phenomena causes them to forget that the cause must be greater than the effect, that the cart cannot be put before the horse. The idea of infinity or of sanctity or of the numinous must *precede* the desire for it, for nothing in nature and the information of our senses can produce that desire.

And that leads us to the second thing that Lewis argues requires a supernatural source: our very desire *for* the supernatural. All people, if they are honest, will recognize times in their life, especially when they are younger, when they have felt an overwhelming desire for something beyond our physical, natural, material world. That yearning, which Lewis variously refers to by the German word *sehnsucht* or the English word *joy*, can be set off by almost anything: a landscape, a tune, a line of poetry. But whatever the trigger, the quality that makes the joy unique is that it points us toward a something that is beyond nature.

Now, Lewis reasons, the fact that we get hungry proves—or at least strongly suggests—that we are creatures made for eating. Likewise, the fact that we experience thirst proves that we are creatures made for drinking. We may be denied those things, we may even die if we are denied them for a long enough period of time, but it would be a strange thing indeed if we lived in a world where neither food nor drink existed. The desire we experience to marry a girl does not in itself guarantee that we will get the girl, but it would be passing strange if that desire existed in a sexless world. In the same way, the fact that we desire things that our physical world cannot supply, or even know anything about, seems to prove that we are creatures meant for another, supernatural world.

What Descartes says about infinity is echoed, whether consciously or unconsciously, in an argument that Lewis makes in the final chapter of *Reflections on the Psalms*. Why is it, Lewis asks, that we are continually surprised by the passage of time? Though we have all, whatever age or culture we were born into, felt that sense of surprise and bewilderment when we suddenly realize that we have reached the age of fifty or that our kids have grown and left the house or that the baby we are holding in our hands is not our son but the son of our son, it is a decidedly odd thing that we should feel it. After all, we have lived our whole lives in time; we have never known anything but past, present, and future. And yet in the face of our daily sense experience, we feel out of sorts when we become conscious of the passage of time.

For temporal creatures like ourselves, to be continually surprised by time would be like a fish being continually surprised by the wetness of water. Now, water is the element in which a fish spends its entire life; it knows nothing else. So, yes, it would be a strange thing if a fish were to be continually surprised by the wetness of water—unless, of course, that fish were destined someday to be a land animal. Just so, we were not made for time but for eternity, not for finitude but for infinitude. Our sense of discomfort in time does not proceed from Locke's two-step empirical process of sensation and reflection, but from the fact that our soul bears within it an innate sense of that infinite eternity for which we were made.

> For Lewis and Chesterton, neither our sense of the numinous nor our experiences of joy and longing could have evolved; both demand a supernatural source.

Postscript

In his argument by joy, Lewis not only echoes Descartes's meditation on infinity and Solomon's meditation on eternity (Ecclesiastes 3:11), but a sentence and a phrase from two great Christian apologists whose longing for God was as intense as their desire to defend the divine origin of that longing.

The sentence comes from the opening paragraph of Augustine's *Confessions*: "You stir man to take pleasure in praising you [God], because you have made us for yourself, and our heart is restless until it rests in you." The phrase comes from Pascal's *Pensées*, where he argues that we all have within our hearts what modern commentators have termed a "God-shaped vacuum" that aches and longs until it is filled by God: "What else does this craving, and this helplessness, proclaim but that there was once in man a true happiness, of which all that now remains is the empty print and trace? This he tries in vain to fill with everything around him, seeking in things that are not there the help he cannot find in those that are, though none can help, since this infinite abyss can be filled only with an infinite and immutable object; in other words by God himself."

In both cases, only God can satisfy the very hunger that he inspires within us. Wordsworth surely spoke the truth when he proclaimed that "not in utter nakedness, / But trailing clouds of glory do we come / From God, who is our home."

Despite the fears of the radio evangelist mentioned at the beginning of this chapter, I intend to continue reading fiction. Not so much because it is entertaining as because it has a powerful way of rattling my God-shaped vacuum and setting me off yearning for the numinous and the infinite.

CHAPTER FIVE

The Good, the True, and the Beautiful

Being what they called a "serious" student, I wanted to make good use of that final childhood summer that began with my high school graduation and ended with the start of my freshman year in college. Since I already knew that I would be majoring in literature, I decided I would spend my summer reading those two fat Russian novels that all liberal-arts-educated students are supposed to have read: *War and Peace* and *The Brothers Karamazov*. Though I enjoyed the first, it was the second that changed my life.

In many ways, that most cerebral of novels is really, at its core, a detective story. Old man Karamazov is killed, and suspicion immediately falls on his hotheaded son Dmitry. After all, the murder couldn't have been committed by either of his other sons: the saintly Alyosha or the brainy Ivan. Or could it? Though I loved Alyosha the monk, I immediately became intrigued by the thoughtful, well-read Ivan and his intellectual struggles. I was still a new Christian at the time, and so I was drawn to Ivan's agonizing doubts over the goodness of God in the face of evil and injustice. Though I didn't agree with Ivan's position, I could follow his train of thought as he rejected not only God but any higher standards of right and wrong that rely on God's existence and his holiness.

And then came the shock that woke up Ivan, and me, to the moral nature of our universe. As it turned out, Ivan's father had not been killed by any of his three sons. It was, rather, his illegitimate son Smerdyakov who had done the deed. Now, throughout the novel, this Smerdyakov had been a disciple of Ivan and of his rejection of moral absolutes. If God is dead, Ivan had taught his half-brother, then all things are permissible. For Ivan, such statements were only part of an intellectual game; Smerdyakov, in sharp contrast, took them deadly seriously. In fact, it was precisely by following out to their logical conclusion the theories of Ivan that he came to kill the father he hated.

Almost at the same moment, Ivan and I were struck by the same revelation: Ideas are not neutral; they carry with them real, sometimes terrible consequences. If there really are no standards of right and wrong, if the good, the true, and the beautiful are nothing but words, then theft, adultery, and murder are no longer crimes, and both individuals and society lose the right to judge abhorrent behavior. If all moral, intellectual, and aesthetic standards are man-made and change radically from age to age and culture to culture, then there was no reason that Ivan should have been troubled by the evil and injustice in the world. Indeed, if Ivan had not been born, as we all have been born, with an innate sense of right and wrong inscribed in his soul, then he would not have been able to *recognize* that the world was filled with evil and injustice.

That revelation brought Ivan to his knees in prayer and confession. As for me, I vowed then and there that I would not engage in the kind of "mental masturbation" so common in modern universities. I would treat ideas with respect and learn to trace them back to their foundational assumptions and forward to their necessary outcomes.

The Legacy of the Sophists

Serendipitously, I had already begun that process of analyzing truth claims six months earlier. At the start of my senior year, I had made a comment to my favorite English teacher and mentor about Plato. I no longer remember what my comment was, but I remember vividly the reply of my teacher: "You can't make that statement unless you have read all of Plato's *Republic*." Half out of cockiness and half out of real interest, I took up his challenge and devoured the book over Christmas break. Since then, Plato has been the key figure in my intellectual, spiritual, and aesthetic growth, matched only by Dante and C.S. Lewis.

Although I considered then, and still consider today, the Bible to be the final authority on matters of Truth, I was pleased to learn that, four centuries before Christ, Plato had already addressed and, to my mind at least, defeated the claims of moral relativism. The new atheists may fancy that they have been the ones to "free us" from absolute standards, but any critiques they have offered were already laid on the table some 2,500 years ago by those most infamous citizens of the golden age of Athens, the sophists.

Along with most of the Pre-Socratics, the fifth-century BC sophists were pragmatists and materialists who kept their eyes firmly fixed on the ground. They didn't seek to overthrow religion per se, but they were of the settled opinion that moral-ethical law codes were man-made products that changed from one city-state (*polis* in Greek) to the next. They made their living, often a good one, by teaching the sons of the rich how to use rhetoric and oratory to defeat their social, economic, judicial, or political rivals. Often that meant teaching them how to so manipulate logic as to make the weaker argument appear to be the stronger.

Unlike Socrates, who used the dialectical method of question and answer as a method for drawing his students away from false ideas of courage or friendship and toward absolute truths that transcend time, place, and culture, the sophists taught their pupils that ethical actions, philosophical principles, and aesthetic standards are relative and shift, sometimes radically, from polis to polis. The goal of the sophists, therefore, was not to direct their students toward divine, eternal truths but to teach them a technique for navigating and manipulating whatever the favored virtues and fashionable outrage of the moment happened to be. Since truth was a man-made, polis-endorsed thing, there was little point in spending time looking for nonexistent divine standards.

One way of expressing this ethos is to say, along with Protagoras the sophist (c. 485–415 BC), that man is the measure of all things. But there is a far darker, antitheistic way of expressing it. Protagoras's motto did, after all, help inspire true Christian humanism in the early Renaissance. Not so the motto of another sophist named Gorgias (c. 483–375 BC), a motto expressed through three propositions that anticipate not only the modern materialism and moral relativism of the new atheists, but the postmodern deconstruction of thinkers like Jacques Derrida and Michel Foucault.

According to the first of Gorgias's propositions, nothing exists. That is not to say that the world is an illusion, but that there are no absolute standards that are true for all people at all times and that can thus act as a stable center for philosophy, theology, and ethics. Besides, continued Gorgias in his second proposition, even if some kind of divine touchstone existed, it wouldn't make a difference because we could not know it. No such metaphysical bridge exists that could convey that absolute standard to us. To make matters worse, Gorgias concludes in his third proposition that even if we could somehow know it, we would not be able to communicate it to others. Human language does not possess the capacity for containing or expressing truths that surpass the limits of our physical, material, natural world.

In one sense, Gorgias's three propositions prefigure Locke's rejection of innate knowledge—for Locke not only dismissed the existence of such knowledge; he did not allow for any kind of epistemological faculty by which we could know or communicate that knowledge. With Hume, the epistemological pathway to God is closed off altogether. Hume would not have called himself an atheist, but he is, surely, a functional atheist—one for whom God, even if he does exist, has no ultimate bearing on the way we live our lives. Increasingly since Hume, there has been a long line of atheists and functional atheists who have refused to acknowledge any moral-ethical-philosophical standards beyond those constructed by human beings; a short list would include T.H. Huxley, John Stuart Mill, Nietzsche, Bertrand Russell, A.J. Ayer, Carl Sagan, Richard Dawkins, and Christopher Hitchens.

But the dark legacy of Gorgias's propositions does not stop there. Since Derrida (1930–2004), postmodernists have gone further than simply rejecting our ability to access higher standards; they have pronounced language itself an unfit tool for conveying any kind of stable meaning. Atheists like Marx and Freud built systems that could take the place of revealed religion; Derrida and his heirs have rejected all systems and structures that claim to provide a fixed center of truth or purpose. We are alone in a world with no signposts whatsoever.

> The sophists believed, as do their heirs, that ethical actions, philosophical principles, and aesthetic standards are relative and shift radically from polis to polis.

From the Sophists to Socrates to Plato

But now I fear I have digressed too far from my main topic. You'll forgive me for doing so. Gorgias's three propositions, you see, controlled a good deal of what I learned (or unlearned) in my nine years as a college student. About two-thirds of my professors, I'm sorry to say, had bought into either (1) the modernist skepticism against all claims to transcendent goodness, truth, or beauty; or (2) the postmodernist rejection of language as a meaning-bearing tool; or (3) both. Most felt that they were being very progressive in doing so, not realizing—or not wanting to realize—that their skepticism, far from being newly fashioned, was as old-fashioned as the sophists of the fifth century BC.

Incidentally, very, very few of my skeptical professors denied God outright; they didn't have to. In the absence of divine standards, or at least of our ability to know and communicate them, the existence of God becomes a nonissue. Sure, students can believe in God by clinging to their nonrational, a-logical faith, but that faith does not and cannot have any bearing on the classroom. And that stricture holds true in the modern secular academy even when studying a book like Plato's *Republic* that rests squarely on the philosophical contention that our limited, earthbound definitions of goodness, truth, and beauty are pale imitations of the real Goodness, Truth, and Beauty that we can only glimpse by committing ourselves to the discipline and training of philosophy.

When one considers the fact that a philosopher is, etymologically speaking, a "friend of wisdom," Gorgian, Humean, Nietzschean, and Derridean philosophy all become tragic oxymorons. Why be a friend of wisdom if no such wisdom exists, or if we are utterly incapable of finding, perceiving, and sharing it? Socrates certainly felt this way; that is why he pushed his students and his

fellow Athenian citizens to examine themselves and their definitions of such key nouns as virtue, friendship, and the good.

Given this central aspect of his teaching, it might seem at first
that Socrates agreed with the sophists that our definitions are man-
made and relative. But the similarity is deceptive. Socrates arrived
at the relativistic nature of our man-made definitions not from
the perspective of Gorgias's three propositions, but from the perspective of Truth. Or to put it another way: Socrates was skilled at
exploding false definitions not because he thought everything was
relative, but because he had something absolute to measure the
false definitions against.

Now, it is most likely the case that the historical Socrates rarely,
if ever, offered an absolute definition himself. His philosophical
mission was mostly negative: to wipe away the false definitions—
what Francis Bacon would later call the "idols of the marketplace"—so as to prepare the way for the pursuit of the true. Once
that was done, the road was clear for his star pupil, Plato, to move
on from the negative task of exposing philosophical idols to the
positive task of formulating definitions that transcend the individual, the polis, and even Greece itself.

> Socrates and Plato agreed with the sophists that our
> definitions of goodness, truth, and beauty are
> man-made and relative, but that is only because they
> believed that absolute standards existed against
> which the relative ones could be measured.

The Nature of Justice

Socrates is one of my chief heroes and has long been one of
my role models, but he is not enough on his own. Though I enjoy
the early dialogues of Plato, I find them frustrating and ultimately

unfulfilling. That is because the early dialogues seem to present Socrates just as he was, without Plato stepping in to direct things. What that means is that the early dialogues do a thorough job of wiping away false definitions, but then stop dead in their tracks before going on to posit true ones. Not so *The Republic*, which belongs to Plato's middle dialogues when the pupil began to move past his teacher.

The Republic is a long book, especially when compared to Plato's other middle dialogues (*Symposium, Phaedrus, Phaedo, Critias, Timaeus, Protagoras, Meno, Gorgias*, etc.), but it is carefully organized around a single task: to define justice. Plato's lengthy and at times wildly imaginative creation of an ideal state consumes over half of *The Republic*, but it is not carried out simply as an end in itself. Everything in the dialogue is there to further the goal of discerning and articulating the exact nature of justice. Just as Pythagoras sought and found a numerical formula that captured and expressed the already existing relationship between the three sides of a right triangle, so Plato seeks, through the Socratic method of question and answer, to identify and put into words the real, eternal, absolute quality of Justice that surpasses any one constitution or the laws and decrees of any one ruler.

If he can do so successfully, then Plato will have answered the sophist rejection of absolute standards. And yet the very fact that he can write a dialogue like *The Republic* itself furnishes significant proof that those standards exist. In Book I, Polemarchus, the son of Socrates's host, suggests that justice means doing good to your friends and evil to your enemies. At first, this sounds like a solid, common-sense definition—until Socrates begins to test it as one might test the sharpness of a blade or the sturdiness of a table. If a just man, Socrates reasons, were to injure his enemy, he would be making that enemy less excellent, less good, and less just. But how can that be? How can a just man make others less just? Granted that this argument is not airtight (a just king could sentence a traitor to the death penalty to ensure the maintenance of justice in his state), the fact that it can be stated, debated, and understood demonstrates that those engaged in the dialogue already possess a basic sense of justice inscribed within their soul. Only the existence of a real sense of justice behind their conversation would enable them to contemplate the problems inherent in a just man doing an action that renders others unjust.

Of course, I realize that my own argument here leaves me open to the charge of naivety. Socrates and his dialectical circle are merely products of a democratic ethos, the ancient or modern sophist will reply; were they from Sparta or Persia, their sense of justice would be radically different. This critique is a strong one, but it does not frighten me away, for it is this very critique that drives *The Republic* and makes it relevant to twenty-first century Christians and others who would defend absolute truth from its new-atheist detractors.

No sooner does Socrates invalidate Polemarchus's definition than the headstrong young sophist Thrasymachus leaps up and argues with great force that justice does not embody some kind of divine standard but is nothing more than the interest of the stronger. Or, to put it in common parlance, might makes right. For Thrasymachus and his heirs (in particular, Machiavelli, Nietzsche, and Michel Foucault), the winners not only write the history books; they get to define for their society the meaning of justice—and, with it, mercy, law, honor, virtue, and happiness.

After Thrasymachus dumps all this on Socrates and company, Socrates patiently demonstrates to him that unjust men inevitably betray each other and incite civil war. Worse yet, the unjust man produces civil war in his own soul, leading not to excellence but to defect, disease, and death. Injustice, far from creating and maintaining strength, breeds division and disunity—both of which breed misery rather than happiness.

> *The Republic* begins with Socrates tearing apart two
> conventional definitions of justice: that it means
> doing good to friends and bad to enemies, and that it
> is nothing more than the will of the stronger.

Justice in the State and in the Soul

That is how Book I ends, and that is where I expected *The Republic* itself to end. But, thankfully, Plato refuses to leave the dialogue in limbo with the true nature of justice shrouded in uncertainty. And so rather than conclude with the defeat (and quick exit) of Thrasymachus, Plato begins Book II by having his own brother, Glaucon, challenge Socrates to answer Thrasymachus's critique on a much higher and deeper level. Though Glaucon agrees with Socrates, he decides to play the role of devil's advocate and push Socrates to truly defend justice by showing that it is better *for its own sake*, whether or not it leads to fame and fortune or poverty and prison.

This decision prompts Glaucon to set up two hypothetical cases which most people would look to as proof that justice is not a good thing in and of itself. Imagine, Glaucon says, two contrasting men: one is perfectly unjust, so much so that he convinces everyone that he is just and goes on to win power, wealth, and the accolades of all; the second is a perfectly just man who is rejected, reviled, and killed by the people. Of this second man, Glaucon says that he must be

> stripped of everything but justice…Though the best of
> men, he must be thought the worst. Then let him be
> put to the test to see whether he will continue resolute
> in the service of justice, even though all the while he

must suffer the opprobrium of an evil reputation. Let
him so persevere—just in actuality but unjust in reputation—until death itself (361c-d).

In constructing this just-man-who-is-accused-of-injustice, Plato
certainly had in mind Socrates himself, who was condemned and
executed by the citizens of Athens in 399 BC, and yet the descrip-
tion uncannily reads like a pagan prophecy of Christ.

Still, regardless of its links to the Gospels, Plato's parable of
the perfectly just man illuminates a foundational tenet of what
might be called metaphysical realism: There exists an eternal, cross-
cultural standard of justice that is written into the fabric of the
universe and that transcends practical, pragmatic concerns. That
standard is inscribed as well in our conscience; it is, in fact, the
source, *not the product*, of our innate yearning for goodness, rightness, and wholeness.

Socrates begins to look for that absolute Justice in the soul, but
then decides that it would be easier to seek it first on a larger scale:
not in a single human soul (microcosm), but in a perfectly ordered
state (macrocosm). Hence the long digression that gives the dialogue its name and that establishes the various parts of the well-
run state that must work in harmony and cooperation if justice is
to exist. In the absence of that harmony and cooperation, in which
each part of the state performs its proper function and practices its
proper virtue, justice is perverted into injustice and the state falls
prey to civil war. In the same way, when the three parts of the soul—
the rational part that leads us upward toward the divine, the appetitive part that leads us downward toward the beast, and the spirited
part that mediates between the two—lose their harmony, injustice
ensues and the soul wars against itself.

When true justice rules, it brings order and health to state and individual alike. Justice is not something that man makes up, but that he recognizes and participates with. When a man gives in to injustice, he does more than play around with words; he literally "starve[s] the human being within him to the point where he can be dragged wherever the other parts of his soul want to go" (589a). When, for example, he steals gold, he does more than break a man-made law; he "enslave[s] the most divine part of himself to what is most unclean and shameful" (589e). The absolute tyrant turns out, in the end, to be the most abject of slaves, for his embrace of injustice enthralls him, literally, to the appetitive part of his soul. The just man, on the other hand, even if he is condemned, is free, for all the parts of his soul exist in the proper harmony.

> True Justice is not something that man makes up but that he recognizes; it is the source, *not the product*, of his innate yearning for goodness, rightness, and wholeness.

Escaping the Cave

Plato convinced me that Justice exists and is a kind of harmony or balance, but can it be accessed? If Gorgias's second proposition is correct—that even if Something exists, it cannot be known—then we end up with a dry, dead deism: an absentee God who does nothing but exist. Such a faith borders on functional atheism because the God of deism makes no demands on us, has no plans or desires for our lives, and is not moving history toward any *telos* (purposeful end). To say that God exists but that we are cut off entirely from any and all knowledge of him and his Holiness-Love-Mercy-Justice is finally the same thing as to say that he does not exist—or to say, with Spinoza, that God is the same thing as nature or the universe.

That will not do. Not only have the great Christian philosophers and theologians fought against this position for 2,000 years; the God of the Bible, I firmly believe, raised up the pagan, pre-Christian Plato to fight it out with the new atheists of his day (the sophists) four centuries before the birth of Christ. It was the genius of Plato that he glimpsed the nature of our world in an allegory (or metaphor or parable or myth) about prisoners trapped in a deep, dark cave.

From birth, these prisoners have been chained to chairs that keep them ever staring forward at the back of the cave. Behind them burns a roaring fire, and between them and the fire puppeteers parade wooden images of all the real things that exist outside the cave. As they parade their imitations of trees and stones, fish and birds, dogs and lions, the fire casts the shadows of the puppets onto the cave wall. The prisoners, not knowing any better, believe that those shadows represent reality.

And then something wonderful happens. One of the prisoners breaks his chains and turns around to face the fire. At first he is blinded by the light and confused by the puppets. But in time, he realizes the true nature of his condition and struggles his way out of the cave. Eventually he comes to see that what he had thought was real was only a shadow of a shadow, a pale imitation of the true nature of reality. For a while, he enjoys his freedom in the upper air of light and truth, but he cannot escape the duty he feels within himself to return to the cave and liberate the other prisoners not only physically, but mentally and spiritually as well.

In Plato's allegory, the cave represents our physical, temporal World of Becoming while the land outside the cave represents the unchanging, heavenly World of Being where dwell the Forms. We ourselves are the prisoners in the cave, while the one prisoner who breaks his chains, escapes, and then returns is both the true Socratic philosopher and the perfectly just man. I don't base that comparison on a hunch. Plato makes the comparison himself, for he says that the prisoner who returns to the cave and tries to enlighten his fellow prisoners will most likely be rejected by them and, if he persists and attempts to drag them out of their chains, killed by them.

Such is the danger the perfectly just man faces; yet Plato does not hesitate to argue that it is precisely this type of philosopher who must be forced to rule his republic. The reason for this is that only a philosopher-king who has knowledge of Justice in its perfect form can properly judge and steer his polis. But no one can know the Forms, the sophist (ancient or modern) cries out. To the contrary, Plato replies, all of us have the potential to escape from the cave and catch sight of the Forms. It is, in fact, the proper role of education to make philosophers of citizens.

In chapter 4, I explained that *educate* comes from the Latin for "to draw out." In keeping with that notion, Plato has Socrates state:

> We assert that this power [of gaining true knowledge] is already in the soul of everyone. The way each of us learns compares with what happens to the eye: it cannot be turned away from darkness to face the light without turning the whole body. So it is with our capacity to know; together with the entire soul one must turn away from the world of transient things toward the world of perpetual being, until finally one learns to endure the sight of its most radiant manifestation (518c-d).

To gain sight of Justice, not to mention the Good, the True, and the Beautiful, in its absolute form takes effort, training, and discipline. It can be achieved, but not through empirical observation of the world; indeed, if we focus our eyes only on this world, we will decrease, not increase, our ability to see that which is eternal and absolute.

Our eyes and our soul must be turned from "the world of change to the world of eternal things" (521d) if we are to gain sight of the Forms. But once we do that, we must return and help those who live their lives in the shadows. This, Socrates insists, is what we must tell the philosopher:

> Because you have seen the reality of beauty, justice, and goodness, you will be able to know idols and shadows for what they are. Together and wide awake, you and we will govern our city, far differently from most cities today whose inhabitants are ruled darkly as in a dream by men who will fight with each other over shadows and use faction in order to rule, as if that were some great good (520d).

Influenced first by Plato and Aristotle and then later by Christianity, the Mediterranean world adopted this high view of the philosopher as one who guides others toward the light, toward the true standards that transcend man-made laws.

> The true philosopher is one who turns his gaze away from our world of change toward the eternal Forms, and then returns to our world to guide others out of the cave.

Realism vs. Nominalism

Though many today see Plato's philosopher-king as a kind of fairy tale, the fact is that from the early church through to the Renaissance, Europe was guided and essentially ruled by bishops, priests, and monks who dedicated most of their time and energy to meditating on the Good, the True, and the Beautiful. They showed their fitness to rule, not by their power or wealth or practical skills, but by their wisdom—that is, by their knowledge of the Forms.

That is not to say that the medievals believed literally that there were Forms of Goodness, Truth, Beauty, Justice, Courage, and Love stored up in the World of Being. But they did believe, as most people still believe—or at least take for granted—today, that behind our words for goodness, truth, beauty, justice, courage, and love there exists a real meaning that has universal value. Aristotle did not believe literally in the Forms, but he did believe that all things have a *telos* and an essence inscribed within them from birth. Augustine came up with the supreme Christian solution: He put Plato's Forms into the Mind of God. It is not only our universe that needs an Unmoved Mover; our words, our virtues, and our truths also call out for a transcendent origin.

By a strange quirk of etymology, the empiricists who have cut us off from the Forms have convinced moderns that they are the realistic ones who see the world as it is and don't harbor any silly superstitions about eternal or innate or absolute ideas. I call this a quirk of etymology because throughout the Middle Ages the Platonic-Augustinian position was known as *realism*—for those who followed it believed that our words and ideas were backed up by real concepts that transcended time and culture. Those who believed otherwise—who, like the sophists before them, taught that our words were just man-made names, particulars behind which we could not identify any type of universal—referred to their position as *nominalism* (from the Greek word translated "name").

Writing with reference to notions of beauty in the Middle Ages, Umberto Eco describes succinctly and powerfully the negative influence that the nominalist theories of William of Ockham (c. 1285–1347) had on the arts:

> According to Ockham, created things are absolutely contingent, and there is no regulation of things by Eternal Ideas in the mind of God. There is no stable cosmic order to which things conform, or which governs our mental dispositions, or which might inspire the craftsman…The concept of the organising form of a thing, as a rational principle which informs it but is distinct from its constitutive parts, had gone…The reality of universals, which was necessary to the concept of *integritas*, was dissolved by nominalism. The problem of the transcendental status of beauty, and of the distinctions which specify beauty, can scarcely be posed in a system in which there are no such distinctions, neither formal nor virtual. All that remains is the intuition of particulars, a knowledge of existent objects whose visible proportions are analysed empirically.

What Eco writes here about the deleterious effect of nominalism on beauty (aesthetics) holds true for its equally deleterious effect on goodness (ethics and morality) and truth (philosophy and theology) as well. In a world reduced to empirical observation, there can be no ultimate standard to appeal to, no form or pattern or organizing principle to give shape to our desire for beauty, our yearning for truth, and our longing for goodness.

It should be obvious that no civilization can last for long if it throws off all standards, but even individuals cannot live fully in a world devoid of the Good, the True, and the Beautiful. Of course, there have been and continue to be individuals and societies that reject universals and yet continue to thrive, but that is only because they cheat. Both the Nazis and the Soviets rejected God-ordained standards, but then they substituted them with an idolatrous worship of racial purity and equality, secular dogmas which they pretended were absolute and self-evident, mandated by natural, Darwinian forces. The western democracies of Europe have also slowly separated themselves from revealed, Judeo-Christian ethical laws, all the while fooling themselves into believing that they can manufacture a fixed, unwavering commitment to tolerance and human dignity out of moral and cultural relativism.

> Whereas realists like Plato and Augustine taught that there were real, eternal ideas behind such words as *goodness*, *truth*, and *beauty*, nominalists like William of Ockham treated such words as particular names cut out from transcendent universals.

Christian Cross-Examination #1: C.S. Lewis on the Tao

As the seemingly eternal Roman Empire crumbled around him, Augustine wrote his magnum opus, *The City of God*, as a way of laying out God's eternal vision for human society. As WWII raged across Europe, C.S. Lewis was asked by the BBC to deliver a series of talks over the radio to explain to the British population exactly why they should fight to the death against Hitler. After all, if the cultural relativists were right and there really were no standards for moral-ethical behavior, then why should they think democratic ethics were superior to fascistic ones? Could there really be standards that transcended the respective cultures of Britain and Germany, Russia and Italy, America and Japan?

The fact that, after the war ended, the Allies were able to hold the Nuremburg trials to try Nazi war criminals certainly seems to prove that universal standards exist. Otherwise, by what measure of right and wrong, good and evil could they have judged people from another culture who claimed they were just following orders? Although Lewis put together his broadcast talks (1941–1944) several years before the Nuremberg trials, he argues forcefully in his earliest broadcasts—which were later gathered together and published as book 1 of *Mere Christianity* (1952)—that God's existence could be proven precisely by the fact that we all share a common, cross-cultural understating of morality that has been written into our conscience. In *The Abolition of Man* (1943), Lewis gives a name to that universal law code: the Tao.

For Lewis, the existence of the Tao is subtly proven each time two people argue over something. Whether they realize it or not, the two people could not argue if they didn't agree, often unconsciously, to a standard that transcends both of them. If they didn't accept that standard, they could not argue; they could only fight. The uniquely human act of arguing demands a higher standard; the point of the argument is to decide which person's "side" comes closest to that standard. No standard, no argument.

But that argument does not only take place between two people; just as often, it takes place within the mind-heart-soul of each of us. When a person wrestles internally over a course of action, he invariably uses the word *ought* or *should*: "I know that I *ought* to do this, but I'd rather do that"; "I don't want to do what I know that I *should* do." Though the sophists of the world don't like to admit it, the very existence of words like *ought* and *should* offers evidence that standards exist of which we are aware and accountable—even, and especially, when we decide not to follow them.

Indeed, there are two things that all people know, whether or not they are willing to own up to it: (1) we should live in a certain way; and (2) we do not, and cannot, do so. In terms of Christian salvation, this recognition of our own sinfulness is what leads us to Christ and his atoning sacrifice. However, it also highlights something about the nature of reality: Goodness is not a man-made thing. Like the mathematical tables, it is something we discover rather than invent.

Despite the writings of anthropologists like Margaret Mead, morality does not change radically from culture to culture. We all know the Tao; it's the way we expect other people and other nations to treat us. Should anyone doubt the universality of the Tao, Lewis includes a lengthy appendix in *The Abolition of Man* in which he lines up the law codes of such ancient peoples as the Greeks, Romans, Babylonians, Egyptians, Norseman, Native American Indians, and Chinese. By doing so he reveals that cultures across time and space share a basic understanding of the biblical Ten Commandments. So close is that shared understanding of basic moral-ethical behavior that when a would-be prophet or holy man (Reverend Moon, Jim Jones, David Koresh, Osama bin Laden) starts to preach a moral code that deviates from the Tao, he is quickly recognized as a false prophet by everyone outside his tight-knit group.

To repeat what I said a moment ago: Morality (Plato's Form of Goodness that Augustine put in the Mind of God) is not invented but discovered. But might not that discovery rise up from primal urges and instincts that we inherited from primitive man? Man, after all, is not the only animal with a built-in instinct for survival, procreation, and the defense of the tribe. True enough, but man is unique in his ability to choose between instinctual urges. As soon as we step back from the urges and ask ourselves what we *ought* to do, we step out of the merely physical to touch upon a supernatural standard that transcends ourselves, our culture, and our age.

> A universal standard of morality exists that does not change from culture to culture, that was not made up by human religious leaders, and that transcends our instinctual urges for survival and procreation.

Christian Cross-Examination #2: Alvin Plantinga on the *Sensus Divinitatis*

For Lewis, clear proof that an absolute standard of Goodness exists, and behind it a divine lawmaker, can be found in the way our conscience recognizes a binding set of moral laws that it should obey. A more recent philosopher-apologist, Alvin Plantinga, working from the writings of Aquinas and Calvin, has found proof not only that such standards exist but that an epistemological mechanism exists by which God can and does convey those standards to us. That is to say, Plantinga has shown that Gorgias and his heirs are in error when they argue that even if something exists it cannot be known.

Our belief in God and our perceptions of his moral, philosophical, and aesthetic standards are not delusions, as Marx argued, or wish fulfillments, as Freud argued. Rather, we all possess a *sensus divinitatis* (Latin for a "sense of the divine") that is as real and as functional as any of our senses or cognitive faculties. That *sensus* does not, in and of itself, furnish proof for the existence of God. However, once the existence of God has been established by other arguments (like those presented above and in the previous four chapters), then the *sensus* naturally presents itself as the means by which an eternal, omnipresent God might communicate with mortal, time/space-bound creatures.

Critics as far back as the sophists and Pre-Socratics have complained—as more recent ones from Hume to John Stuart Mill to Richard Dawkins have complained—that if God were real, he would have announced himself to us in a much clearer way. But Plantinga reminds us that one of the central teachings of the Christian worldview is that we and our world are fallen. Not just our bodies, but our cognitive systems as well are broken, flawed, and fragmented. Part of that brokenness is revealed in our rejection of what our inner *sensus divinitatis* demands of us, a rejection that sometimes manifests itself as a desperate wish fulfillment *against* the existence of God! Again and again, we rage against the conviction we feel, but we are unable to evade or elude it; it is just too deeply engraved in our psyche.

In contrast to our five senses, our innate and ineradicable *sensus divinitatis* allows us to arrive at a knowledge of God that is immediate; unlike empirical-based knowledge, it does not proceed by inference or argument. To the secular empiricist who takes as an unproven given that innate ideas do not exist and that experience and the five senses are the only avenues to truth, our *sensus* will appear irrational and unwarranted. But that is only because he rejects out of hand, without any empirical proof to substantiate his rejection, the possibility of revelation. Once we allow that possibility, it becomes quite reasonable to suppose that we would possess an intuitive, not rational, power that can perceive revelation from a supernatural source invisible to the senses.

> All people possess a *sensus divinitatis* ("sense of the divine") that allows them to receive directly and intuitively—apart from the five senses—revelation from God.

Postscript

Lewis's Tao and Plantinga's *sensus divinitatis* convinced my mind that supernatural, metaphysical standards exist and can be known, but it was not until I read *The Silver Chair* that I felt in my bones the truth of that statement. In that wonderful novel, one of Lewis's seven Chronicles of Narnia, two children from our world are carried by magic into Narnia to help rescue Prince Rilian, who has long been held as a prisoner in the underground lair of an evil green witch.

Although the children successfully rescue Rilian, before they can return with him to the upper world, the witch catches them. Rather than kill them, she does her best to enchant them into believing that Narnia does not exist, that there is no such thing as the sun or lions—especially not Aslan, the Christ figure of Narnia. What they call "sun" and "lion," she tries to convince them, is nothing more than a concept they invented by extrapolating upward from a torch or a cat they once saw. To put that in the terms of this chapter, she almost makes them believe, as the prisoners in Plato's cave believe, that the shadows they see are real things and that nothing else exists above or beyond them. A sort of medieval nominalist with a vengeance, she tricks them into believing that "sun" and "lion" are nothing more than names; they do not point to a reality outside themselves.

Just in the nick of time, one of their companions sticks his foot in a fire, breaking the intoxicating spell of the witch and waking them all up to the truth: It is the greater things (the sun and the lion) that are the originals, not the lesser things (the torch and the cat). Freud was wrong when he argued that divine fatherhood is a projection upward from earthly fatherhood; it is God the Father who is the Source, the Cause, the Original. Earthly fatherhood is a falling away from and a lesser reality than divine fatherhood.

Though I say it with fear and trembling, Lewis here outdoes Plato's allegory of the cave. Unlike Plato's prisoners, who have been fooled since birth by shadows, Lewis's heroes have had direct experience of the sun and of Aslan the lion. They *know* those things are

real and substantial—far more real and substantial than torches
and cats—yet the witch is able, in a matter of minutes, to convince
them that what they know is true is not, that what they know to
be an origin and a cause is nothing more than a copy and an effect.
Like the witch, a growing army of secular philosophers, social scientists, and educators have striven hard to convince everyone in the
West that the Good, the True, and the Beautiful are only words that
have no real, separate existence.

They have not succeeded.

PART THREE:

The Nature of God

CHAPTER SIX

More Moral Than God?

Although I am an English professor whose learning has come mostly from books, I am an avid movie watcher (I've seen close to 4,000 of them) who owes many of his deepest insights to film. Usually that insight comes from the film's ability to draw me closer to goodness, truth, or beauty...but not always. There are times when a movie, usually in conjunction with one or two others, opens my eyes to lies and errors that have led individuals, groups, even whole cultures astray. The experience is not always a pleasant one, but it is essential if one is to understand the fullness of the human condition.

In the fall of 2015, I watched two movies in close proximity that ripped away the veil from a modern orientation toward God that, though it has roots in the past, has reached epidemic proportions over the last several decades. The first was a lavishly produced postmodern reworking of the Cecil B. De Mille epic *The Ten Commandments*; the second was a modestly budgeted British-made TV movie shot mostly on one set.

In the first, *Exodus: Gods and Kings* (2014), directed by Ridley Scott and starring Christian Bale, the audience follows the story of Moses as he flees Egypt, is called by God, wrestles with his calling, and leads the Jews to freedom. Many have rightly

faulted the film for its lackluster characters, its plodding narrative structure, and its jarring shifts in mood. But what is most disturbing about *Exodus: Gods and Kings* is its depiction of God. To
my horror, I watched as the Almighty Yahweh, maker of heaven
and earth, was reduced to a petulant boy who, by the end of the
movie, comes across as less holy and less loving than the confused
and erratic Moses.

In the second, *God on Trial* (2008), written by Frank Cottrell
Boyce and directed by Andy de Emmony, the audience is carried
away to a Nazi concentration camp where a group of Jews awaiting
execution literally put God on trial for breaking his covenant with
the Jewish people. The trial is gut-wrenching and effectively highlights some of the most difficult issues in religion, but it climaxes
with a pronouncement on the nature of God that chilled me to the
bone. After reviewing the various "atrocities" perpetrated by God
in the Old Testament—from the flood to the plagues on Egypt to
the conquest of Canaan—the most intelligent and passionate of
the witnesses declares that God is *not* good. He only *seemed* good
to the Jews of the Old Testament because he was on their side.

I had been sensing the problem for about five years, but I could
not put my finger on it. Watching *Exodus: Gods and Kings* and
God on Trial in the same week helped me to give expression to my
growing sense of dread: We are raising a generation of young people who consider themselves to be morally superior to the God of
the Old Testament.

Of Heresy and Creeds

Modern man is squeamish about words like *heretic* and *heresy*;
unfortunately, that squeamishness, of which we are falsely proud,
has led us to fall back into heresies that the church fathers defeated
1700 years ago. Because we no longer study church history—at

least we don't study it to learn from it—we end up having to fight the same theological battles over and over again. Our modern disease with the violent sections of the Old Testament is not, as we like to suppose, a testament to our greater sensitivity. It is merely a return to a major second-century heresy whose proponent, Marcion, we have allowed ourselves to forget.

A heretic is not someone whom we dislike; he is someone who knowingly twists a central teaching of Christian theology. Those teachings, which are clearly laid out in the Nicene Creed, include the following:

- that the earth was created out of nothing (*ex nihilo*) by a single God who is all-powerful, all-knowing, all-present, and all-loving

- that the one God exists eternally as three divine persons: the Father, the Son, and the Holy Spirit

- that we were created in God's image but disobeyed him and fell (became separated from him)

- that Jesus Christ is the incarnate Son of God, fully human and fully divine

- that Christ died on the cross to atone for our sins

- that he was resurrected on the third day and now sits enthroned at the right hand of God the Father

- that he will come again to judge the living and the dead, after which our bodies too will be resurrected

Though this list is not exhaustive, nearly all heresies in the church have arisen out of a denial or twisting of one or more of these tenets of the faith.

There are many today who argue that this Christian creed was "made up" at the Council of Nicea (325) and enforced by the emperor Constantine, who crushed an earlier, more authentic form of Christianity. This notion is utterly false to history. We have numerous letters written by such early Christians as Clement (written about 96) and Ignatius (written about 110)—not to mention the work of such second-century apologists as Justin Martyr, Irenaeus, and Tertullian—that attest to the fullness of Christian theology. Nicea did not make up theology but put into official statements what had long been believed and taught by the apostles and their successors.

Why then did they feel the need to put together the creed? To protect the church from enemies without (the pagans) and from within (the heretics). Chief among those heretics were the Arians, who taught that Jesus was not divine (he was just a God-ordained, God-inspired man), and the Gnostics, who taught that Jesus was not human (he only appeared to have a body). Neither group could accept the earth-shattering implications of the incarnation: that God would deign to take on human flesh and live as a man. That Jesus of Nazareth could be fully human and fully divine, 100 percent man and 100 percent God was foolishness to most of the heretics. In the face of attacks from Arians and Gnostics, the church was forced to protect the true and unique teachings of the apostles by encapsulating those teachings in a standard theological and philosophical language.

Interestingly, those who incorrectly charge Constantine and his cronies with imposing a creed upon fourth-century Christians that was not true to Jesus and his original followers tend also to charge the church with tyrannically imposing a scriptural canon that suppressed all writings that, like the Gnostic gospel of Thomas, did not reflect the official teaching of the church. But this charge also obscures the historical motivation for the formation of the canon.

With only a few exceptions (2 Peter, 2 and 3 John, and Jude, and, to a lesser extent, James and Revelation), the authority of the New Testament books, especially the four Gospels and the epistles of Paul, was universally accepted by the early church. The books of the Old Testament were also accepted as canonical and are quoted often by Clement and Ignatius. But then an influential Gnostic heretic rose up in the middle decades of the second century and began to deny the authority not only of the Old Testament, but of those books in the New Testament that relied heavily on and quoted often from the Old.

His name was Marcion, and his influence convinced the church of the need to establish an official canon—not by making it up out of whole cloth, but by giving their authoritative imprimatur to what already was accepted by the faithful. It later convinced Tertullian (c. 155–240) of the need to write a detailed refutation of Marcion's heretical understanding of the Old Testament and his even more heretical understanding of God.

> The Nicene Creed did not invent Christian orthodoxy; rather, it responded to heretical teachings within the church by putting into clear theological/philosophical language what was already believed by the apostles and their successors.

Marcionism Then and Now

I can understand, and even sympathize with, Marcion's fall into heresy. My first superficial reading of the Old and New Testaments left me with the uneasy feeling that I had been introduced to two different Gods: one who was perpetually angry and liked to zap people who stepped out of line, and one who was lovingly merciful and who never fought back or defended himself. Indeed, I would suggest that every Christian has, at one time or another, struggled with this seeming dichotomy between God the Father and Jesus Christ.

That uneasiness slowly lifted, however, as I read the Bible more closely, noticing the compassion that the God of the Old Testament offers to such non-Jews as Rahab the harlot, Ruth, and the repentant people of Nineveh, and the wrath that the God of the New Testament unleashes on the Pharisees and Sadducees in the Gospels and on the full unbelieving world in Revelation. God's justice and mercy were inextricably intertwined and could not be arbitrarily torn apart. The very same God whose holiness demanded that he punish sin allowed the full penalty of that sin to fall upon his Son. His righteous anger against those who willfully violate his standards is as much a part of who he is as his self-sacrificial love for sinners who repent of their sin and seek his forgiveness.

Sadly, the inseparable nature of God's justice and mercy was something Marcion found himself unable (or unwilling) to understand or accept. As Tertullian explains in *Against Marcion* (c. 208), Marcion taught his followers that the Gods of the Old and New Testaments not only seemed to be two different Gods; they *were*, in fact, two separate deities: "one judicial, harsh, mighty in war; the other mild, placid, and simply good and excellent" (Book I, Chapter 6). Not much has changed since Marcion preached his heretical views. Though no one today speaks, literally, of two gods, people inside and outside the church have continued to drive a wedge between Yahweh, the angry tribal deity who thunders on Mount Sinai, and Jesus meek and mild preaching a gospel of permissiveness and inclusivism.

Ignoring the fact that God blessed Abraham (and his Jewish descendants) *so that* all peoples would be blessed through him

(Genesis 12:2-3), the modern mind, starting with the Jewish Spinoza, has rejected, often vehemently, the possibility that God could have been so narrow and exclusivist as to care only for one people group. The very notion that God could hate some things, and some people, and love others does not sit well with our modern egalitarian beliefs. Because we have lost the ability to distinguish between fairness (treating everyone the same) and true justice (giving to each what is his proper due), between weak-kneed tolerance (that wiggles and squiggles like unformed Jell-O) and pure holiness (that consumes like a raging fire), we find ourselves increasingly unable to embrace the Old Testament and to grasp the unity and fullness of the triune God who speaks to us and acts in human history from the first chapter of Genesis to the last chapter of Revelation.

Indeed, I would argue that our lost ability to make that distinction and grasp that unity has given the new atheists their strongest argument. Actually, if truth be told, it has given them their *only* argument. The newest discoveries in science; the return of philosophy to its theistic roots; the latest research on the historicity of the Gospels, the Pauline epistles, and the resurrection; and the work of Christian sociologists and psychologists who have reclaimed the social sciences from their secular humanistic roots has laid to rest most of the stock arguments of Dawkins, Hitchens, and company. I believe the new atheists are aware of this; that is why they have been getting bolder and nastier in their attacks on God himself. Oh, they have no problem domesticating and defanging Jesus, but the God of the Old Testament who chooses, judges, and kills has got to go! Which means that Christianity—true, orthodox, Nicene Christianity—must go as well.

The new Marcionism has been expressed most fully and unapologetically in the infamous opening paragraph of chapter 2 of Richard Dawkins's *The God Delusion*:

The God of the Old Testament is arguably the most
unpleasant character in all fiction: jealous and proud
of it; a petty, unjust, unforgiving control-freak; a vin-
dictive, bloodthirsty ethnic cleanser; a misogynistic,
homophobic, racist, infanticidal, genocidal, filicidal,
pestilential, megalomaniacal, sadomasochistic, capri-
ciously malevolent bully.

Marcion himself could not have said it better. In the previous
chapter, I argued, alongside C.S. Lewis, that a divine, universal,
cross-cultural standard of right and wrong exists (the Tao) which
we know we must follow but which we nevertheless break. Here,
Dawkins reverses the favor: constructing his own Western, twenty-
first century man-made code and then judging God against that
code—and finding him wanting.

But are Marcion and Dawkins correct? Is the God of the Old
Testament really inconsistent with that of the New? Or, to put it
more pointedly, can we tear Jesus away from Yahweh and still have
a Jesus who can in any way have the power or desire to save us?
Some 1,800 years ago, Tertullian answered that question with a
decisive no. We would do well today to heed his reasons.

> From the earliest days of Christianity, heretics have
> tried, unsuccessfully, to drive a wedge between the
> God of the Old Testament and the New, between an
> angry tribal deity and a meek and mild Savior.

The Impotent God of Marcion (and Dawkins)

To maintain, as Marcion does, that Yahweh and Jesus are two
separate gods, we must imagine that the latter and loving God just
sat on his hands for thousands of years while the former and judg-
mental God blasted away at us. If Jesus was truly a God of pure

goodness and love, Tertullian asks, then why didn't he intervene immediately after the Fall and save Adam and Eve? Of course, in orthodox Christianity, Yahweh *does* immediately offer provision—prophesying that a time will come when a son of Eve will crush the head of the serpent at the cost of his own pain (Genesis 3:15). But Marcion can't accept that because he throws out the Old Testament and its prophecies of the Messiah.

Marcionism, past and present, conveniently obscures the clear teaching of the Bible: that the God of the Old Testament is the same God who promised and then sent his Son into the world to save us. Yahweh and Jesus are not two competing Gods, but the same God (the first and second persons of the Trinity) who both judges and saves, who both condemns us for violating the law and then takes the punishment of the violation upon himself. Our modern age wants a user-friendly God who affirms all that we do, either by turning a blind eye to our sins or by graciously redefining them so they are no longer sinful. But such a God would by definition be a tyrant, for he would break his own laws whenever it was expedient or it made him feel good about himself.

The God that Marcion (and his heirs) wants—a God who loves without judging—is an impossibility. How is it possible, Tertullian asks, that this God

> should issue commands, if he does not mean to execute them; or forbid sins, if he intends not to punish them, but rather to decline the functions of the judge, as being a stranger to all notions of severity and judicial chastisement? For why does he forbid the commission of that which he punishes not when perpetrated? (Book I, Chapter 26).

One can't be a judge and not a judge at the same time and in the same way. One can't be a just God and not uphold justice when it is violated.

The God we say we want—even if he could logically exist— would be a weak, impotent God who would not deserve and could not win our obedience or trust. Such a God, Tertullian explains, would be utterly listless,

> since he takes no offense at the doing of what he dis- likes to be done, although displeasure ought to be the companion of his violated will. Now, if he is offended, he ought to be angry; if angry, he ought to inflict pun- ishment. For such infliction is the just fruit of anger, and anger is the debt of displeasure, and displeasure… is the companion of a violated will. However, he inflicts no punishment; therefore he takes no offense (I.26).

Remarkably, Tertullian describes here exactly the kind of God so many modern people, Christian or otherwise, desire—one who is never offended and never punishes. But such a God is not wor- thy of worship or even respect.

He is not even the kind of God we *really* want. Though we like the fact that he turns a blind eye to our sins and those of our group, we are enraged when his abdication-of-responsibility ethos causes him to turn a blind eye as well toward the slaveholders of the old South, the perpetrators of the Holocaust, the architects of apart- heid, and the 9/11 terrorists. We don't want justice against our pet sins, but we very much want justice against those crimes that we consider the most heinous.

Whether we want it to or not, our conscience cries out that Ter- tullian is correct when he writes that nothing is so unworthy of the Divine Being as not to execute retribution on what He has disliked and forbidden. *First*, He owes the infliction of chastisement to whatever sentence or law He promulgates, for the vindication of His authority and the maintenance of submission to it; *secondly*, because hostile opposition is inevitable to what He has disliked to be done, and by that dislike forbidden. Moreover, it would be a more unworthy course for God to spare the evil-doer than to punish him, especially in the most good and holy God, who is not otherwise fully good than as the enemy of evil, and *that* to such a degree as to display His love of good by the hatred of evil, and to fulfill His defense of the former by the extirpation of the latter (I.26).

The God of the Bible, Yahweh and Jesus alike, is a holy God who hates evil. Our moral outrage is puny compared to his. It is puny and inconsistent, for it comes and goes, depending on what party we belong to, what news channel we watch, what we ate the night before, and what kinds of behaviors we engaged in when we were in college.

> Like Marcion, many today want a user-friendly God who loves but does not judge—until something we consider evil occurs. Then we cry out for a God of justice.

Moralistic Therapeutic Deism

In chapter 3 of *The Problem of Pain*, C.S. Lewis says that while we all claim to want a Father in heaven, what we really want is "a grandfather in heaven—a senile benevolence who, as they say, 'liked to see young people enjoying themselves,' and whose plan for the universe was simply that it might be truly said at the end of each day, 'a good time was had by all.'" I'd like to say Lewis is exaggerating, but he isn't. In fact, his words are far truer today than they were when he wrote them at the outset of WWII.

We simply do not know what we are asking for when we ask for Marcion's Jesus. But Tertullian knew, and he explains it in words that are as searingly relevant today as when he first wrote them. Consider again, Tertullian implores us, what an exclusively meek and mild Jesus really means:

> Again, he plainly judges evil by not willing it, and condemns it by prohibiting it; while, on the other hand, he acquits it by not avenging it, and lets it go free by not punishing it. What a prevaricator of truth is such a god! What a dissembler with his own decision! Afraid to condemn what he really condemns, afraid to hate what he does not love, permitting that to be done which he does not allow, choosing to indicate what he dislikes rather than deeply examine it! This will turn out an imaginary goodness, a phantom of discipline, perfunctory in duty, careless in sin (I.27).

Is this really the God we want? Is this really the God that our *sensus divinitatis* points us toward? The God to whom we would appeal in the face of evil and injustice? Mercy has no power and no meaning if it is separated from justice. It is neither strong nor honest; it is not even, by any real measure, good. What kind of Savior is this who is afraid to discipline, afraid to act, afraid even to judge?

Yet we persist in wanting him to be our God. In a wonderful burst of rhetorical sarcasm, Tertullian tells the followers of

Marcion—and through them, us—exactly why we want this impossible, impotent God:

> Listen, you sinners; and you who have not yet come
> to this, hear, that you may attain to such a pass! A bet-
> ter god has been discovered, who never takes offense,
> is never angry, never inflicts punishment, who has pre-
> pared no fire in hell, no gnashing of teeth in the outer
> darkness! He is purely and simply good. He indeed
> forbids all delinquency, but only in word. He is in you,
> if you are willing to pay him homage, for the sake of
> appearances, that you may seem to honor God; for
> your fear he does not want (I.27).

What Tertullian (anachronistically) describes here is what soci-ologists Christian Smith and Melinda Lundquist Denton found when they interviewed 3,000 Americans teenagers on their reli-gious beliefs. Whether or not they identified as Christian, most teenagers ascribed to a religion Smith and Denton dubbed Moral-istic Therapeutic Deism (MTD).

Like Tertullian's Marcionites, practitioners of MTD believe in God, which, on the surface, sets them apart from Dawkins and the new atheists. But that God bears only a slight resemblance to the God of the Bible. The goal of MTD is not to stand in awe before the all-holy, all-powerful Creator of the universe or even to feel a profound sense of remorse and gratitude for what Christ suffered on our behalf, but to be happy and to feel good about ourselves. God is in control on the macro level, but we need to call on him only when we have a problem. As long as we are good and nice and fair to those around us, God will leave us alone and take us to heaven when we die.

According to the proverbial wisdom of the Bible, the fear of the

Lord is the beginning of wisdom (Job 28:28; Psalm 111:10; Proverbs 1:7). In Marcionism, MTD, and new atheism, that vital fear of the Lord is lost. As Tertullian goes on to explain:

> And so satisfied are the Marcionites with such pretences, that they have no fear of their god at all. They say it is only a bad man who will be feared, a good man will be loved. Foolish man, do you say that he whom you call Lord ought not to be feared, while the very title you give him indicates a power which must itself be feared? But how are you going to love, without some fear that you do not love? Surely (such a god) is neither your Father, towards whom your love for duty's sake should be consistent with fear because of His power; nor your proper Lord, whom you should love for His humanity and fear as your teacher (I.27).

Lewis, like Tertullian, saw the advent of MTD; both sensed our desire for a grandfather in heaven whom we need not fear, whom we can manipulate and patronize at will. But a true Father, like a true Lord, is to be loved *and* feared, a universal, cross-cultural pillar of the Tao for which our egalitarian age has little sympathy or patience.

> Moralistic Therapeutic Deism, like Marcionism, seeks not a just, holy Father in heaven but an indulgent grandfather in heaven, someone who will make us feel good about ourselves and take us to heaven when we die.

Anthropomorphism

The true God, argues Tertullian in Book II, Chapter 1 of *Against Marcion*, "ought to be worshiped rather than judged; served reverentially rather than handled critically, or even dreaded for His severity." This advice our age has not heeded. We would stand in judgment over God and the Bible rather than let them stand in judgment over us. Despite the seemingly ubiquitous presence of the new atheists, a very small minority of people are able to convince themselves that there is no God. What most do instead, Tertullian goes on to explain in chapter 2, is to censure God on the basis of their own sense experience of the world and of themselves.

I remember speaking to a fellow Christian once who expressed severe doubt as to whether God would actually send someone to hell. Here was his logic: (1) I would not send someone to hell; (2) surely God is more merciful than I am; therefore, (3) God would not send someone to hell. Ironically, my friend's method for tempering God's justice and accommodating it to modern—or, to be more accurate, postmodern—sensibilities would have been attacked by Lucretius, Spinoza, and Hume alike as a fallacious example of anthropomorphism—that is to say, of projecting our own human characteristics on to God. Nearly every critic, past and present, of the Old Testament who shares Marcion's animus against Yahweh will, at some point, make use of the anthropomorphism attack. Such critics simply take for granted that whenever God is described as having or acting in accordance with human-type emotions that the biblical writer is anthropomorphizing.

In one sense I would agree with this critique. Marcionism, MTD, and my friend's critique of hell all proceed out of a subtle form of anthropomorphism that begins with this unproven assumption: God must be as singularly focused as I am on tolerance and inclusivism or he wouldn't be a fit deity. But this is not what we encounter in the Old Testament. If God appears to display human emotions in the Bible, that is not because we have made him in our image, but because we were made in his. We, unique among animals, possess consciousness, rationality, and free will, because we alone were made in the image of a conscious, rational, free God.

Because Tertullian realized that this misunderstanding of anthropomorphism was central to the Marcion heresy, he addresses it head-on in his refutation of Marcion:

> Furthermore, although you allow, with others, that man was inbreathed by God into a living soul, not God by man, it is yet palpably absurd of you to be placing human characteristics in God rather than divine ones in man, and clothing God in the likeness of man, instead of man in the image of God. And this, therefore, is to be deemed the likeness of God in man, that the human soul has the same emotions and sensations as God, although they are not of the same kind; differing as they do both in their conditions and their issues according to their nature. Then, again, with respect to the opposite sensations—I mean meekness, patience, mercy, and the very parent of them all, goodness— why do you form your opinion of the divine displays of these (from the human qualities)? For we indeed do not possess them in perfection, because it is God alone who is perfect. So also in regard to those others—namely, anger and irritation, we are not affected by them in so happy a manner, because God alone is truly happy, by reason of His property of incorruptibility. Angry He will possibly be, but not irritated, nor dangerously tempted; He will be moved, but not subverted (II.16).

In sharp contrast to Greek mythology, where Zeus's lust and wrath *do* represent human lust and wrath taken to the extreme by a being who is immune from weakness, disease, and death, the anger that Yahweh expresses in the Old Testament is not human anger magnified and writ large on a cosmic scale. To the contrary, it is our human anger that represents a corruption of the pure, righteous anger of the One who made us in his image.

It is *our* morality, not God's, that is flawed and broken. Human jealousy is nearly always marred by pettiness, rancor, hypocrisy, or wrath. Even if the jealousy is justified, we too often use that justification as a cover for pride, bitterness, resentment, and injustice. Not so God's jealousy, which is perfect and pure.

It is right that a man should feel jealous if his wife commits adultery on him; if he did not, he could hardly be said to truly love her or to take seriously their marriage vows. God's love for his bride (first Israel and later the church) is real and total; if he did not react with jealousy when his bride committed spiritual adultery with the world, then the purity of his love would be thrown into question. What would you think of a man who did not feel righteous anger toward the atrocities committed by the Nazis? Just so, God's judgment on the Egyptians, the Canaanites, the Assyrians, the Babylonians, the Philistines, and the Phoenicians is in keeping with the evil of their deeds.

> The reason God is depicted as having human-like emotions in the Bible is not because the writers projected their emotions on to God, but because our emotions are a lesser, broken reflection of that which is perfect and whole in God.

Christian Cross-Examination #1: Evil Originated in a Misuse of Free Will

But why, the Marcionite of yesterday or today asks, does God react with wrath and jealousy when he himself is the origin of human wickedness? What choice did Adam and Eve really have? Surely God must have known that we would disobey and fall. If he did not, then he is not truly sovereign; if he did, then he must be the ultimate cause of that fall, and of all the evil that it ushered into the world.

The answer to this conundrum, resolved by Tertullian and countless apologists after him, is simply this: Evil was ushered into the world by a misuse of free will. Genesis makes it clear that we were made in God's image. If we are not truly free, if we cannot choose between good and evil, obedience and rebellion, then we do not bear the image of God. Tertullian explains this with his signature clarity and directness:

> ...man was by God constituted free, master of his own
> will and power; indicating the presence of God's image
> and likeness in him by nothing so well as by this con-
> stitution of his nature. For it was not by his face, and
> by the lineaments of his body, though they were so
> varied in his human nature, that he expressed his like-
> ness to the form of God; but he showed his stamp in
> that essence which he derived from God Himself (that
> is, the spiritual, which answered to the form of God),
> and in the freedom and power of his will. This his state
> was confirmed even by the very law which God then
> imposed upon him. For a law would not be imposed
> upon one who had it not in his power to render that
> obedience which is due to law; nor again, would the

penalty of death be threatened against sin, if a contempt of the law were impossible to man in the liberty of his will. So in the Creator's subsequent laws also you will find, when He sets before man good and evil, life and death, that the entire course of discipline is arranged in precepts by God's calling men from sin, and threatening and exhorting them; and this on no other ground than that man is free, with a will either for obedience or resistance (II.5).

I must apologize for these lengthy quotes, but once one begins on a passage from Tertullian, it's hard to know when to stop. Besides, Tertullian's *Against Marcion* lies at the very core of the vision and purpose of this book. As I've tried to make clear in the previous chapters, not only the attacks against theism and Christianity but the rebuttals to those attacks have been with us for thousands of years. Man did not "evolve" from faith to skepticism; both options have been available for millennia and the debate—sometimes friendly, sometimes heated—has continued unabated for all those years. True, atheism in its various forms has made a number of attempts to put Christianity (or at least theism) on trial. But Christianity, more often than not, has returned the favor, mounting skillful arguments and cross-examinations that have silenced the champions of atheism.

There is no expiration date on the long passage I just quoted. It was either true or false when it was written, and it continues to be so today. To be made in God's image is to be a free moral-ethical agent, but that freedom has no meaning unless we have something to choose. Just as God's law presupposes that we are volitional beings who are capable of making real choices, so the fact that he appends punishments to the breaking of that law presupposes that we can make the free choice to break it. The fact that God, because he dwells outside of time, knew from the beginning the (bad) choice we would make does not nullify the reality of the choice. To the contrary, it is the proof that God, in his love, made us free and separate agents who could choose to violate his will.

Very well, the skeptic might reply, I see that as creatures made in God's image, we necessarily share in his divine freedom. But why then do we not also share in his divine goodness? Shouldn't evil be impossible to one made in the image of a good God? No, Tertullian replies, because there is a difference between God's goodness and ours:

> Now, God alone is good by nature. For He, who has that which is without beginning, has it not by creation, but by nature. Man, however, who exists entirely by creation, having a beginning, along with that beginning obtained the form in which he exists; and thus he is not by nature disposed to good, but by creation, not having it as his own attribute to be good, because (as we have said), it is not by nature, but by creation, that he is disposed to good, according to the appointment of his good Creator, even the Author of all good (II.6).

God *is* good; we, in contrast, possess the *capacity* for goodness. Just as our emotions are, unlike those of God, subject to corruption, so our goodness can be compromised and even forfeited by our willful choice to reject the laws of our Creator.

Sadly, one of the results of our disobedience and the subsequent corruption of our goodness is a deep-seated refusal to allow our fallen sense of goodness to be judged by and measured against God's perfect goodness. Instead, we convince ourselves that it is

God's goodness that should be judged by and measured against our sense of the way things ought to be. We don't understand the fullness of God's holiness: partly out of ignorance because our loss of original goodness has blinded us to the full nature of the divine and spotless holiness; and partly out of arrogance because we consider our goodness to be more godly, more tolerant, and more enlightened than his holiness.

> The fact that God imposed a law upon Adam and Eve and that he assigned punishments for the breaking of that law offers strong evidence not only that the freedom God gave them was real, but that they possessed the power to disobey him and his laws.

Christian Cross-Examination #2: God's Goodness and Justice Are Intertwined

"Up to the fall of man," writes Tertullian, "from the beginning God was simply good; after that He became a judge both severe and, as the Marcionites will have it, cruel" (II.11). Since we currently stand in a relationship of rebellion toward God and his law, God's goodness is now, of necessity, mixed up with his justice—for violations of God's holy law demand retribution. Which is not to say that God was not just before the Fall; merely, that that part of God's nature was altered and took on a different character *toward us* as a consequence of the Fall.

In the beginning, before the Fall, God's goodness and justice "advanced together. His goodness created, His justice arranged, the world; and in this process it even then decreed that the world should be formed of good materials, because it took counsel with goodness" (II.12). A quick glance over Genesis 1 will confirm that much of what God does during the creation week is a work of sifting and discerning, of separating the light from the darkness, the earth from the sky, the dry land from the waters. In our modern day, the word *discrimination* has almost been banished from the language; yet God demonstrated his original pre-Fall justice through a process of discrimination—of ordering, distinguishing, and putting things in their proper hierarchical categories.

Alas, Tertullian continues, after we fell,

> …and the goodness of God began now to have an adversary to contend against, God's justice also acquired another function, even that of directing His goodness according to men's application for it. And this is the result: the divine goodness, being interrupted in that free course whereby God was spontaneously good, is now dispensed according to the deserts of every man; it is offered to the worthy, denied to the unworthy, taken away from the unthankful, and also avenged on all its enemies. Thus the entire office of justice in this respect becomes an agency for goodness: whatever it condemns by its judgment, whatever it chastises by its condemnation, whatever (to use your phrase) it ruthlessly pursues, it, in fact, benefits with good instead of injuring. Indeed, the fear of judgment contributes to good, not to evil (II.13).

These words are as hard for modern ears to hear as they were for the ears of the Marcionites. But they must be heard. For it is God's justice that not only stems the tide of evil but builds in us that fear of the Lord which is the beginning of wisdom. And it is only that fear of the Lord that keeps us on track, that prevents us from falling further into moral entropy and self-destruction.

Critics from Marcion to Dawkins who rail against the severity of God's justice must be reminded of God's holiness, of our fallen state, and the evil that is in the world:

> We dread the Creator's tremendous threats, and yet scarcely turn away from evil. What if He threatened not? Will you call this justice an evil, when it is all unfavorable to evil? Will you deny it to be a good, when it has its eye towards good? What sort of being ought you to wish God to be? Would it be right to prefer that He should be such, that sins might flourish under Him, and the devil mock Him? Would you suppose Him to be a good God, who should be able to make a man worse by security in sin? Who is the author of good, but He who also requires it?...justice is the very fullness of the Deity Himself, manifesting God as both a perfect father and a perfect master: a father in His mercy, a master in His discipline; a father in the mildness of His power, a master in its severity; a father who must be loved with dutiful affection, a master who must needs be feared (II.13).

What do we want? That sin and evil should get the upper hand? That God should be mocked by the devil? It is not enough for us to love God; we must fear him as well, ascribing to him the proper reverence that is his due. It is not enough for God to show only his mercy. If he is to deal with evil, he must show his justice as well.

As Tertullian goes on to explain in chapters 14 and 15, the severity of God is remedial in nature, meant to break through the hardness of our sin. It may result in what appears to us as evil, but it is of a wholly different kind than the evil we encounter in the world. God's "evils" are penal in nature, while those from the devil are sinful through and through. The end of God's justice is goodness, wholeness, and life, while the devil seeks only to steal, to kill, and to destroy (John 10:10).

> God's justice not only stems the tide of evil; it builds in us that fear of the Lord, which is the beginning of wisdom.

Postscript

As I was constructing this chapter and choosing those arguments from Tertullian that best retain their power in our at-once modern and postmodern world, I was struck by how many of his arguments are echoed, probably unconsciously, by a great English poet and essayist who lived more than 1,500 years after Tertullian. I speak of John Milton, author of the epic *Paradise Lost* and of one of the greatest defenses of the freedom of the press, "Areopagitica."

In the former work, Milton offers the same analysis, albeit in poetry, of the origin of evil, carefully exonerating God of any guilt for our fall into sin. As God himself explains to the angels as he watches Satan fly toward Eden to tempt Adam and Eve,

And now

Through all restraint broke loose [Satan] wings his way
Not far off heav'n, in the precincts of light,
Directly towards the new-created world,
And man there placed, with purpose to assay
If him by force he can destroy, or worse,
By some false guile pervert; and shall pervert
For man will hearken to his glozing lies,
And easily transgress the sole command,
Sole pledge of his obedience: so will fall,
He and his faithless progeny: whose fault?

Whose but his own? Ingrate, he had of me
All he could have; I made him just and right,
Sufficient to have stood, though free to fall.
Such I created all th' ethereal Powers
And Spirits, both them who stood and them who
    failed;
Freely they stood who stood, and fell who fell.
Not free, what proof could they have given sincere
Of true allegiance, constant faith or love,
Where only what they needs must do, appeared,
Not what they would? What praise could they receive?
What pleasure I from such obedience paid,
When will and reason (reason also is choice)
Useless and vain, of freedom both despoiled,
Made passive both, had served necessity,
Not me. They therefore as to right belonged,
So were created, nor can justly accuse
Their maker, or their making, or their fate,
As if predestination over-ruled
Their will, disposed by absolute decree
Or high foreknowledge; they themselves decreed
Their own revolt, not I: if I foreknew,
Foreknowledge had no influence on their fault,
Which had no less proved certain unforeknown
(III.86-119).

Paradise Lost is not an easy poem, but here Milton speaks clearly
and directly. The fault for the Fall is ours, for God *did* make us sufficient to resist temptation. Our choice to disobey God's just com-
mands was a free one, as was the choice of Satan and the other
fallen angels who rebelled against God.

How could it have been otherwise? Had our will not been free, then we could not have obeyed God or shown any true loyalty and allegiance to him. If our choice was not real, then our obedience would have been forced and therefore neither sincere nor meritorious. Without free will, we would have served necessity rather than God; just so, animals act on the basis of instinct rather than moral-ethical choice. As Milton makes clear, reason, will, and choice are inextricably bound together. We would not be rational creatures if we were not also volitional creatures. That, in part, is what it means to be made in the image of God.

It is true that God foreknew what our choice would be, but that foreknowledge did not affect our free choice to disobey. The author of evil is not God, but our misuse of the free will we were given at our creation. As to whether God was right to give us free will, that is not a question we can answer from our limited perspective. God's goodness assures us of the rightness of his decision to gift us with freedom, even as his justice works to stem the consequences of our foolish and thankless misuse of that precious gift.

And what of those consequences? From Tertullian I learned how the Fall brought a change to the function and manifestation of God's justice in the world, ushering in a new kind of penal evil that brings with it real pain and suffering even as it furthers the workings of God's justice. From Milton's "Areopagitica," I learned something similar, but more far-reaching. Milton the Puritan revolutionary fought against all forms of censorship, for he understood that the Fall robbed our human sphere, temporarily, at least, of pure goodness, truth, and beauty:

> Good and evil we know in the field of this world grow
> up together almost inseparably; and the knowledge of

good is so involved and interwoven with the knowledge of evil, and in so many cunning resemblances hardly to be discerned, that those confused seeds which were imposed upon Psyche as an incessant labor to cull out, and sort asunder, were not more intermixed. It was from out the rind of one apple tasted, that the knowledge of good and evil, as two twins cleaving together, leaped forth into the world. And perhaps this is that doom which Adam fell into of knowing good and evil, that is to say of knowing good by evil. As therefore the state of man is, what wisdom can there be to choose, what continence to forbear, without the knowledge of evil? He that can apprehend and consider vice with all her baits and seeming pleasures, and yet abstain, and yet distinguish, and yet prefer that which is truly better, he is the true wayfaring Christian.

We live in a messy, fragmented world, where good and evil grow, not only side by side, but intertwined with each other. Indeed, so intertwined are they that we must often go *through* evil to get to the good.

The growing number of people today who consider themselves to be more moral than the God of the Old Testament would do well to remember that good and evil are no longer capable of being simply and cleanly discerned and separated. As a professor at a Christian school, I have found that the two most common reasons that my church-raised students distance themselves from the God who revealed himself to Moses—and thereby stray from the Christian faith, since that God is also the Father of our Lord and Savior Jesus Christ—are the conquest of Canaan (recorded in

Joshua) and the wide-ranging issues surrounding homosexuality and transgenderism.

The first they dismiss as a form of ethnic cleansing, forgetting the degree of evil to which the Canaanites had sunk and the centuries that God patiently waited to allow them time either to repent or to reach the fullness of their depravity. When an entire nation turns to evil, there are no easy solutions; one can't surgically remove the "baddest" of the bad people and leave the rest untouched. Given the degree of sin and moral confusion that reigns in our fallen world, there are no global game plans that don't carry with them devastating collateral damage. We live in a world where both the blessings and the sins of the fathers are visited on their sons to the third and fourth generation.

As for the champions of gay marriage and the arbitrary choosing of one's gender, their smugness and self-righteousness are almost too much to bear. Such "enlightened" thinkers are not only convinced of their moral superiority to Yahweh; they think they are absolutely, unequivocally right in holding a position that no civilized (or primitive) group or nation could have even conceived of before the closing decades of the twentieth century. Yes, there is a beauty to modern tolerance and inclusivism, but they cannot be as easily disassociated from evil and depravity as their advocates seem to think. The gay-transgender lifestyle carries with it remarkably high levels of depression, substance abuse, and suicide not because of social scorn but because those who participate in it are setting themselves against their created nature, treating disordered desires as if they were pure fountains flowing from a pure source.

Much goodness, truth, and beauty have been brought into the world by those trapped, through a mixture of heredity, environment, and choice, in the LGBT lifestyle; those contributions should be accepted and their contributors thanked and protected from abuse. But we must not confuse the inherent value of the contribution and the contributor with the brokenness of the lifestyle. If we do not know the proper nature and function of a thing, we will misuse, injure, or break it. Our Creator alone knows what that nature and function are; if we set ourselves against him or replace his standards and definitions with our own, then we will bring ruin upon ourselves, our families, and our society.

CHAPTER SEVEN

The Problem of Pain

I remember well the first time I sat down to tackle Thomas Aquinas's monumental *Summa Theologica*. I was used to reading dense philosophical tomes by then, but was unprepared for Aquinas's decidedly odd way of framing his philosophical proofs. He begins innocuously enough with a question that demands a yes or no answer. Then he moves on to offer, in a fair-minded, non-biased way, two or more objections to the answer he intends to offer. Then he answers those objections by way of authority (usually the Bible or Aristotle); then he gives his own view on the matter; then he looks again more closely at each objection to see how and why it falls short of total truth.

When I reached Part I, Question 2, Article 3, and saw that Aquinas would tackle right off the bat the question of whether or not God existed, I was eager to see how many objections to the existence of God Aquinas would come up with. Shockingly, he offered two, *and only two*, reasons for denying God's existence! Aquinas, one of the greatest minds in human history, could identify only two reasons why a rational person would choose the atheist position.

In chapters 1, 2, and 3, I already discussed the first of those reasons: that everything in the world can be explained by natural processes. I would now like to consider the second reason: the problem of pain.

The Problem Posed

In the previous chapter, I argued, with the help of Tertullian and Milton, that evil was not caused or created by God but was ushered into the world through our misuse of the free will with which God gifted us. Traditionally, this response to the origin of evil also provides the central theological-philosophical answer to the problem of pain, to why there is so much suffering and injustice in the world. Still, as the problem of pain is arguably the strongest and most ubiquitous argument leveled against Christianity today—not to mention the argument that touches individual seekers on the most personal level—it deserves to have a chapter devoted to it alone.

On several occasions now, I have had recourse to quote from the founder of Epicureanism, Epicurus, and from one of the chief architects of empiricism, David Hume. Interestingly, when it comes to wielding the problem of pain as a weapon against belief in a personal, holy, historically active God to whom we are accountable, Epicurus and Hume, though separated by two millennia, speak as one voice.

Indeed, when Hume, in his *Dialogues Concerning Natural Religion*, states the problem of pain as one of his knockout punches against Christian theism, he does it via a reference to Epicurus. Hume seems willing to entertain a severely limited theism in which God has nothing to do but exist. However, as I mentioned in chapter 4, there is nothing specifically Christian about Hume's *Dialogues*; the words *Trinity*, *incarnation*, *atonement*, and *resurrection*

are never mentioned, and the words *Christian* and *revelation* appear
only once and at the very end.

What neither Epicurus nor Hume (nor Spinoza) can abide is
the (to them) ridiculous and even offensive notion that God might
be a personal God, that he might have likes and dislikes, that he
might be intentionally holy and merciful. Any suggestion that God
might have these qualities—that he could really make covenants
with people groups and desire our good—would be dismissed as
anthropomorphic thinking, as a primitive projection of our own
human emotions on to God.

Here, then, are the words that Hume puts in the mouth of his
spokesman, Philo, as he tries to convince the rational Cleanthes—
who favors the argument by design—that God, even if he exists,
cannot be the kind of loving, active God Christians claim he is:

> And is it possible, *Cleanthes*, said *Philo*, that after all
> these reflections, and infinitely more, which might be
> suggested, you can still persevere in your anthropo-
> morphism, and assert the moral attributes of the deity,
> his justice, benevolence, mercy, and rectitude, to be of
> the same nature with these virtues in human creatures?
> His power we allow infinite: Whatever he wills is exe-
> cuted: But neither man nor any other animal is happy:
> Therefore he does not will their happiness. His wis-
> dom is infinite: He is never mistaken in choosing the
> means to any end: But the course of nature tends not
> to human or animal felicity: Therefore it is not estab-
> lished for that purpose. Through the whole compass of
> human knowledge, there are no inferences more cer-
> tain and infallible than these. In what respect, then, do

his benevolence and mercy resemble the benevolence
and mercy of men?

Epicurus's old questions are yet unanswered. Is he
willing to prevent evil, but not able? then is he impotent. Is he able, but not willing? then is he malevolent. Is he both able and willing? whence then is evil?
(Part X).

There is the argument in a nutshell. It has not changed for thousands of years, and it continues to be offered up by new atheists as
sufficient reason to dismiss the God of the Bible.

Please be clear: The problem of pain emerges at the precise
moment we begin speaking of the God revealed in the Bible. If
God were impersonal, if he were nothing more than the God of
Spinoza (that is, equivalent to nature), then there would be no
problem of pain. If God were like the petty, cruel gods of Greco-
Roman mythology, then there would likewise be no problem. Pain
only becomes a problem if we accept the biblical revelation that
God is omnipotent (all-powerful) and omnibenevolent (all-loving).

As C.S. Lewis himself makes clear in the introductory chapter
of his *The Problem of Pain*, it is ludicrous to imagine that early man,
looking at the world around him, would have inferred an omnibenevolent God in the face of so much suffering and death. Again,
pain *only* becomes a problem when we accept the Bible's revelation
of God's mercy and personal love for the creatures he made.

> According to the problem of pain, human suffering
> suggests that God is either too weak to do away with it
> or lacks the loving desire to eliminate it. In either
> case, it is only a problem if God is conceived to be
> all-powerful and all-loving.

The God of the Philosophers

Like all the major arguments against God, particularly the Christian God, the problem of pain has been with us for thousands of years; and yet, when it comes to this specific argument, there is a great irony. In the early church and Middle Ages, when disease and mortality rates were much higher and the overall level of pain and suffering more acute, there was far less outcry against God and far less use of the problem of pain as a means of disproving his existence or denying his biblical traits.

It was not until the Enlightenment that the problem of pain became a major sticking point, and not until the modern world that it became the argument one most often hears leveled against God and Christianity. In fact, I don't think it an exaggeration to say that those groups that are the most shielded from suffering—think well-educated, upper-middle-class white Americans and Europeans—tend to be the ones who trumpet most loudly the problem of pain. It seems that the more our pain decreases, the more our sense of entitlement and outrage increases, rather than our humility and gratitude.

But the irony goes deeper than this. The rise in the strength and shrillness of the problem of pain argument not only tracks with a general lessening in human suffering; it tracks as well with the slow ascendancy of the Enlightenment God of the Philosophers. Unlike the God of the Bible, who takes an active role in the affairs of nature and of man, who is holy *and* merciful, and who loves some things and hates others, the God of the Philosophers is more of a hypothetical construct, a divine idea whose chief, if only, function is to serve as a theoretical stay against infinite regress.

Although Bacon, Descartes, and Spinoza—the three philosophers who laid the foundation for that Enlightenment thinking that would reach its climax in Locke, Hume, and Kant—disagreed on a number of key issues, their various methods and theories all worked toward the same effect of depersonalizing God. Yes, their God exists and he may even have power, but he is not the covenant God of Israel, nor is he the holy God who cannot have sin in his presence, nor is he the jealous but compassionate God who weeps over adulterous Jerusalem, nor is he the courageous God who enters our world as a man, nor is he the self-sacrificing God who gave his Son for the life of the world.

At this point, careful readers may have spotted a seeming contradiction in my treatment of the problem of pain. Did I not say a moment ago that the problem of pain only becomes a problem when we are dealing with the God of the Bible? And does not Hume all but admit that the deistic God of the Philosophers—on account of his not embodying or reflecting anything like human standards of "justice, benevolence, mercy, and rectitude"—is relatively immune from the problem of pain?

Well, yes. But here is where one layer of irony gets inscribed over another. Critics of Christianity since the Enlightenment—especially the new atheists of today—want to have their cake and eat it too. They first reduce the biblical God to the God of the Philosophers, and then turn around and attack that emasculated God for not coming to their rescue. They remind me of countless Americans I know who proclaim loudly and continuously that the government needs to get off of their backs; but then the second the slightest thing goes wrong, they complain even more loudly, "Where was the government, and why didn't it protect me?"

Let me state this in a different way. Most philosophers and theologians since the Enlightenment throw around words like *omnipotent, omnibenevolent, omnipresent,* and *omniscient* without investing them with anything close to their full biblical meaning.

They are just terms: adjectives to describe a hypothetical deity rather than verbs offering a glimpse into the cosmic activity of a creative God intimately involved in his creation. When they speak of a loving God, they do not mean the triune God of orthodox Christianity in which the eternal Father has eternally loved the eternal Son; they only mean love as a vague idea, an impersonal Platonic Form. Love in the Bible has little to do with some philosopher's abstract notion of "niceness" or "fair play." The love that we encounter in Genesis and then in the Gospels is a dynamic divine force that moves out of itself—first to create the world, and then to enter it.

Perhaps the best way to get behind the competing languages spoken by the Enlightenment philosopher and the orthodox Christian is through a story I once heard about Mother Teresa. In the story, whose source I can no longer locate, a self-satisfied businessman approaches Mother Teresa and asks her a theoretical question that reflects perfectly the impersonal nature of the God of the Philosophers: "Where is God when a child is dying in the streets?" Rather than answer him in terms of his reductive view of God, Mother Teresa boldly transcends the narrow limits of his abstract, uninvolved deity to offer a glimpse of a truly compassionate God who literally feels and shares our pain: "God is *with* that child."

But she does not end the dialogue there. Her God, the God of the Bible, is more real than the philosopher's God of the businessman and, as such, he has the right and the power to make demands upon our lives, to hold us accountable. "The real question," she goes on to say, "is where are you?" We become like the gods we serve: cold, removed, and self-protective, or filled with compassion and empathy. The great hospitals, orphanages, charity houses, and universities were not built by atheists preaching a

religion of humanity, nor were they built by Enlightenment philosophers dispensing abstract notions of love. They were built by
Christians actively serving and loving an actively serving and loving Savior.

> Although the God of the Philosophers is an abstract,
> uninvolved, impersonal deity, Enlightenment skeptics
> and new atheists alike attack him for not rescuing us.

The Best of All Possible Worlds

Earlier in my career, I had the opportunity to teach, on numerous occasions, a two-semester survey of European literature. The
second semester began with the Enlightenment and included a
study of Voltaire's satirical novel *Candide* (1759). I quickly learned
that Voltaire had written his amusing but often scathing satire in
response to the influential—if obscure—philosophical theories of
Leibniz (1646–1716), specifically his belief that we live in the best
of all possible worlds.

As a highly rational philosopher and mathematician, Leibniz
wrote in the tradition of Descartes and Spinoza. He was a maker
of systems in search of universal harmony, and he conceived of
God as the one who held that harmony together. God could have
arranged the universe, and man's place in it, in an infinite number of ways, but Leibniz believed that God *must*, in keeping with
his perfect nature, have done so in the optimal way. If we were
tempted by the existence of pain and suffering to doubt the existence of a good God, then that was only because we were looking
at the picture too closely. We had to step back and see God's greater
design, a design that necessitated millions of working parts per-
forming their proper, optimal functions. Evil and pain play a part
in that function, even if our limited knowledge prevents us from

understanding that function and causes us now to suffer, now to inflict much of that evil and pain.

Unlike Spinoza, Leibniz the philosopher accepted the revelation of the Scriptures. Unlike Descartes, he worked harder (at least to my mind) to integrate Christian revelation with the findings of human reason. Still, there is no getting around the fact that the God of Leibniz, for all his sincere attempts to honor the God of the Bible, is very much the God of the Philosophers. He is a grand designer and orchestrator, to be sure, a God to be held in awe and reverence. But he is not the adventurous God who risked tearing apart the very fabric of reality by becoming a man and dying on a cross.

Leibniz's God, like that of most of his fellow Enlightenment thinkers (Pascal would be one major exception), is the God of the Philosophers; as such, he makes an easy target for the satirical pen of Voltaire (1694–1778). Voltaire thinks that all he needs to do to dismiss orthodox, biblical, creedal Christianity is to poke holes in Leibniz's best of all possible worlds. This he does with narrative and philosophical panache. He allows his delighted, if sometimes scandalized readers to watch as Pangloss, Voltaire's mouthpiece for Leibniz, is systematically hanged, dissected, beaten, and condemned to the galleys. And the same endless atrocities befall his romantic couple as well; even when they marry, Voltaire makes sure to inform us that our once-lovely heroine is now hideously ugly! There is nothing harmonious or optimal or providential about the world of *Candide*. The only solution Voltaire offers his readers is to withdraw from the madness, stop indulging in idle philosophy and theology, and cultivate our own little plot of land.

Of all the atrocities that we encounter in the novel, the one that is most central—the one that inspired Voltaire to write *Candide* in the first place—is the historical earthquake that occurred in Lisbon, Portugal, in 1755 and killed more than 30,000 people. Although, as I said earlier, the problem of pain has always been with us. While skeptics and believers alike have always pondered the meaning of natural disasters, Voltaire's use of the Lisbon earthquake as some kind of proof positive against the claims of Christianity started an unfortunate trend that is still with us today. With a kind of adolescent abandon that would be considered distasteful in any other context, a long line of skeptics and atheists from Voltaire to Richard Dawkins have reveled in the face of disasters, for it has allowed them to point their fingers, wag their tongues, and say with a trumped-up look of outrage, "Where was this so-called God of love of yours when all those people died?" In doing so, they come uncomfortably close to mimicking their supposedly extreme opposites: legalistic, self-righteous Christians who, whenever there is a tsunami or earthquake or terrorist attack, take it upon themselves to prophetically declare what specific social sin was the cause of the disaster.

My friend, let us not be swayed by the tasteless glee of either the Pharisee or the new atheist. Let us, as well, move beyond the cold, stoic, impassive God of the Philosophers. We are not playing some sandbox game of theological name-calling. We are talking about and struggling with life in a fallen and fragmented world, a world run by a loving God but which has been thrown out of whack. Most importantly of all, we are talking about and struggling with a God who does not snap his fingers and erase all the consequences of sin, but who fixes the brokenness in his own broken flesh. Over against a suffering humanity, the Bible holds up a suffering God. In answer to millions of people around the globe who look up at the sky and ask, "Why me?" the Bible offers a Savior praying intensely in the Garden of Gethsemane, begging the Father to take away the suffering he is about to endure (see Luke 22:39-46).

We're talking about real life here, not philosophical mind games.

> Though Voltaire's *Candide* effectively explodes a simplistic understanding of Leibniz's best of all possible worlds, it is powerless to address either the broken nature of our world or the drastic measures God took to set things to right.

Christian Cross-Examination #1: The Only Possible *Kind* of World

Some two centuries after Voltaire took aim at the theories of Leibniz, C.S. Lewis—writing under the shadow of the Nazi bombing of London—resuscitated the notion of the best of all possible worlds, but from a creative angle befitting a man who would, ten years later, create the world of Narnia. Here's how he works it out in chapter 2 of *The Problem of Pain* (1940):

1. God chose from the beginning to give us free will. That does not mean we can do anything we want or that we have the right to reinvent ourselves at will, but that we are, at the core, moral-ethical creatures whose choices matter. Lewis even goes so far as to depict God as carrying out a free-will experiment: not frivolously, but in keeping with his serious divine desire that we should be separate, rational creatures who freely obey our Creator. God is sovereign, and, because he dwells outside time and space, knows what we will choose; but that knowledge does not thereby violate our ability to choose, nor does it sweep under the rug the very real consequences that accompany our choices.

2. Since God gave us free will, he can't turn around in the next breath and take it away from us. Just as our choices carry

consequences with them, so the choice to give us choice carries consequences: namely, that some sort of neutral playing field exists against which we can enact our free will. The earth that God created for us is just such a playing field. It is fixed in nature and cannot be manipulated by the various players of the game. As such, it is hard and resilient and cannot help but bring physical injury (pain) to those who butt up against it. That is to say, even before the fall of man, the possibility for some pain existed simply because of the solidity of nature.

3. Some might ask why we can't alter nature so as to prevent ourselves from being hurt, but, if we could do that at will (change the playing field), then we would be robbing others of their free will. Well then, why doesn't God change nature to prevent us from being injured? As a matter of fact, he *does* do that now and then when he performs a miracle. But miracles, by their very nature, must be rare. If miracles sprang up every second to protect people from harm, the game *as a game* could no longer be played.

4. This may not, Lewis concludes, be the best of all possible worlds, but it just may be the only possible *kind* of world that God could have created to enable his free-will experiment. Needless to say, after the Fall ushered sin into both human society and the natural world, the tendency of reality to collide with our desires and bring pain and suffering was greatly magnified. Still, the possibility of pain was there from the beginning, inscribed into the very nature of the physical world.

In working out this four-step argument, Lewis makes use of a logical progression of reasoning. God, for whom all times are now, has no need of such step-by-step thinking or acting. When he created the universe to accommodate his free-will experiment, he did it in a flash of creative power that defies the sequential logic of the human mind. Human philosophers like Leibniz must think in terms of parts working together; for God, who sees the forest in the acorn, all is unified. Even the creation week of Genesis 1, though it unfolds over six days, exists as a unity in the mind of the Creator.

We must not, Lewis writes near the end of chapter 2, "think of God arguing, as we do, from an end (co-existence of free spirits) to the conditions involved in it, but rather of a single, utterly self-consistent act of creation which to us appears, at first sight, as the creation of many independent things, and then, as the creation of things mutually necessary." Though he does not say so directly, Lewis almost surely was influenced by a comment Augustine makes in Book XII, Chapter 15 of *Confessions* during his lengthy meditation on Genesis 1: God "does not will one thing at one time, and another thing at another time. Once and for all and simultaneously, he wills everything that he wills."

I belabor this point, for too often suffering people who experience intense pain torment themselves by trying to trace every cause, event, and seeming coincidence that converged in the painful experience. I know that I myself do this far more often than is good for my spirit. Voltaire plays this game on numerous occasions in *Candide*, not as a way of getting at the truth, but of satirizing those who try. But the game does not work—either as a method of consolation or as a critique of the God of the Bible. God's overarching plan is too complexly unified to be broken down into a chain of causes and effects. All occurs simultaneously in the mind of God: providence and free will, energy and entropy, beauty and pain. We have no choice but to watch things unfold in time and space. That limitation, however, is not imposed upon God.

When the Bible asks us to have faith in God's plans and purposes, it does not invite us to manufacture clever scenarios for how "bad event A" is a necessary ingredient in "good event B." Our faith does not rest on a series of clever twists and turns, but in a God who holds all things and all times in his hand, and who thought it worth the risk to endow us with choice. Remember that this personal God who plans and purposes is not a removed, dispassionate God, but one who is intimately involved in his creation. He's not an armchair general calling the shots while his men take all the risks. He himself risked everything by entering our fallen world. That's why the ultimate answer to the problem of pain is not the divine plan behind creation but the God-Man who hung on the cross.

> This may not be the best of all possible worlds, argues
> C.S. Lewis, but it may be the only possible *kind* of
> world to allow God to enact his free-will experiment.

Christian Cross-Examination #2: We're Not Here to Have Fun

Once we accept—*really* accept—that God gave us free will from the beginning, then the need for pain, or at least the potential for pain, becomes somewhat clearer. It becomes even clearer, Lewis argues in chapter 3, when we consider more fully exactly *why* God created us. At the core of God's free-will experiment is his desire not that we should have fun, but that we should grow into the people that he intended us to be. The medieval theologians often spoke of our earth as a vale of soul-making; that does not mean our earth is *merely* a testing ground, but it should remind us that we are here for a purpose beyond our own amusement and entertainment.

Lewis was strongly influenced by the Greek Orthodox doctrine of *theosis*: the belief that, in the incarnate Jesus, God became like us so that we could become like him. God's overall plan is not to save us by the skin of our teeth—though, in his mercy and condescension, he will do so—but to make us into gods. No, we will *not* literally become gods, but it is the greater will of our Creator that we be raised up to share in his eternal, indestructible, triune life. Salvation is more than a get-out-of-hell-free card; it is the first step in a process meant to make us perfect, even as our heavenly Father is perfect.

Today, we have so reduced the meaning of the Christian virtue of love that it means little more than tolerance: leaving people alone to decide for themselves who and what they are and will be. Our love is passive rather than active. It doesn't build up; it simply lets go. Our weak-kneed love does not care whether its object becomes good and noble. Rather, it only cares that it be happy and not have to suffer too much.

How different, writes Lewis, is the fiery, uncompromising love of God from the feeble, apathetic kindness of men:

> It is for people whom we care nothing about that we demand happiness on any terms: with our friends, our lovers, our children, we are exacting and would rather see them suffer much than be happy in contemptible and estranging modes. If God is Love, He is, by definition, something more than mere kindness. And it appears, from all the records, that though He has often rebuked us and condemned us, He has never regarded us with contempt. He has paid us the intolerable compliment of loving us, in the deepest, most tragic, most inexorable sense.

There are many, many times when I, along with *all* people, do not want this kind of God. We would very much like to be left alone to our own devices and self-pity. But, Lewis reminds us, if we ask God to stop loving us in this inexorable way, then we are asking him to stop loving us.

All over the world, when parents have to discipline their children in order to form their character and steer them away from willful disobedience, they say something like this: "This is hurting me worse than it's hurting you." Now, that is one of those phrases that children do not believe when it is said to them, but which magically comes to makes sense when, years later, they must say it to their own rebellious and recalcitrant children. In this case, finding the proper perspective makes all the difference. Without some pain, without proper resistance, there can be no growth.

That's how it would have been if Adam and Eve had not fallen, for even in the Garden the call to obedience meant a denial of our desire to eat of the forbidden fruit and to trust to our own wisdom and autonomy. After they disobeyed, however, all future obedience became infinitely harder and far less pleasant. Before the Fall, Lewis explains in chapter 5, surrendering to God "meant no struggle but only the delicious overcoming of an infinitesimal self-adherence which delighted to be overcome." Alas, since the Fall, the act of turning to God in self-surrender calls for "painful effort."

Let me offer my own analogy to draw out Lewis's point. Though the experience of pain in our body is not pleasant, it more often than not protects us from disease and further injury. If we get a speck of something in our eye, it hurts intensely, forcing us to do whatever we must to clean out our eye. Imagine if we did not feel that pain. We would not remove the speck, leaving our body open to infection, disease, and possible blindness. And the same goes for pains that afflict our limbs and our organs. The pain signals to us that something is wrong and needs to be repaired.

In our moral lives, painful feelings of guilt and shame play a similar role. The guilt signals to us that there is something broken and damaged not in our body, but in our soul. If we do not attend to the guilt and alter our choices and our behaviors, we risk moral infection and disease—a cancerous process that, if not stopped through confession, repentance, penance, and deep moral change, will transform us into monsters.

Both pain and guilt are signals that something is wrong and needs to be fixed. All things being equal, the system works well for the maintenance of our physical and spiritual health. But not always. We live in a broken world that has been subjected to futility. Because of that, the signals often go awry. Someone with cancer or with PTSD will be flooded with a type of pain and guilt that is unhealthy and that needs to be dealt with through drugs and therapy.

So yes, pain and evil come ultimately from man's misuse of the free will given him by God, and yes, the vast majority of suffering on our planet is caused by human sin. Still, God is in control, and there is purpose in the excessive pain that now afflicts us and our world—even if it is so deeply woven into God's grand design that it is all but invisible to human eyes. The famous promise in Romans 8:28 that all things work together for good to those who love God must be taken together with the whole chapter, particularly with the painful list in verse 35 of all the terrible things that seek with devilish glee to separate us from the love of God.

But all the pain and suffering the world can dish out will not prevail over those who make God their refuge and who offer up even the smallest grain of willing faith to participate in God's plan. And we can trust that promise not because it squares with the rational arguments of the God of the Philosophers but because the promise was made by a personal, passionate, supremely involved God who did not spare his own Son from the harsh discipline of pain (verse 32).

Postscript

I have attempted throughout this chapter to shift attention away from the God of the Philosophers and keep it focused on the active, loving, risk-taking God of the Bible. Nevertheless, I would be remiss if I concluded without sharing something that should be more widely known. Despite the protestations of new atheists and aggressive secular bloggers, serious philosophers—whether religious or secular—have given up on using the problem of pain as a simple, Humean defeater of Christian theism. That is because Alvin Plantinga, one of the foremost living philosophers, exploded it more than forty years ago in his *God, Freedom, and Evil* (1974).

Even if we remain within the limits of the God of the Philosophers, Hume's contention that a belief in God's omnipotence and omnibenevolence is inconsistent with the pain we encounter is untenable as a logical proposition. Hume and his heirs seem to think that a simple assertion of God's power and benevolence is enough to invoke the problem of pain and bring down theism. But it is not. As Plantinga demonstrates, the mere assertion of omnipotence and omnibenevolence is not enough. For the presence of pain, evil, and suffering to disqualify the existence of an all-powerful, all-loving God, two further premises need to be proven: (1) that God's power allows him to do anything he wants; and (2) that God's love would impel him, *in all cases*, to eliminate suffering.

But, as we have already seen, God cannot do anything he wants. He cannot, for example, give us free will and take it away from us at the same time. God certainly can put restraints upon himself. Indeed, as Lewis so powerfully argues in *The Problem of Pain*, God's decision to give us free will carried with it the need for a fixed nature that itself carried with it the potential for pain.

As for the second expanded premise, God's ability to bring good out of evil, all of which is woven into his overarching plan, highlights the fact that a good God might have legitimate reasons for not eliminating suffering in certain situations. I should add that in making his philosophical argument, Plantinga insists that he need not provide a list of bad things that lead to good; the mere possibility that God might allow or even cause suffering for a deeper, more loving purpose is enough to explode the seeming strength of Hume's argument.

Alas, as I noted above, the modern Western world has so reduced and desiccated the meaning of the word *love* that we have lost our collective ability to discern in the midst of our pain the same intimate, self-sacrificing, God-making love that brought the eternal God into a dangerous world and onto a cruel cross.

CHAPTER EIGHT

The Watchmaker God

Like most of my fellow apologists and evangelists, I enjoy quoting all those wonderful surveys that proclaim the statistical fact that more than 90 percent of people believe in God. And while it's gratifying to quote such surveys, I know in my heart that they are inaccurate. Oh yes, more than 90 percent of people *say* they believe in God. But what kind of God do they believe in?

Scratch under the surface, and you will find that many people who say they believe in the God of the Bible are actually deists: That is to say, they believe in a watchmaker God who may have kicked things off in the beginning but who is uninvolved in our world and our lives. For others, the being they call God is an amorphous force that runs through all things; or, even worse, is indistinguishable from nature. Yet others mean by God little more than the God portion of their brain.

If that's all God is, then what's the point? Really, I mean that! What's the point? Such a God cannot really love us, nor can he have any real impact on our lives. He certainly is not a God to whom we are accountable, in whose name or for whose sake we might actually change our beliefs or our behaviors. We can take him or leave him depending on how we feel that day. Like the God of the Philosophers, he's a great topic for debate—he might even help supply a missing premise in our logical proof—but we need not fear that we will have to stand before him on judgment day and give an account of our lives. It's not so much God as our religion, our culture, and our traditions before which we stand in awe and with which we desire to be reconciled and have communion.

Transcendence vs. Immanence

It wasn't until I learned and understood the real meaning of two philosophical-theological terms—*transcendence* and *immanence*—that I was able to grasp the true uniqueness of the triune God of the Bible.

To speak of God as transcendent is to say that he is totally separate from the world, that he exists outside of time and space. As such, he is wholly other from us; he is the sky God or the mountain God who dwells far above us and whom we cannot approach. He may rage, or he may be indifferent, but he is nevertheless unapproachable. Ultimately we can know nothing positive about this removed deity; we can serve and obey him but not in any kind of personal or intimate way. He has power, but he doesn't really communicate; he's not the type to make promises or to dirty himself with the world and its inhabitants.

Those, in contrast, who believe in an immanent God see him not as the Creator of nature and the universe, but as being one *with* nature and the universe. It's not just that there are many different gods (polytheism), but that everything *is* god (pantheism): the trees, the grass, the sky, the rivers, and we ourselves if we only knew it. God is in all and of all and through all; his being is spread out through everything we see and everything we cannot see. We can pray to him, but to pray to him is no different, finally, from praying to nature or to ourselves. We may say we are going to follow his standards, but he has no standards, for he is one with nature.

Followers of the fully immanent God generally live by some kind of moral law, but they can't trace that law back to God.

Where, I asked myself, did the God of Abraham, Isaac, and Jacob—the triune God who sent his Son into the world and whose Holy Spirit indwells those who serve him—fit on this sliding scale between transcendence and immanence? Somewhere in the middle. He is primarily a transcendent God: He created the world out of nothing and is separate from it. He is himself the standard of all that is Good, True, and Beautiful. He is holy and dwells in irreproachable light, and we cannot fathom his being or his glory.

But he is also an immanent God. His eternal, indestructible life underlies all that is; were he to remove his animating presence from the universe, it would collapse and be no more. He is intimately involved in all that happens in the universe, especially on planet Earth. Again and again, he comes down to communicate with us and to make his presence known. He meets with Moses at the burning bush, then meets him again on Mount Sinai to give him— *personally*—his laws, commandments, and promises. He speaks through the prophets and performs miracles. He knows and wants to be known by the rational creatures he made in his own image.

Then, were that not enough, he entered into the world he created and became a man. He didn't just *appear* to be a man; he *became* a flesh-and-blood human being. The God who is not bounded by either time or space took on flesh at a specific point in history. His name was Jesus ("Savior"), but he had a deeper name foretold by the prophet Isaiah (7:14): Immanuel, "God with us."

God the Father, who has never been seen by human eyes (John 1:18), is radically transcendent; God the Holy Spirit, who dwells within the hearts of all believers and empowers the church, is radically immanent. God the Son, the incarnate Christ, is both transcendent and immanent, the great bridge between God and man.

Through Christ, the invisible, unknowable God can be seen and known. In his transcendence, God is wholly other; in his immanence, he indwells us through his Spirit.

This is the paradoxical God revealed in the Bible. It is not the man-made God of human religion. When man makes up religion, he either makes God fully transcendent or fully immanent. That is to say, he either gravitates toward some form of deism or Unitarianism, especially if he lives in the West. Or if he lives in the East, toward pantheism or monism.

> The God of the Bible is unique, for he is both transcendent, separate from the world he created, and immanent, intimately involved in the world he created—so much so that he entered it as a man.

Too Close for Comfort

Though I am an evangelical Protestant, I was deeply moved and instructed when, back in the 1990s, I worked my way through Pope John Paul II's *Crossing the Threshold of Hope*. I remember in particular reading his answer to the question of why God, if he exists, hides himself from us. As I expected, the Pope explained in clear terms that God, far from hiding himself, had become incarnate in the person of Jesus Christ. But he didn't stop there. To my surprise, Pope John Paul II went on to explain that though people often *say* they want a close and intimate God, most fear and shun that intimacy.

In one sense, he writes, God could not have gone any further to reveal himself than he did in the incarnation, crucifixion, and resurrection. And yet, in another sense,

> God has gone too far! Didn't Christ perhaps become
> "a stumbling block to Jews and foolishness to Gentiles"

(1 Cor 1:23)? Precisely because He called God His
Father, because He revealed Him so openly in Himself, He could not but elicit the impression that it was
too much…Man was no longer able to tolerate such
closeness, and thus the protests began.

*This great protest has precise names—first it is called
the Synagogue, and then Islam.* Neither can accept a
God who is so human. "It is not suitable to speak
of God in this way," they protest. "He must remain
absolutely transcendent; He must remain pure Majesty. Majesty full of mercy, certainly, but not to the
point of paying for the faults of His own creatures, for
their sins."

From one point of view it is right to say that God
revealed too much of Himself to man, too much of
that which is most divine, that which is His intimate
life; He revealed Himself in His Mystery. He was not
mindful of the fact that such an *unveiling would in a
certain way obscure Him in the eyes of man, because man
is not capable of withstanding an excess of the Mystery.*
He does not want to be pervaded and overwhelmed by
it. Yes, man knows that God is the One in whom "we
live and move and have our being" (Acts 17:28); but
why must that be confirmed by His Death and Resurrection? Yet Saint Paul writes: "If Christ has not been
raised, then empty is our preaching; empty, too, your
faith" (1 Cor 15:14).

I apologize for the lengthy quote, but John Paul II touches on
something here that is so vital that it merits the space I have given it.
Though most people will say they want to be closer to God, many

who say that don't really want it. They want to keep God at arm's length. Oh, they might be willing to obey a few laws, but a God that's *that* close?

Although all the original Christians were Jewish, the Jews as a people and as a religious group—the historical children of Isaac—chose to deny "a God who is so human." Six hundred years later, Mohammed "purified" Christianity by denying the Trinity, the incarnation, the crucifixion, and the resurrection and returning the sons of Ishmael to a fully transcendent God who is wholly other, utterly removed from this physical earth and its inhabitants. True, for the Muslim ("one who submits"), religion and the law pervade every aspect of his life—there is no separation of church and state in Islam. But God as an immanent deity who can be known and loved intimately plays little to no role in Islam. Perhaps to account for the radical Unitarian transcendence of the God of Judaism and Islam, both religions have evolved a mystical sect (Cabbalism and Sufism, respectively) that allows for more intimate communion with the divine.

I do not mean here to disparage Judaism, Islam, or any other religion. I only mean to point out, in keeping with the above quote from Pope John Paul II, that there is something in man that resists a God who is too close. At the end of the day, many who identify as Christian actually share the same Unitarian view of God found in Judaism and Islam. Jesus for them is a good prophet who taught good precepts, but he is not God-in-human-flesh. The default religion of man, at least in the West, is deism: the lonely, distant watch-maker God who does not meddle. Give us laws, give us rituals, give us traditions, but don't give us a God who invades our space.

> Though many people *say* they want God to come close, most fear the divine intimacy of the incarnation. We prefer to keep God at arm's length.

Arians

In many ways, the greatest threat to the early church did not come from the outside, from Roman persecution, but from the inside, from heretics who sought to twist Christianity away from its central doctrines. In chapter 6, we looked closely at the heresy of Marcionism, which attempted to sever the New Testament from the Old, and strip God of his holiness and his righteous wrath against sin. That heresy is still with us today, preventing modern people from seeing and grasping the fullness of God's nature.

But there was an even greater threat to the early church, one that has also persisted into the twenty-first century. Actually, that threat was a dual one, coming as it did from two opposite directions; yet both heresies worked toward the same goal: to deny that Jesus Christ was fully God and fully man, 100 percent divine and 100 percent human. On the one side were the Arians, who denied the deity of Christ, arguing that he was an enlightened man chosen by God and holding some authority but in no way a member of the triune Godhead. On the other were the Gnostics, who said, as odd as it may sound to modern ears, that Christ was God but was not a man.

In both cases, the ludicrous, offensive notion that God could be both transcendent and immanent was categorically rejected. The proto-Muslim Arians, Unitarians to the core, could not accept or even fathom that God could be three-in-one or Jesus two-in-one. From their point of view, they were, like Mohammed after them, protecting the honor and dignity of God. In a very real sense, neither Arians nor Muslims have a theology to speak of. God is God and that is it! No mystery, no paradox, no miracles even. God is God: submit and obey! At least the (transcendent) Jewish creed, the *Shemah* ("Hear, O Israel: The Lord our God, the Lord is one"), is followed by these tender (immanent) words of intimacy: "You

shall love the Lord your God with all your heart and with all your
soul and with all your might" (Deuteronomy 6:4-5). The Muslim creed ("There is no God but Allah, and Mohammed is his
prophet") stops there and goes no further. But then the Jewish
creed looks forward to the fuller revelation of the Trinity and the
incarnation, while the Muslim creed marks a deliberate rejection
of that revelation.

It should come as no surprise that Arianism and Islam were popular with soldiers, spreading like wildfire through military camps
across the Roman Empire and the Middle East. What soldier can
really respect and worship a God who would become a poor, weak
man and then die a traitor's death on a cross! Revisionist histori-
ans who like to present the church as having all the power on her
side over against the weak underdog heretics are playing fast and
loose with history. It was the Arians who had most of the military
power and who came very close to crushing Trinitarian orthodoxy.

It should also come as no surprise that Islam forbids all images,
as the Arians would most surely have done had they succeeded
in seizing control of the church and remaking her apostolic doctrines. For Muslims, God is not to be depicted in any way, for
he is utterly other, holy, and ineffable. Similar restrictions held
in the Old Testament, though even there God made himself visible in such things as the burning bush and the glory that hung
about the Ark of the Covenant. But when God became incarnate
in Christ, all that changed. Christians realized that the incarnation
had, quite literally, baptized the physical world as a fit receptacle for
God's divine presence. With amazing rapidity, icons—depictions
of Christ or Mary or one of the saints made on wood, plaster, glass,
etc.—appeared in catacombs and churches…and that despite the
fact that Judaism forbade all such graven images.

And so it went for more than half a millennia until the armies of Islam ravaged their way across the Byzantine Empire in the seventh and eighth centuries. As the Muslims seized greater and greater control, it instigated a crisis within the Eastern Orthodox Church. A movement to destroy all images, a movement known as iconoclasm, spread through the empire, with its strongest, most vocal proponents being—you guessed it—in the army. In 726, Byzantine emperor Leo III ordered the destruction of all icons in his realm, a ban that lasted until 843, when Orthodoxy triumphed once more. Why did the Orthodox fight so hard for their icons? Because the icon is a visual proclaimer of the incarnation, of the radical belief that the transcendent God became immanent in Christ.

Throughout her history, the church—Catholic, Orthodox, and Protestant alike—has fought long and hard to preserve the supreme theological truth of the incarnation, and with it the belief that though God is wholly other and outside the universe, he is actively involved in the world, so much so that he entered it as a man. I apologize if I seem to be repeating myself, but it is, finally, *this* God, *not* the God of the deists and Unitarians, who provokes such wrath from Enlightenment skeptics and new atheists alike. For it is only this God, transcendent and immanent, exceedingly distant and profoundly close, that must be wrestled with, that must be accepted or rejected, obeyed or defied. Not rituals or laws or religion, but a personal, passionate God who would know and be known.

> For Arians and Muslims alike, God is God, period! They offer no Trinity, no incarnation, no mystery, no intimacy, no miracles, and, ultimately, no theology.

Gnostics

Such is Arianism, both then and now. But what of the other heresy that fought with equal vigor against the doctrine of the incarnation? Like the Arians, the Gnostics saw themselves as defenders of God's pure transcendence, but from a different and more radical point of view.

According to the Gnostics, physical matter, including and especially flesh, is inherently fallen and evil. The goal of religion is to escape the physical, not to redeem it through the incarnation and resurrection of God. For the Gnostics, no thought could be more insane, more odious than that God, dwelling in eternal, immaterial perfection, would willingly take on flesh. No, it was impossible. If God were to become a man, he would dirty himself, compromise his holiness.

Indeed, so much did the Gnostics look down on physical matter that they believed our universe itself was created by a lesser, even an evil god. Genesis was wrong to say that God made us and our world good but that we then fell through disobedience. The real truth, known only to the Gnostics (Greek for "knowers"), was that creation was itself the Fall. Salvation meant escaping from matter altogether. Though most Gnostics did not have a problem with sex per se, most were opposed to marriage and procreation. What could be worse than bringing more flesh and matter into an inherently fallen world?

During the second and third centuries, some of the Gnostic sects composed their own gospels, many of which have been trumpeted by modern theological liberals as being equally, if not more, historical than the four canonical Gospels of Matthew, Mark, Luke, and John. That they could make such a claim almost defies belief. Read, say, the Gnostic Gospel of Thomas and try this thought experiment: Take Jesus and replace him with Confucius or Buddha or Socrates. You will find that the change does not alter the text in any real way. Why? Because the Gnostic gospels are *anti*-historical. They do not present an incarnate Savior who entered the world at a specific time and place (during the reigns of Caesar Augustus and Herod the Great), but a mouthpiece for secret sayings that only the elect can understand. Whereas the transcendent-immanent God of Christianity works through human history to redeem it, Gnosticism seeks to escape from history even as it seeks to escape from matter and the flesh.

One of the earliest Gnostic sects was the Docetists, a name derived from the Greek verb translated "to seem." They called themselves that because they believed Jesus only *seemed* to be a man. Yes, Jesus was divine, but he was not human; he only wore the flesh as someone might wear a suit of clothes. One Gnostic, Valentinus, writing around 140, even invented elaborate mythologies about (nonincarnational) divine emanations. All Gnostics saw the body as a prison house of the soul from which one should seek to be liberated. The Manicheans, a sect which counted the young preconverted Augustine in its ranks, believed that by eating certain fruits they could help release trapped spirits!

How ironic that many today attack the early church both for stamping out Gnosticism and for promoting a low view of the body. This is ironic because the very reason the church suppressed Gnosticism is because it taught—contra Christ, the Bible, and the apostolic tradition—that the flesh is inherently evil. It is a further irony that many modern feminists have hailed Gnosticism as embodying an earlier, more authentic form of Christianity. Because of their low view of the body and of procreation, the Gnostics tended toward misogyny. In fact, the Gnostic Gospel of Thomas ends with Jesus promising Mary Magdalene that if she behaves herself, she will one day become male!

Gnostics rejected the incarnation because they believed that matter was inherently evil; to them, it was unthinkable that God should ally himself with the flesh.

Christian Cross-Examination #1: Athanasius on the Incarnation

Against the Arians and the Gnostics, the great Christian apologists of the last two millennia have held up the incarnation, not only as a true doctrine of the church but as a statement about the nature of God, man, and reality itself. Together with the Trinity, the incarnation reveals a God who is not a cold, aloof watchmaker unwilling to sully himself with matter and flesh, but an actively loving God who moves out of himself toward the rational creatures he made in his own image.

It took me many long years of study, prayer, and reflection to realize that the incarnation not only had ramifications for the nature of God but for the nature of man as well. For there is a sense in which, like Christ, we are incarnational beings—we are fully spiritual and fully physical. We are not souls trapped in bodies, as Gnostics then and now believe, but enfleshed souls. The relationship—or, better, marriage—between our body and soul, our brain and our mind is profoundly incarnational: that is to say, the two are separate and one at the same time.

Later in this chapter, I will return to the incarnational nature of man. For now, I would like to consider how one of the early Christian apologists defended the incarnation against its many detractors. Although Tertullian, Irenaeus, and Justin Martyr all bore witness to Christ's dual nature in their apologetical writings, first place must go to Athanasius, Bishop of Alexandria (293–373), whose defense of the incarnation helped pave the way for the Nicene Creed. In standing up against the Arians and the Gnostics, the young Athanasius—he was in his twenties when he wrote *On the Incarnation*—faced considerable persecution. Still, he would not compromise the central truth revealed in Christ and the New Testament and passed down by the apostles. Jesus was neither an enlightened human prophet nor God in a flesh suit; he was the second person of the Trinity, the incarnate Son, the unique God-Man.

In the previous chapter, I made reference to the Orthodox doctrine of theosis: the belief that, in the incarnate Jesus, God became like us so that we could become like him. Athanasius is one of the chief architects of that doctrine; in fact, the classic summation of theosis is to be found in chapter 54 of *On the Incarnation*: "For he [Christ] was made man that we might be made God; and he manifested himself by a body that we might receive the idea of the unseen Father; and he endured the insolence of men that we might inherit immortality." What Athanasius here presents is a God who wants to be known, no matter the cost to himself. He is unseen (transcendent), yet becomes seen in the incarnate Christ (immanent); he does not hoard his immortality, but shares it with us. He does not scorn to share our flesh, nor does he grudge us participation in his eternal, triune life.

No, Athanasius argues: Neither the Jews (who share the radical Unitarian monotheism of the Arians and the later Muslims) nor the Gentiles (who share the Gnostic, neo-Platonic belief that matter and flesh are inherently evil) should have been shocked by the incarnation. Had the Jews studied more carefully the Old Testament, they would have recognized that Christ fulfilled all the prophecies from Genesis to Malachi. But the Gentiles too would have recognized the incarnate Savior had they attended more to their own pagan philosophers; for they taught that the universe is a great body in which the Word (Logos) dwells, and if

the Word of God is in the universe, which is a body,
and has united himself with the whole and with all its
parts, what is there surprising or absurd if we say that
he has united himself with man also…if it be unseemly
for a part to have been adopted as his instrument to
teach men of his Godhead, it must be most absurd
that he should be made known even by the whole universe (Chapter 41).

What Athanasius does in this incisive passage is similar to what
Paul does before the Stoic and Epicurean philosophers in Athens
(Acts 17:16-34; Athanasius, in fact, quotes verse 28 in Chapter 42):
forge a connection between limited pagan wisdom and the fuller
revelation of Christianity. Though they lacked the Hebrew Scriptures, Athanasius, together with Paul, argues that the Gentiles
possessed traces of the truth. Athanasius does not mention any philosophers by name, but he most likely has the Pre-Socratic Anaxagoras in mind. Anaxagoras, as I explained in chapter 2, taught that
the universe was composed of eternal bits of matter (seeds) ordered
by an eternal, universal mind (*nous* in Greek). Now, Anaxagoras's
God was finally a deistic watchmaker God, but Athanasius locates
in the impersonal God of the Pre-Socratics an inkling of the truth
to come: that a God who moves and inhabits the universe will one
day move and inhabit a human body.

The Greek philosophers *should* have known this, but they
blinded themselves to how intimate the connection is between
God and his creation. As a result, God had to take more drastic
measures. Since "men were not able to recognize him as ordering and guiding the whole, he [God] takes to himself as an instrument a part of the whole, his human body, and unites himself with
that, in order that since men could not recognize him in the whole,

they should not fail to know him in the part" (43). The partial god glimpsed by the Pre-Socratics and the true God revealed in Christ are the same God. Though none of the Gentiles, even ones as wise as Plato and Aristotle, could have fully predicted or understood that greater revelation to come, they should have recognized it when it came.

Of course, God the Son did not become incarnate on the earth merely to reveal his presence in the universe. In order to save us and our world, to bring us back into a right relationship with God the Father, and to effect our rebirth and theosis, it was necessary that "the incorporeal and incorruptible and immaterial Word of God [come] to our realm, howbeit he was not far from us before. For no part of creation is left void of him: he has filled all things everywhere, remaining present with his own Father" (8). The fully transcendent God was fully immanent before *and* after the incarnation; there is no part of the cosmos that is not alive with his presence. Even when he was incarnate on earth, he remained fully present with his Father.

"But wait," the Gnostic cries out. "How could the holy God have remained holy when he became a man? Once he took on our flesh, would he not be corrupted by it?" Not at all, Athanasius replies: The "all-Holy Word of God, maker and lord also of the sun [was not] defiled by being made known in the body; on the contrary, being incorruptible, he quickened and cleansed the body also, which was in itself mortal" (17). Though it is true that in our world of physical and moral entropy corruption naturally spreads and infects that which is incorrupt, it was the prerogative of the all-holy transcendent-immanent God to reverse that process in the incarnation. That is why the proper way to view the incarnation is not as the lowering of the divine into the human, but as the taking up of the human into the divine.

> The incarnation, Athanasius shows, not only marks the
> fulfillment of Jewish prophecy, but reveals in full what
> the Gentiles could only see in part.

Pantheism and Monism

While those in the West lean toward a fully transcendent God
who remains aloof from the world he created, those in the East lean
toward a fully immanent God who dwells within nature. For the
Hindu and the Buddhist, God (or the gods) does not stand outside the world but is disseminated through it. Although this may
suggest the potential for intimacy between God and man, it is far
less intimate than deism. At least the removed watchmaker God
has some kind of personal integrity. By contrast, the God who is
spread out through nature has no personality whatsoever. He (it)
cannot be known, for there is no one to know.

It is customary to speak of Hinduism and Buddhism as holding a pantheistic view of the world, a belief that all of nature is
pervaded and animated by the divine. Though this is true on a
surface level, when Hinduism and Buddhism are traced down to
their deepest and most mystical philosophical-theological level, a
different truth emerges. It's not that the divine pervades the natural (pantheism) but that there is finally no difference between the
divine, the natural, and the human: All is one (monism).

There are many holy books in Hinduism, but the one that is
most often cited as expressing Hinduism in its purest form is the
Bhagavad-Gita, or *Gita* for short. Representing but an interlude in
the midst of the lengthy national epic of India, the *Mahabharata*,
the *Gita* recounts a conversation between an Achilles-like warrior
named Arjuna and Krishna, a human embodiment (or avatar) of
the god Vishnu. Krishna teaches Arjuna many things, particularly

the importance of duty, but the main revelation he shares is the secret truth, known only to the elect, that Brahman is Atman.

For the *Gita*, Brahman (not to be confused with the creator god Brahma) signifies the all, the impersonal force which has no beginning or end and which extends through all things. Atman, in contrast, signifies the individual soul. Though we like to think that our soul is separate from the world, the truth is that it is merely a part of Brahman. The final goal of contemplation is to realize that we are but a drop in the ocean of Brahman. Salvation is achieved not by putting one's faith in the incarnate God-Man, but by having one's eyes cleansed and seeing that, despite deceptive appearances—in Hinduism, the physical world is *maya* ("illusion")—Atman and Brahman are one and the same.

To help Arjuna achieve this enlightenment, Krishna vouchsafes him a vision that is truly apocalyptic (a Greek word that means "uncovering" or "unveiling"). In a sublimely poetic passage, Arjuna's mask of ignorance is ripped away—a mask that covers us when we trust to our senses and the *maya* they perceive—and he looks upon Krishna in his full glory. What he sees in that mystical moment is that Krishna is not just an avatar of Vishnu, but is all the gods combined. More than that, he is all the elements and natural forces—thought, life, and intelligence; the generative life-force of all things; the deathless one that speaks through a thousand eyes and mouths. In short, he is all that exists on earth and in heaven.

In the last two chapters of the biblical book of Revelation, heaven is described as a great marriage between Christ and the church. Just as marriage in the Bible is defined as two into one flesh, so heaven means a state of pure joy in which we retain our own selfhood yet are also, paradoxically, one with God. Not so Hinduism, where to achieve heaven is to move beyond both pleasure and pain, to lose one's self in the all that is Brahman, to achieve a state of passionless and personless bliss. In heaven, the Bible promises, we will see our Savior face to face (1 Corinthians 13:12). There is no seeing face to face in the Buddhist nirvana (which signifies the blowing out of a candle)—only a final joining with the all that is equivalent to the extinction of the self.

> Hinduism and Buddhism, in their purest form, are not pantheistic (all of nature is pervaded by God) but monistic (nature, God, and man are one and the same).

From Parmenides to Spinoza

Although monism today is identified with the East, it did have at least one great proponent in the West: the Pre-Socratic philosopher Parmenides, who flourished around 470 BC. For Parmenides, reality was not plural and in constant change—as it was for the Pre-Socratic Heraclitus, who famously declared that a man cannot step in the same river twice—but one and unchanging. Yes, our senses *suggest* that things are in perpetual motion and flux, but we cannot trust our senses. Our senses, which rest on custom, only supply us with opinions; if we want true knowledge, we must turn to nature and to speculative reason.

Whereas opinion tells us that all things change and move (pluralism), reason dictates that all is one (monism). Here is how Parmenides reasons himself to this counterintuitive conclusion. Being, he argues, is perfect and complete, and, as such, cannot change—for to change would be to move into a less-perfect state. Meanwhile, there is no such thing, and cannot be any such thing, as non-Being. But if there is no non-Being (no void), then there is no empty space for Being to move around in. Furthermore, Being must be eternal, for, if it came into being at some point in time, then it could only have come out of non-Being, and non-Being does not exist. Nothing can come from nothing; Being exists and has always existed in a state of unchanged perfection. All is one, even if our senses, enslaved to opinion, fool themselves into believing that things change and move and are distinct, one from the other.

Ultimately, Parmenides arrives at the same secret wisdom as the *Gita*: that the individual (Atman) is but a piece of that unchanging Being that is not only *in* all but that *is* all (Brahman). God, too, is part of that all and is indistinguishable from nature and man. In the monism of Parmenides and the *Gita*, God loses his transcendence, for nothing exists outside Being, outside Brahman, outside the one that is all.

In the end, the West chose not to follow the monist path laid out by Parmenides, though Plato integrated Parmenides into his philosophical system, arguing that while the earth below (the World of Becoming) is in constant change and flux, the heavens above the moon (the World of Being) exist in a state of unchanging perfection. Still, Plato and those who followed him—orthodox Christian theologians like Augustine, neo-Platonic philosophers like Plotinus, and Gnostic heretics like the Manicheans alike—kept alive the belief that God was transcendent, separate from the world, whether or not that transcendent God involved himself in the physical world of matter and flesh.

True, Europe has had her share of pagan nature worshipers, most of them living in the countryside (*pagan* means "hillbilly"), but the central tradition of the West has leaned toward transcendence and away from immanence. That is, until monism reared its head again in the most unlikely of places: in the writings of the Portuguese-Dutch-Jewish Spinoza. As I explained in chapter 2, Spinoza (1632–1677) taught that both God and nature were eternal. More than that, he taught that the two were indistinguishable.

Though Spinoza does not directly reference Parmenides, he comes very close to quoting him in the Scholium to Proposition 15 of Part I of *The Ethics*:

> If therefore we consider quantity as it is presented in the imagination—and this is what we more frequently and readily do—we find it to be finite, divisible, and made up of parts. But if we consider it intellectually and conceive it in so far as it is substance—and this is very difficult—then it will be found to be infinite, one, and indivisible, as we have already sufficiently proved.

Spinoza here uses "imagination" in precisely the same way that Parmenides uses "senses" and "opinion," and "intellectually" the same way he uses "reason" and "true knowledge." He further uses "substance" in a way that comes close to Parmenides's "Being." While our imagination suggests that things are finite and divisible (pluralism), our intellect tells us that they are actually infinite, one, and indivisible (monism).

And Spinoza extends this monism of substance (Being) to man himself. Whereas Descartes offered a dualistic view of man, with body and mind as radically separate (the Cartesian split, as it is known to philosophers), Spinoza, in conscious reaction against Descartes, argued that mind and body are one and the same. Making use of Cartesian terminology that linked the body to extension and the mind to thought, Spinoza boldly asserts that "the idea of the body and the body itself—that is, mind and body—are one and the same individual thing, conceived now under the attribute of Thought and now under the attribute of Extension" (Part II, Scholium to Proposition 21).

In the radical monism of Spinoza, God and nature, God and man, mind and body are all one and the same. Spinoza's vision of reality, that is to say, is identical to that revealed in the *Gita*—but with one important difference. For the Hindu, Brahman (the All) is spiritual; for Spinoza, that universal substance in which there is no distinction between God and nature, God and man, and mind and body is physical, natural, and material. There is no mind separate from body in Spinoza because there is no spiritual essence that transcends matter, just as there is no God separate from nature and its laws.

> For Parmenides and Spinoza alike, our senses deceive us when they posit a distinction between God and nature, mind and body; true reason tells us they are one.

Christian Cross-Examination #2: Man, like Christ, is Incarnational

Though I firmly believe Spinoza's monistic vision of mind and body is wrong, I applaud him for the courage he showed in attacking the Cartesian split. Descartes *needed* to be challenged on this point, but the obscurity in which Spinoza lived and wrote prevented his ideas from exerting a needed check on those of Descartes. As a result, the West has been infected with a dualistic vision of man that has left its mark, especially in America, in the form of a semi-Gnostic view of the body as negative and even shameful and unseemly. The rise of pornography over the twentieth century has not, as the Hugh Hefners of the world would have us believe, restored the high status of the body; to the contrary, it has made the body an object of consumerist value rather than eternal value.

It has also led, I would argue, to the popularizing among Christians of a view of the afterlife that is both unscriptural and anti-creedal: namely, that when we die we become angels. In the Platonic, neo-Platonic, and Gnostic traditions, death frees the soul from the body. Not so in orthodox Christianity, where we are promised resurrection bodies like the one that now clothes Jesus. Just as Jesus was, on earth, fully God and fully man, so in heaven he continues to be fully God and fully man. When he ascended into heaven, God the Son did not go back to being pure spirit like God the Father and God the Holy Spirit. To the contrary, he rose in a resurrection body that was like his earthly body, only redeemed and glorified.

It is the grand promise of Scripture that our bodies too will be redeemed on the last day and that, in heaven, we will continue to be what we are on earth: enfleshed souls who are 100 percent physical and 100 percent spiritual. The word *cemetery* means "sleeping place." When Christians say that a departed believer has fallen asleep in the Lord, they are not indulging in euphemistic language. The body sleeps in the grave until it is awakened on that final day when the earth and the sea shall give up their dead, and the redeemed soul and the redeemed body will be joined in an eternal, incarnational union.

It should come as no surprise that Hinduism and Buddhism, based as they are on a pantheistic-monistic view of reality, teach reincarnation. Since there is no incarnational link between body and soul in these religions, there is no reason why a single soul can't inhabit numerous different bodies, both male and female, human and animal. Plato, influenced by Parmenides and Pythagoras, toyed with the notion of the transmigration of souls, for his dualistic vision of body and soul did not allow for an incarnational view of man or of heaven. Christianity rejects utterly any form of reincarnation; perhaps, as I discussed in chapter 4, our soul pre-existed our body, but that soul nevertheless is linked incarnationally with one and only one body.

What has this mini-lesson in the Christian theology of heaven to do with Spinoza and Descartes? A great deal! Spinoza, along with a growing number of people today, wrongly believed that the only response to Cartesian dualism was a materialistic monism that broke down any distinction between body and soul, brain and mind. What he did not see is that there is a middle position between dualism and monism: incarnation, both that of man and that of Christ, in whose image we were made. Incarnation is more than a dry bit of dogma to be fought over by theologians; it is a statement about the nature of reality.

Spinoza, who denied the afterlife, formulated his materialistic monism on his own. His heirs, who live on this side of Darwin and Freud, feel confident that Darwinian evolution and Freud's "scientific" exploration of the psyche have somehow proven that not only our body but our mind, soul, and consciousness as well could have evolved solely by natural, physical, material processes. These things have in no way been proven; they have merely been assumed because they *must* be assumed.

The arguments made by neuroscience often border on the comical. Emboldened by discoveries in cognitive science and evolutionary biology, writers from Oliver Sacks to Antonio Damasio to Steven Pinker seem to think they can dismiss the existence of a supernatural soul and a metaphysical mind—one, that is, that transcends the physical, material mechanisms of the body and the brain—by reminding us that when our physical brain is damaged or manipulated, it affects our behaviors, emotions, and feelings.

Well, of course it does! We are incarnational beings. Though our brain and mind are not the same thing, they are as intimately linked as our body and soul. Even the incarnate Jesus, though he was fully God, got tired and hungry and had to sleep and eat to survive.

Our ability to analyze and reflect upon our lives and choices cannot be accounted for merely by chemical and mechanical processes. We can only do so because we possess, unique among animals, the prior ability to step outside of our physical brains and look back—but that is precisely what Sacks, Damasio, Pinker, and a host of other "materialist monists" will not allow us to do. The heirs of Spinoza, Darwin, and Freud will not accept a realm beyond the physical: Nature is all there is; what we call soul-mind is part of that all-encompassing nature. Like the materialists and atheists I discussed in chapter 2, cognitive scientists want to have their cake and eat it too. They want neat little "scientific" (that is, materialist) explanations for our consciousness, our choices, and our emotions, but they want to retain the ability to step outside of the natural cage of their brains to assert the truth of their theories.

Let me say this as clearly as I know how. Anyone who has taken care of a parent or grandparent with Alzheimer's can attest to those brief but magical moments when the real person peeks out from behind his damaged neurons. Yes, the physical brain is damaged, and yes, that damage has the power to hold the person in a cage. But then there *is* a person in that cage, a person who transcends the limits put upon him by that horrible and terrifying disease that we call Alzheimer's. But, praise God, that prison is a temporary one. If Christianity is true, then a time will come when body and soul together will be redeemed and the true marriage of brain and mind will be restored and perfected.

> Though body and soul, brain and mind are not the
> same thing, they are deeply and incarnationally
> linked; even Jesus got tired and hungry and had to eat
> and sleep.

Postscript

Although it has always been Athanasius's great defense of the incarnation that has guided my understanding of Christ the God-Man, I have also been influenced by another eastern father of the church who stood up for the Trinity and the incarnation in the decades following the formation of the Nicene Creed, just as Athanasius had stood up for them in the decades leading up to the great council at Nicea. His name was Gregory of Nazianzus (c. 330–389), and he boldly defended orthodoxy from the Arians and Gnostics in a series of Five Theological Orations. Like Athanasius before him, he helped the church, and later me, to see that Christ, in the incarnation, assumed our full humanity. The incarnation was not just a necessary prelude to the crucifixion and the atonement; in and of itself, it broke down the walls between God and man and began the process of theosis.

But it was a passage in one of Gregory's letters (#101) on the Apollinarian controversy that summed up for me the unsurpassed richness of the doctrine of the incarnation. Arguing against the Apollinarians, a sect that denied the full divinity and humanity of Christ, Gregory has this to say of Christ:

> For we do not sever the man from the Godhead, but
> we lay down as a dogma the unity and identity [of per-
> son], who of old was not man but God, and the only
> Son before all ages, unmingled with body or anything
> corporeal; but who in these last days has assumed

> manhood also for our salvation; passible in his flesh,
> impassible in his Godhead; circumscript in the body,
> uncircumscript in the Spirit; at once earthly and heav-
> enly, tangible and intangible, comprehensible and
> incomprehensible; that by one and the same [person],
> who was perfect man and also God, the entire human-
> ity fallen through sin might be created anew.

There it is, the full paradox of the incarnation: the nexus point where God and man, heaven and earth, boundless and bounded, spiritual and physical, unknowable and knowable, impervious and vulnerable, transcendent and immanent meet and join hands.

This is the great mystery of the ages that none could guess or comprehend, but which, once revealed, provided the answer to all the greatest longings of Jew and Gentile alike. Arians and Gnostics, whether past or present, flee from this mystery and refuse to com-prehend it. In doing so, they close their hearts to the very key that unlocks the truth about God, man, and the universe.

Just as Gregory lived one generation after Athanasius, so Augus-tine (354–430) lived one generation after Gregory. But his spiritual journey was far more difficult than that of Gregory or Athanasius. Before becoming a bishop and a saint, he spent many years among the Gnostic Manicheans and neo-Platonists. In his *Confessions*, he documents his road from heresy to orthodoxy with honesty and passion. Many parts of his memoir remain vivid in my mind, but the passage that helped me finally to understand the link between Greek philosophy (for which I have always had a deep love) and the incarnation came in Book VII as Augustine moved out of the strange practices of the Manicheans and into the more serene phi-losophy of the neo-Platonists.

In Book VII, Chapter 9, Augustine confesses that from the

essentially Gnostic teachings of the neo-Platonists he was able to learn that the Logos (the Word) was God, that it had come to its own, and that it had brought light and life. That is to say, the pagans had taught him truths that squared with the opening verses of the Gospel of John (1:1-9). What he did not learn, however, from the neo-Platonists was the greater truth revealed in John 1:14: namely, that the Word was made flesh and dwelt among us.

The hints were there to all who had eyes to see and ears to hear, but the reality could not be grasped without direct revelation from the triune God. Apart from that revelation, man could only reach as far as the deistic watchmaker or the pantheistic-monistic god who is all (and therefore nothing). Many today still cannot move beyond those man-made options. And yet, as Deuteronomy 30:11-14 and Romans 10:6-9 promise, he is not far from any of us; nay, he, the God who became man, is as close as our hearts and our mouths. We need only believe and confess.

PART FOUR

The Nature of Man

CHAPTER NINE

The Illusion of Choice

I came of age in the 1970s and '80s during the closing decades of the Cold War. As a proud American and loyal devotee of representational democracy and free-market capitalism, I looked upon the Soviets as the great enemy and nodded my head in full agreement when Ronald Reagan accurately labeled them as the Evil Empire. And then I actually sat down and read Marx.

You might think that reading Marx would soften my antipathy toward Marxism. To the contrary, it convinced me of a single truth that I state here without apology: Marx was the most evil and destructive thinker of all time. Indeed, if I were given the power to, for the sake of mankind, prevent the birth of one person, I would not choose Hitler or Stalin or Mao. Rather, I would choose the fountainhead of the poisonous ideas that made Nazi Germany, Soviet Russia, and Communist China possible: Karl Marx.

Marx's Dark Legacy

In chapter 2, I described how Marx (1818–1883) infected Europe with a belief that history was moving blindly and yet somehow unstoppably toward pure Communism. Marx believed this because he was a rigid determinist who worshiped, if he worshiped anything, the iron laws of nature and the unswerving patterns of history. I call Marx an evil thinker because he was profoundly anti-humanistic. He may be painted by some as a humanitarian who felt love and pity for the poor; in actuality, he, like the forces that drive Darwinian natural selection, had neither regard nor compassion for the individual. Only groups and classes mattered: worker and boss, poor and rich, proletariat and bourgeoisie.

But Marx's antihumanism went even deeper than that. Not only did he reduce all people to their class (Marx is the true founder of modern identity politics); he reduced us even further to mere products of our socioeconomic milieu. In the materialist world-view that undergirds Marxism, *everything* in society, from politics to art to religion, is a product of deep economic forces: what Marx dubbed the means and modes of economic production. In this lengthy but seminal passage from the author's preface to *A Contribution to the Critique of Political Economy*, Marx establishes a pyramid with the means and modes of production forming the base (or structure) and everything else forming layers, or superstructures, upon that base:

> In the social productions which men carry on they enter into definite relations that are indispensable and independent of their will; these relations of production correspond to a definite stage of development of their material powers of production. The sum total of these relations of production constitutes the economic structure of society—the real foundation, on which rise legal and political superstructures and to which correspond definite forms of social consciousness. The mode of production in material life determines the general character of the social, political and spiritual processes of

life. It is not the consciousness of men that determines their existence, but, on the contrary, their social existence determines their consciousness. At a certain stage of their development, the material forces of production in society come in conflict with the existing relations of production, or—what is but a legal expression for the same thing—with the property relations within which they had been at work before. From forms of development of the forces of production these relations turn into their fetters. Then comes the period of social revolution. With the change of the economic foundation the entire immense super-structure is more or less rapidly transformed. In considering such transformations the distinction should always be made between the material transformation of the economic conditions of production which can be determined with the precision of natural science, and the legal, political, religious, aesthetic or philosophic—in short ideological forms in which men become conscious of this conflict and fight it out. Just as our opinion of an individual is not based on what he thinks of himself, so can we not judge of such a period of transformation by its own consciousness; on the contrary, this consciousness must rather be explained from the contradictions of material life, from the existing conflict between social forces of production and the relations of production.

Ideas have consequences, and I do not exaggerate when I say that the ideas expressed in this single paragraph played a considerable role in laying waste the twentieth century.

I could say much more about the links between this passage

and the rise of totalitarianism, but my focus henceforth will be anthropological rather than political. That is, my focus will be on what Marx has to say not about the nature or politics or society or religion, but about the nature of man. Every time I read the above passage I do a double take. Did Marx really say that? More to the point, did he really believe it? The answer, sadly, is yes; he believed, and preached to the world, that it "is not the consciousness of men that determines their existence, but, on the contrary, their social existence [that] determines their consciousness."

Please read that sentence again slowly and wrap your mind around what it is saying about man. For Marx, it is not just our ideas or our beliefs or our passions that are determined by socioeconomic forces; it is our consciousness itself. We are not just *influenced* by social and economic factors; we are *made* by them. Here is a materialistic monism that surpasses even that of Spinoza, Darwin, and Freud, an utter reduction of the soul-mind to physical forces and mechanisms. No silly illusions here about being the makers of our own destiny or rising above our circumstances. We are the products of blind, purposeless, materialistic forces over which we have no control.

Yes, Marx was a destructive thinker, but at least he had the courage of his convictions. He knew and was unashamed to preach the natural consequences of a radical materialism that allows for no transcendence of any kind. If the brain and the mind are the same thing, if consciousness evolved by the same process as the body and has no status separate from the physical matter of our brain, then it must be the case that our consciousness was created and shaped by socioeconomic forces and not vice versa.

> For Marx, it's not just our ideas, beliefs, and passions that are determined by our socioeconomic milieu; our consciousness too is a product of materialistic forces.

Epicureans in Search of Free Will

It's time we traveled back again to the Epicureans, all of whom based their philosophies on the science of atomism, on the belief that all that exists are atoms moving ceaselessly through the void. Simply by definition, to be an atomist is to be a determinist. Since everything, including the human soul and mind, is made up of atoms there can ultimately be no choice. All is determined by the mindless motion of the atoms.

Or so it would seem. The two greatest Epicureans, Lucretius and Epicurus himself, though they accepted fully the atomic worldview, balked at the idea of rigid determinism. Both Epicurus and Lucretius were, after all, moralistic writers who sought to teach their followers/readers how to live a better life. Their goal was to achieve freedom, balance, harmony, and a maximization of pleasure over pain. But how could they actively seek such ends if all human actions and decisions are determined by physical motions outside of our control?

Here is Epicurus in the conclusion of his "Letter to Menoeceus" consciously refusing to accept the implications of his own atomism: "It would be better to accept the myth about the gods than to be a slave to the determinism of the physicists [that is, the atomists]; for the myth hints at hope for grace through honors paid to the gods, but the necessity of determinism is inescapable." How's that for an admission! What Epicurus says here is directly equivalent to Richard Dawkins saying, "I'd rather be a Christian who puts his faith in the promises of the gospel, than follow out my materialistic beliefs to their logical end and admit that man has no free will." My comparison is neither forced nor facetious. Epicurus was just as scornful and dismissive of those who put their faith in the gods as the new atheists are of those who put their faith in the incarnate, risen Christ.

Determinism is intolerable to the human mind, even and especially to materialists who advocate a worldview that robs man of
his volition, his unique status, and his dignity. So the materialist
must cheat and evade and turn to just-so stories in order to find
a loophole, a way out of the black hole of determinism. Epicurus
thought he could find a place for freedom within the tightly closed
system of atomism by focusing attention on the random swerve of
atoms that cause them to collide with other atoms and form new
compounds. Surely there, in the swerve of the atom, there was a
space for freedom?

Following in the footsteps of his great master, Lucretius incor-
porated this swerve-based freedom into his epic vision of the cosmos. In Book II of *On the Nature of Things* he writes that if

> all movement is connected,
> (new movement coming from old in strict descent)
> and atoms never, by swerving, make a start
> on movement that would break the bonds of fate
> and the endless chain of cause succeeding cause,
> whence comes the freedom for us who live on earth?
> Whence rises, I say, that will torn free from fate,
> through which we follow wherever pleasure leads,
> and likewise swerve aside at times and places
> not foreordained, but as our mind suggests?

Lucretius, like Spinoza after him, *did* believe in endless material chains of causation. Yet in this passage he proves unwilling to
accept where his own beliefs want to lead him. He cannot shake his
deep-set faith in human freedom, in man's ability to break himself
free from fate and seek after pleasure. So he convinces himself of
something that really makes no sense: that the random swerve of

atoms moving through space is somehow a sufficient instrument for creating and preserving free will.

Though I applaud Epicurus and Lucretius for their ingenious, imaginative, poetic attempts to guarantee the reality of volition, it just doesn't hold water. We cannot make a real choice unless we can step back and truly inspect our options. But atomism gives us no place to step back to. There are only atoms and the void; even the soul is made of atoms—atoms that disperse at death, leaving no trace of the person who once possessed it.

> Refusing to accept the determinism implicit in their atomist beliefs, Epicurus and Lucretius claimed to locate human freedom in the random swerve of the atom.

A Victorian Epicurean

T.H. Huxley, Darwin's bulldog and something of a Victorian Epicurean, makes the same dodge, the same bait-and-switch in his famous lecture "On the Physical Basis of Life" (1868). Throughout most of his talk, he presents a purely materialistic, reductive view of the world, positing as the universal building block of life—as that sought-after first principle that the Pre-Socratics dubbed the *arche*—not atoms, but something he calls *protoplasm* (Greek for "first form"). Everything can be accounted for by the death, life, and endless rearrangements of this atom-like and infinitely malleable *arche*. In his talk, he makes no room for an eternal soul separate from protoplasm; in fact, he subtly ridicules anyone who would insert some kind of spiritual force or energy beyond the protoplasm.

Slowly, inexorably, Huxley pushes his listeners toward a materialist worldview, and then…he draws back. He knows that the credulous religious believers in his audience will be repelled by the notion that all there is in the universe is matter. So he makes an unexpected about-face and hides behind ridicule:

> The consequence of this great truth [that all there is in the universe is matter] weighs like a nightmare, I believe, upon many of the best minds of these days. They watch what they conceive to be the progress of materialism, in such fear and powerless anger as a savage feels, when, during an eclipse, the great shadow creeps over the face of the sun. The advancing tide of matter threatens to drown their souls; the tightening grasp of law impedes their freedom; they are alarmed lest man's moral nature be debased by the increase of his wisdom.

The new atheist tactic of treating sincere Christian believers as if they were unevolved savages is hardly new. It has been indulged in for millennia, starting with some of the Pre-Socratics and passing through Epicurus and Lucretius on down to Spinoza, Voltaire, Hume, and dozens of others. What makes Huxley's use of it here particularly grating and offensive is that he ridicules religious people for having the gall to take seriously the implications of what he and his fellow Darwinians are trying to hoist on the public.

Yes, Huxley really seems disturbed by the fact that people in his audience might actually follow out his (Huxley's) own theories to their logical conclusion. That will not do! "For my part," he goes on to say, using (unashamedly) the language of the Catholic Church, "I utterly repudiate and anathematise the intruder. Fact I know; and Law I know; but what is this Necessity, save an empty shadow of my own mind's throwing?" Very often, atheists, materialists, and secular humanists are more "religious" than Christians; they have their own tightly held, fiercely guarded orthodoxies and dogmas, and they can be remarkably unflinching about them, even in the face of the facts.

But how can Huxley possibly justify his utter rejection of necessity (that is, of determinism)? He does so, amazingly, by indulging in a logical fallacy known as the argument to ignorance:

> But, if it is certain that we can have no knowledge of the nature of either matter or spirit, and that the notion of necessity is something illegitimately thrust into the perfectly legitimate conception of law, the materialistic position that there is nothing in the world but matter, force, and necessity, is as utterly devoid of justification as the most baseless of theological dogmas. The fundamental doctrines of materialism, like those of spiritualism, and most other "isms," lie outside "the limits of philosophical inquiry," and David Hume's great service to humanity is his irrefragable demonstration of what these limits are.

Always a good move to take refuge in the name of Hume, for Hume, undeservedly, continues to be hailed as the one who decisively disproved miracles, who conclusively proved that the only real knowledge is empirical knowledge based on experience and the senses, and who poked a permanent hole in Christian theism by way of the problem of pain. Although—as I attempted to show in chapters 3, 4, and 7—none of these claims are true, Hume's reputation in academia marches on unscathed.

Though Hume and Huxley, like the new atheists after them, never hesitate to accuse Christians of clinging to a "God of the

gaps"—of covering up their lack of scientific knowledge by ascribing everything they can't understand to God's unseen providence—
they see no problem, or hypocrisy, in covering their own tracks
by appealing to gaps in scientific research. Huxley seems to think
that by excoriating the extremes of that very materialism that he
devoted his life to propagating and comparing it, unfavorably,
to religious dogmatism, that he can escape the necessary consequences of materialistic, nontheistic Darwinism—which *is* precisely what Huxley advocates. He admits as much in the second to
last paragraph of his lecture: "Thus there can be little doubt, that
the further science advances, the more extensively and consistently
will all the phenomena of Nature be represented by materialistic
formulae and symbols."

And yet despite this strong, unwavering statement of materialism, Huxley asserts just three paragraphs earlier that there are two
beliefs of which he is absolutely certain: "the first, that the order of
Nature is ascertainable by our faculties to an extent which is practi-
cally unlimited; the second, that our volition counts for something
as a condition of the course of events." Is Huxley really unaware
that these two beliefs contradict one another? If the order of nature
can be discerned and stated with mathematical precision, then
where is there room for free will? If nature is a machine of which
we are a part, then we can only be cogs in that machine. If all pro-
ceeds from a purely material chain of causes, and if there is no part
of us that transcends that material chain, then freedom, choice,
and free will are all illusions.

Is Huxley aware of this? Perhaps not when he delivered his lecture. But he should at least have been so when he reprinted his
lecture in 1892 as a part of his collected works. In that reprint-
ing, Huxley added a brief note to the passage just quoted that

contradicts the very assertion of human volition to which the note is appended: "Or, to speak more accurately, the physical state of which volition is the expression." There you have it. Huxley wants to assure us that materialism does not necessitate determinism ("our volition counts for something as a condition of the course of events"), and yet he admits in his note that *if* we have volition, the mechanism *through which* that volition arises must itself be purely physical, natural, and material. But if it is purely material, then it is but one more cog in the machine of nature, and if it is no more than a cog, then it lacks the transcendence and the freedom to act against the machine of which it is a part.

> Like Epicurus and Lucretius, T.H. Huxley refused to admit that his materialist worldview necessitated the very determinism that he so deeply despised.

Christian Cross-Examination #1: Atheists Must Act as if Christianity Were True

I am pleased to say that over the last decade or so an increasing number of Christian apologists have picked up on this central contradiction in the writings of atheists and secular humanists and called them to the table for it. Those who would do away with God can't, in the same breath, preserve attributes that only God can give. I continue to be amazed with what untroubled insouciance evolutionists of all stripes speak of nature, chance, and evolution as if they were volitional agents. Oh yes, like Richard Dawkins, they are always quick to remind us that the design we see in nature is only the "appearance" of design. But then, having said that, they immediately return to speaking of mindless, purposeless evolutionary forces as if they were consciously and purposely leading us somewhere.

Let's be clear about something: nature possesses neither consciousness nor conscience nor free will. She is not aware of herself, is not a moral-ethical agent, and has no choice but to follow the iron laws that define her. And the same goes for the plant and animal kingdoms. How is it, then, that we alone possess self-awareness, an inbuilt sense of right and wrong, and the ability to choose between those options? Only of human beings do the words *should* and *ought* have any meaning.

Of the recent apologists who have exposed the inherent inconsistencies in the materialist worldview and free-will rhetoric of the new atheists and their fellow travelers, the one I have found most helpful also happens to be one of my colleagues at Houston Baptist University, Nancy Pearcey. In *Finding Truth*, Pearcey shows how those who replace God with blind evolutionary forces inevitably end up reducing man from a free individual made in God's image to a determined and dehumanized unit in nature.

They may speak rapturously of the complexities of human life, but their naturalist presuppositions cannot begin to account for that complexity. As a result, they are forced to import notions of free will and moral accountability from the very Christian worldview they ridicule and reject. Borrowing a phrase from Kant, Pearcey explains that materialists are forced to act *as if* free will and moral accountability are true, even if their system cannot support such an assertion.

But she does more than explain. To back up her thesis—that materialism cannot live with the consequences of its beliefs—Pearcey provides a series of quotes from influential secular humanists who themselves have admitted their inability to order their lives and choices around their own materialist worldviews. Here are four of my favorites:

Powerful logical or metaphysical reasons for supposing we can't have strong free will keep coming up against equally powerful psychological reasons why we *can't help believing* that we do have it...It seems that we *cannot live* or experience our choices as determined even if determinism is true (Galen Strawson).

No matter that the physical world provides no room for freedom of will; that concept is essential to our models of the mental realm...[We cannot] ever give it up. We're virtually forced to maintain that belief, *even though we know it's false* (Marvin Minsky).

I am compelled to act *as if* free will existed because if I want to live in a civilized society I must act responsibly (Albert Einstein).

At an important and ineradicable level, the idea of my daughter as merely a complex robot carrying my genes into the next generation is both bizarre and repugnant to me...[Such a reductionistic view] inspires in us a kind of emotional resistance and even revulsion (Edward Slingerland).

Pearcey refers to writers like these as "free-loading atheists." Though content to define themselves and their views against Christianity, they are forced to exist parasitically on the very faith they reject.

Consider carefully what these four quotes reveal about the materialist worldview. For Strawson, there is something buried deep in our psychological makeup that cannot help but believe that we have free will, that our actions and beliefs are not completely determined by forces outside of our control. But what is the origin of this unshakeable belief? Blind nature, driven by mechanical laws, can offer no concept of freedom and choice. The source, therefore, must be supernatural and metaphysical. In the same way, if a transcendent idea of justice did not exist, and if that idea were not somehow written in our conscience, we would be unable to ask or even think the question, "Why is there so much injustice in the world?"

As for Minsky, he is equally adamant about the fact that materialism cannot provide a foundation for free will as he is about the inescapable reality that we cannot understand the human mind without recourse to free will. As a result, he will go on blithely believing something he knows is false. But how can he do that? How can he force himself to believe something that contradicts the purely natural forces that made him, unless he possesses the ability to make that choice? The very existence of the dilemma reveals that there is a part of Minsky (and of all of us) that transcends nature.

Einstein's admission—that the moral-ethical behaviors upon which civilization rests rest themselves upon the real existence of free will—is a bit more pragmatic than Minsky's and Strawson's, but it is nonetheless intellectually self-contradictory. How can Einstein harbor the concept of acting responsibly unless he also harbors the concept that there are certain things he ought or ought not to do? But the moment we move into the realm of *oughts*, we move into a divided realm where something beyond Darwinian impulse gives us the ability to step back and analyze that impulse and decide whether or not we should (ought to) follow it.

Finally, in the very personal confession of Slingerland, we get down to the brass tacks. Determinism is not only insupportable to the human psyche; it is both bizarre and repugnant. As a parallel to this insight, consider the natural revulsion most people feel toward the dog-eat-dog ethos of survival of the fittest. If we are indeed made in the image of God, then it is not surprising that we should feel such revulsion. But if the materialists are right, then we ourselves are products of that very process of natural selection that we find so repugnant. How can that be? How could nature breed in us a disgust for the process that formed and shaped us? Likewise, if we are nothing more than cogs in the natural machine, from where does our deep-set abhorrence of determinism rise?

> Though their worldview offers no place for free will, the vast majority of atheists, in contradiction to their materialism, continue to act *as if* free will existed.

Christian Cross-Examination #2: Only the *Imago Dei* Upholds Man's Innate Value

If materialism is true, then free will is, whether we like it or not, an illusion. But free will is not the only casualty of atheism. In the absence of a belief in the *imago dei*, the biblical teaching that we were created in the image of God, we must surrender as well that cherished secular Enlightenment faith on which our country was built: namely, that every individual human being possesses intrinsic value and worth.

It never ceases to amaze me how modern secularists have convinced themselves that it was Enlightenment thinkers who discovered, taught, and propagated the notion of innate human dignity. They did not. They borrowed (stole) it from Christianity, even as they steered Western thought away from the revelation of the Bible and grounded it instead in empiricism. If we are nothing more than products of natural selection, then we do *not* have innate dignity. Period! Some of the ancient Greeks and Romans, especially Plato, Aristotle, and Cicero, were able to reach toward lofty ethical visions. But they lacked the revelation of the Bible, and, because they did, they did not teach that all human beings had essential value.

Of course, that does not mean that Christians who possessed

that knowledge consistently treated all people as fellow creatures equally made in the image of God. But then, as Timothy Keller reminds us in *The Reason for God*, there is no nation or culture that does not have blood on its hands; that is what the Christian doctrine of original sin would expect us to find. All nations, Christian or otherwise, have their atrocities and nearly all have condoned slavery. But let us not forget, argues Keller, that it was the Judeo-Christian worldview, and it alone, that supplied the impetus to abolish the slave trade. The reason for that fact of history is that only Christianity provides a firm, unshakable foundation for the intrinsic worth of every human being. "Identity apart from God is inherently unstable," explains Keller, "Without God, our sense of worth may seem solid on the surface, but it never is—it can desert you in a moment" (164).

The direct link between the *imago dei* and the Enlightenment is best displayed in the American Declaration of Independence. Although in the preamble to this key Enlightenment manifesto Thomas Jefferson makes reference to nature and nature's God, when it comes time for him to assert that we have all been endowed with "inalienable rights" to "life, liberty, and the pursuit of happiness," he is forced to appeal directly to our Creator. A poor man cannot endow someone with great riches; neither can a weak man endow someone with great power. If we are to be granted, as a gift, the rights to life, liberty, and the pursuit of happiness, then that gift must come from someone who possesses those things. That is why nature cannot give them. She might be able to grant us the "right" to participate in the dog-eat-dog struggle of natural selection, but she can't give us life and liberty, for she does not possess those things herself. Likewise, she cannot give us happiness, for that is something that she, being unconscious, can know nothing about.

No, the only real and firm foundation we have for the innate, essential dignity of every human being is that we were made in the image of our Creator. Apart from that, we are nothing more than members of the animal kingdom, products of evolutionary forces that care for species but not for individuals. If the Bible is wrong, then Marx is right, and even our consciousness itself is a product of deep, dark socioeconomic structures over which we have no control.

And yet, even that is not the whole story. The *imago dei* assures us that we are special and that we have some kind of innate worth. But, if we would be assured of our true and eternal value in the eyes of the one who created us, then we must turn from Genesis to the New Testament. For there alone, in the Gospels and epistles, do we find that we are of such worth to our Creator that, even while we were in rebellion against him, he sent his Son to die for us (Romans 5:8).

> The secular Enlightenment was only able to assert the essential dignity of every human being because it borrowed (stole) that concept from the biblical *imago dei*.

Postscript

Before moving on to my final chapter, I feel the need to pause and reflect briefly on a kind of madness that has seized modern America, pushing us, almost overnight, from a Darwinian-Marxist view of personhood that reduces us to our genetic makeup to a radical postmodern view in which we are granted total freedom over our biological identity. This mad shift from determinism to unbounded, standardless free will has taken place within the wider gay rights movement that advocates, quite vociferously, for lesbians, gays, bisexuals, and transgenders (LGBT).

Only a few years ago, genetic determinism was the LGBT

dogma. We were born straight or gay, and there was nothing we could do about it. Our genes made us that way, end of story. Darwin and Marx were their best allies, for they claimed as well that our desires and our consciousness, whether gay or straight, followed our genes.

And then, in the wink of an eye, everything changed. Suddenly, gender was up for grabs; it was not the result of DNA but was something that *we* chose. Our sexual identity was fluid, something that we created ourselves, apart from our body parts, our religious traditions, and our socioeconomic milieu. When it came to issues of gender, we now possessed total freedom...or did we? True liberty is not license, but the liberty to choose that which is right over that which is wrong. Freedom does not come in a vacuum; it is a quality of moral-ethical creatures who possess internal standards, engraved in their conscience, of right and wrong, virtue and vice, good and evil.

Just as materialism offers an illusion of freedom, so the new rallying cry of LGBT offers a false freedom that is detached, fragmented, and ultimately meaningless. We were made to choose wisely, not to live in a free-for-all world without milestones or signposts.

CHAPTER TEN

Good Without God?

Let me begin this final chapter by sharing something that I have confessed to hundreds of students over the years: If it could be proven that Christ did not rise from the dead, I would leave the church and become a Stoic. Yes, I would. Christianity is not a religion that rests on blind faith or that places feelings over truth. It is a historical religion that rises and falls on the basis of its claim that Jesus Christ was the incarnate Son of God who died on a cross and then rose bodily from the grave. If Jesus did not rise from the dead, Paul makes clear, then the Christian faith is empty and vain (1 Corinthians 15:14).

Oh yes, without the resurrection we would still have the moral teachings of Jesus as recorded in the Gospels, but those teachings alone do not guarantee the truth of Christianity. Inasmuch as he was a moral teacher, Jesus's precepts do not vary greatly from those laid down by Moses or Confucius or Buddha or Zoroaster or Socrates. In fact, if Jesus was nothing more than a good rabbi, then we don't need him. There are plenty of prophets and gurus to go around. The problem is not that we don't know how we should behave; the problem is that, knowing good from evil, we still choose to do evil, to go our own way, to disobey the divine law.

But now I'm digressing. I still need to explain my confession. If Jesus did not rise from the dead, then he was not the Son of God, and if he was not the Son of God, then God has never really spoken to us. Oh, yes, he gave the Law to Moses, but if he truly is a God of love passionate for his bride, then where is the proof of that love? If Jesus did not rise, if he was only a man, then we're on our own down here. If Jesus did not conquer death, and, with it, sin and the devil, then all the religious rituals in the world are shams, powerless to save or transform or give new life.

I'm being completely and nakedly honest here. Religion is a man-made thing, our way of finding light in the darkness and meaning in a world that lacks it. If Jesus didn't rise bodily on Easter Sunday, then he was not who he claimed to be; he was just another itinerant preacher peddling another panacea, another warm blanket to keep out the cold. If Jesus didn't walk out of the tomb, then Christianity is the greatest hoax ever played on the human race. And if it is a hoax, then I, for one, would give up on religion.

But where to go if religion proves false? Well, if there is no God, or if he is utterly indifferent, or if he is equivalent to nature, then your best bet is to play it safe: Protect yourself as well as you can from the arbitrary stabs of fate; hold on to what little pleasure you can find in this uncaring world; follow your duty and stay true to your word; foster balance and equanimity of mind; detach yourself from the madness and futility of life.

In a word, become a Stoic.

Stoicism and Utopianism

Walker Percy once wrote that the real religion of the Old American South was Stoicism. In fact, I have been assured by a colleague who knows such things that when Robert E. Lee died, a copy of the *Meditations* of the Stoic emperor Marcus Aurelius was found on his night table. Having lived in Texas now for twenty-five years, I can still see remnants of that heroic Stoicism that, mingled with Christianity, gave the South her honor, her courage, and her sense of duty.

No, I do not think that Stoicism is true in the way that Christianity is true, but I believe it is filled with true things. In the absence of an active, transcendent-immanent God, Stoicism offers, to my mind at least, the most reasonable, practical, manly option. The new atheists would have us believe that if we threw out supernatural Christianity, it would not mark the end of moral-ethical behavior. Man, they assure us, can be moral without God. But they are wrong—wrong because, like Rousseau before them, they deny the biblical doctrine of original sin and fool themselves into believing that man is by nature good. The problem with man, they argue, is not sin, rebellion, and disobedience, but ignorance and poverty. Offer free public education and an equitable economy that provides all people with sufficient food, shelter, and clothing, and utopia will ensue.

Alas, history has proven them wrong. The French Revolution was to bring about that utopia. Throw out superstitious Christianity and replace it with Enlightenment reason, the revolutionaries believed, and we will build a perfect France. Utopia never arrived, but massive bloodshed and tyranny did. Fast-forward a century or so and see how the Bolsheviks were going to build another utopia without God. The Soviet carnage was almost more than one can imagine. Mao's China and Pol Pot's Cambodia fostered similar antireligious utopian dreams. They too ended in a nightmare of repression and slaughter.

Original sin, Chesterton famously argued in chapter 2 of *Orthodoxy*, "is the only part of Christian theology which can really be proved." Can anyone who has carefully studied history, or other people, or himself really believe that we are by nature good, that our bad choices and evil actions are all sociological, that if we were raised in utopia, we would never sin? Aleksandr Solzhenitsyn, longtime prisoner in the Soviet gulag, saw the truth about man to which the utopian Communists had willfully blinded themselves: "Gradually it was disclosed to me that the line separating good and evil passes not through states, nor between classes, nor between political parties either—but right through every human heart—and through all human hearts."

The new atheists are wrong to think that man is by nature good, or at least neutral, and therefore does not need God. And yet in Stoicism, we find that man does possess the tools to achieve a significant level of individual moral growth. The Stoics, who did not fool themselves into believing that men were naturally good, just, and benevolent, often reached successfully after a moderate amount of goodness, justice, and benevolence. Like the Epicureans, they lacked faith in a personal, active God; yet they did manage to leave behind them some real insight into human nature and the human condition.

In this closing chapter, I will pay tribute to the greatest of the Stoics, Marcus Aurelius, and to his classic work the *Meditations*. I will show how he, along with others who share his worldview, possessed a nobility that should be respected, but I will show as well his limitations. Rather than separate out my Christian cross-examinations as I have done in the previous nine chapters, I will weave them into my overview and celebration of the *Meditations*.

Let us, then, enter into the mind of the great Stoic as he wanders over strange seas of thought—marking, as we go, what heights man can achieve, but also acknowledging, Ecclesiastes-like, the essential futility of a life lived without God.

> Whereas utopians believe man is by nature good, and
> then set out, usually with disastrous results, to build
> one, Stoics have a more realistic view of human
> depravity.

Marcus Aurelius

Let me begin by introducing the author of the *Meditations*. Marcus Aurelius, who ruled Rome from 161–180, was an extremely learned and thoughtful emperor, the last of five good emperors who brought stability to the empire in the second century AD: Nerva, Trajan, Hadrian, Antoninus Pius, and Aurelius. In Aurelius's day, Rome had managed to spread order and justice across her vast empire; strife was present on only two frontiers—the Parthians (Persians) to the east and the Germanic barbarians to the north. Aurelius spent much of his reign living on the Germanic border, trying, with the help of his army, to keep the peace. During the long, cold nights, he composed a set of philosophical musings in the mode of the first-century Stoic Seneca. His musings are disjointed and fragmented; they present their reader not with a systematic philosophy, but with a series of freestanding meditations on how to live the Stoic life. Had Aurelius lived today and had access to the Internet and a laptop, his *Meditations* would almost surely have taken the form of a presidential blog.

If the *Meditations* have a central focus, it is Aurelius's yearning for a world united in peace. In pursuit of that high goal, he rejects extravagance and personal glory to serve Rome and defend her from the barbarians who would tear her apart. Seventeen hundred years later, a Victorian Stoic who lived an essentially moral life of public service without harboring any belief in the active, transcendent-immanent God of the Bible would look back to

Aurelius as an ideal and bemoan the fact that Christianity became the official religion of the empire under the brutal, militaristic Constantine rather than the gentle, philosophical Aurelius. "It is a bitter thought," writes John Stuart Mill in chapter 2 of *On Liberty*, "how different a thing the Christianity of the world might have been, if the Christian faith had been adopted as the religion of the empire under the auspices of Marcus Aurelius instead of those of Constantine."

And yet Mill admits—and attempts to justify—that Aurelius, for all his high-minded idealism and ethical behavior, oversaw a persecution of the church:

> Absolute monarch of the whole civilized world, he preserved through life not only the most unblemished justice, but what was less to be expected from his Stoical breeding, the tenderest heart. The few failings which are attributed to him, were all on the side of indulgence: while his writings, the highest ethical product of the ancient mind, differ scarcely perceptibly, if they differ at all, from the most characteristic teachings of Christ. This man, a better Christian in all but the dogmatic sense of the word, than almost any of the ostensibly Christian sovereigns who have since reigned, persecuted Christianity. Placed at the summit of all the previous attainments of humanity, with an open, unfettered intellect, and a character which led him of himself to embody in his moral writings the Christian ideal, he yet failed to see that Christianity was to be a good and not an evil to the world, with his duties to which he was so deeply penetrated. Existing society he knew to be in a deplorable state.

But such as it was, he saw, or thought he saw, that it
was held together, and prevented from being worse,
by belief and reverence of the received divinities. As a
ruler of mankind, he deemed it his duty not to suffer
society to fall in pieces; and saw not how, if its existing
ties were removed, any others could be formed which
could again knit it together. The new religion openly
aimed at dissolving these ties: unless, therefore, it was
his duty to adopt that religion, it seemed to be his duty
to put it down.

Though the utilitarian Mill rejected the supernatural aspects
of Christianity, he did respect the moral teachings of Jesus, particularly the Golden Rule, and saw no problem separating Christ's
teachings from his claims to divinity and his resurrection from the
dead. Were Mill writing today, he would likely avoid the militant
atheism of Richard Dawkins and company, but he would surely
be an outspoken secular humanist committed to reducing Christianity to a generic civil religion with no voice in the public square.

In many ways, I think Mill's assessment of why Aurelius persecuted the church is accurate. Aurelius's Stoic dream of building a universal empire, a world without borders that cut across all
cultures and countries, likely ran afoul of the church's competing
vision of universal brotherhood through faith in the risen Christ.
Constantine, I believe, recognized that fact, for when he, a century and a half later, tried to realize Aurelius's dream of a one-world
empire, he found that Christianity was the only glue that could
hold together the renewed *pax romana* ("peace of Rome") that both
he and Aurelius desired.

But there is something missing from Mill's analysis that gets to
what may be the true reason why Aurelius persecuted the church.

Read carefully through the *Meditations*, and you will find that there is only one reference to Christianity:

> What a soul that is which is ready, if at any moment it must be separated from the body, and ready either to be extinguished or dispersed or continue to exist; but so that this readiness comes from a man's own judgement, not from mere obstinacy, as with the Christians, but considerately and with dignity and in a way to persuade another, without tragic show (Book XI, Chapter 3).

One can almost hear the modern secular humanist or new atheist grinding his teeth and exclaiming with patronizing exasperation: "Why can't these annoying Christians just get with the program? Why can't they let go of their silly, superstitious scruples and help us build our utopia?"

For Aurelius, the phrase "Christian martyr" is an oxymoron. Christians go to their death not out of duty to the state or the gods or even their ancestors, but out of mere obstinacy. They are pigheaded, refusing to embrace the nice civil religion offered them by Aurelius and Rome. You see, Aurelius's Stoicism, despite its ethical enlightenment and humanitarian ethos, insists on a generic spirituality divorced from any ultimate theological claims. Duty, honor, virtue, reverence: welcome into the tent; God in the flesh, dying and rising, claiming to be the one way to God: get out!

Now, as I confessed above, if Aurelius and his heirs are right and God is just a removed watchmaker or a spirit dispersed through nature, then Stoicism is the best option. But what if he is not? What if God has spoken, acted, and even entered into human history? That possibility the Stoic, like the modern secular humanist and new atheist, cannot accept. To do so would be to allow a final authority and arbiter beyond the self.

> Although Marcus Aurelius was an enlightened emperor who served Rome, he persecuted Christianity, probably because he saw it as a rival to his Stoic vision of unity.

Of Branches and Bodies

In the Gospel of John, Jesus compares himself to a vine and his disciples to branches that receive their sustenance from the vine (15:1-8). Apart from that connection and that sustenance, we can produce no real fruit. The apostle Paul says that the church is the body of Christ, with each of us serving as a part or member of that body, however honorable or humble that part may be (1 Corinthians 12:12-31).

Though I do not think that the Stoic Aurelius read the New Testament, he uses imagery that is remarkably similar. "A branch," he muses,

> cut off from the adjacent branch must of necessity be cut off from the whole tree also. So too a man when he is separated from another man has fallen off from the whole social community. Now as to a branch, another cuts it off, but a man by his own act separates himself from his neighbour when he hates him and turns away from him, and he does not know that he has at the same time cut himself off from the whole social system (XI.8).

As for the metaphor of the body, he has this to say:

If thou didst ever see a hand cut off, or a foot, or a
head, lying anywhere apart from the rest of the body,
such does a man make himself, as far as he can, who is
not content with what happens, and separates himself
from others, or does anything unsocial. Suppose that
thou hast detached thyself from the natural unity—for
thou wast made by nature a part, but now thou hast
cut thyself off—yet here there is this beautiful provision, that it is in thy power again to unite thyself. God
has allowed this to no other part, after it has been separated and cut asunder, to come together again. But
consider the kindness by which he has distinguished
man, for he has put it in his power not to be separated
at all from the universal; and when he has been separated, he has allowed him to return and to be united
and to resume his place as a part (VIII.34).

Surely Aurelius's Stoic vision is identical to the Christian vision
of Jesus and Paul. What need have we for miracles, theological par-
adoxes, and people rising from the dead when the essence of Christianity is so perfectly reflected in the secular morality of the Stoics?

This sounds like a compelling argument, but it has one flaw.
There is a subtle but vital difference between the way Aurelius and
the New Testament use the branch and body metaphors. In the
Bible, Christ himself is the vine and the body of which we are
branches and members. Not so in Aurelius. Those who detach
themselves from branch or body are guilty not of violating God's
holiness or his law or his will, but of a social sin.

Unlike the Epicureans, who believed the soul fell apart into its
separate atoms at death, the Stoics believed in something like the
Eastern one soul. In the two passages I quoted from the *Meditations*,

Aurelius treats society as a sort of amorphous one soul of which it is our duty to be a part. Oh, Aurelius grants to man the free will to break off from or reattach himself to the body politic, and for that he is to be commended. But something insidious lurks underneath this seeming affirmation of free will, something that made Soviet Russia, Communist China, and the Cambodia of the Khmer Rouge so horrific.

And that something can be traced back directly to one of the architects of the Enlightenment and of the French Revolution: Jean-Jacques Rousseau. In *The Social Contract* (1762), Rousseau seems to lay the foundation for a truly free state of free individuals able to express themselves through the medium of free speech. There will be no church or monarchy or privileged aristocracy to enforce conformity; man, who is by nature good, will be liberated from the corruption and slavery of ancient social and political structures. Or so it seems.

True, there will be no Pope or king or landlord, but there *will* be something that Rousseau calls the "general will," something that will be arrived at by majority vote but that will then be imposed upon all citizens—so much so, in fact, that they will not only be unable to break it; they will be unable to think outside of it. "Anyone who refuses to obey the general will," writes Rousseau in Book I, Chapter 7 of *The Social Contract*, "shall be compelled to do so by the whole body." If he resists, he will be re-educated. But don't worry, Rousseau assures us in Chapter 8, everyone who is re-educated in accordance with the general will shall "constantly have reason to bless the happy moment when he was drawn out of the state of nature forever and changed from a stupid, short-sighted animal into an intelligent being and man."

This is exactly what happened in the re-education prisons and

camps of the would-be utopias of Stalin, Mao, and Pol Pot. It is
what Aurelius likely would have done to the Christians had he
been "blessed" with modern methods of social engineering. Apart
from a divine standard established by a personal, actively involved
God, the danger remains that society will turn into an octopus
and devour the individual wills of its citizens, transforming them
into a mass of automatons. Do not be fooled: Rigid social conformity is not a product of the Catholic Middle Ages but of the secular Enlightenment. There is far more real conformity of body,
mind, and spirit in twenty-first-century America than there was
in eleventh-century France or England.

> Although Stoicism shares the Christian concern for
> unity, apart from the headship of a personal God, that
> unity can quickly morph into rigid social conformity.

The God Within

But didn't Marcus Aurelius believe in God? Yes and no. Mill
certainly thought he did, and the *Meditations* use the word *God*
often enough, but please remember what I said in the opening
section of chapter 8. Not everyone who says he believes in God
really believes in God. Like the gods of both deism and pantheism,
Aurelius's god is totally impersonal; he neither loves nor wills nor
involves himself in the world.

What, then, does Aurelius believe in? To what does he hold
himself accountable?

Consider these two chapters, which I quote in full from the
Meditations:

> Live with the gods. And he does live with the gods
> who constantly shows to them, his own soul is satis-
> fied with that which is assigned to him, and that it does

all that the daemon wishes, which Zeus hath given to every man for his guardian and guide, a portion of himself. And this is every man's understanding and reason (V.27).

Labour not unwillingly, nor without regard to the common interest, nor without due consideration, nor with distraction; nor let studied ornament set off thy thoughts, and be not either a man of many words, or busy about too many things. And further, let the deity which is in thee be the guardian of a living being, manly and of ripe age, and engaged in matter political, and a Roman, and a ruler, who has taken his post like a man waiting for the signal which summons him from life, and ready to go, having need neither of oath nor of any man's testimony. Be cheerful also, and seek not external help nor the tranquility which others give. A man then must stand erect, not be kept erect by others (III.5).

In these parallel musings, Aurelius lays out two of the cornerstones of his Stoic faith. In each of them, we glimpse the strengths and the weakness, the glories and the failings, the potentials and the limitations of Stoicism as a secular substitute for Christian morality.

Like most people who are ethical without being religious—Spinoza, Hume, Huxley, and Mill among them—Aurelius looks not to shrines or temples for guidance but to his own human breast. He worships not the God which art in heaven but the god who resides within. Not Zeus, but the bit of divine light that Zeus placed inside him as a guide and guardian; not a removed, transcendent deity but a mediating spirit that the Greeks called a daemon. Just as Socrates claimed to have a daemon (or oracle) that resided within him and prevented him from doing things he should not do, so Aurelius claimed to have a daemon that directed him to perform his duty.

In modern parlance, Aurelius's god within is often referred to as the "inner light," a favorite phrase of those who consider themselves ethical but not religious. Both phrases sound spiritual enough, but they carry with them a danger that Chesterton exposed a century ago in chapter 5 of *Orthodoxy*. Speaking with direct reference to Marcus Aurelius and his fellow Stoics, Chesterton boldly proclaims that of all

> conceivable forms of enlightenment the worst is what these people call the Inner Light. Of all horrible religions the most horrible is the worship of the god within. Any one who knows any body knows how it would work; any one who knows any one from the Higher Thought Centre knows how it does work. That Jones shall worship the god within him turns out ultimately to mean that Jones shall worship Jones. Let Jones worship the sun or moon, anything rather than the Inner Light; let Jones worship cats or crocodiles, if he can find any in his street, but not the god within. Christianity came into the world firstly in order to assert with violence that a man had not only to look inwards, but to look outwards, to behold with astonishment and enthusiasm a divine company and a divine captain. The only fun of being a Christian was that a man was not left alone with the Inner Light, but definitely recognized an outer light, fair as the sun, clear as the moon, terrible as an army with banners.

Sorry for the long quote, but one simply can't cut off Chesterton when he is on a roll—especially when that roll involves popping the swelled heads of smug Pharisees.

Christians often speak of looking inward for the power they need, but if those who say such things are true Christians, then they do not mean what you might think they mean. The orthodox Christian looks within because the indwelling Holy Spirit resides within, and it is to God's Spirit, not his own, that the Christian looks for strength. Not so the Buddhist monk or martial artist who, when he looks within for strength, looks not to the Holy Spirit but to the god within, the inner light. Such prolonged inner searching leads to self-absorption and even self-worship rather than true humility and a true love of God and one's neighbor. Excessive introspection, far from making us into saints, makes us psychologically and spiritually unhealthy. The best remedy is not more egocentric meditation, but a trip to the park, a looking outward toward the beauty and wonder of God's creation.

> Stoics worship not a transcendent personal God, but the god within, the inner light; alas, what begins as the worship of the god within usually ends as self-worship.

Sticking to One's Post

In the previous section, I quoted two passages from the *Meditations* that offer a glimpse of two of the cornerstones of Stoicism. The first I identified as the focus on the god within. The second concerns that which the god within impels us to do—namely, to do our duty and stick to our post.

Like Socrates and Cicero before him, to illustrate the essence of duty, Aurelius uses the military metaphor of a soldier who remains at his post no matter what the danger. The true Stoic fulfills the task that has been given to him without allowing anything—fear, emotion, avarice, sloth—to turn him away from the path of duty. Even familial warmth, ties of blood, and personal happiness must be let go if they impede one's duty.

Such duty (or dharma) forms a central tenet of Hinduism, a tenet that finds its supreme expression in the *Gita*. "Do your duty, always," Krishna instructs Arjuna,

> but without attachment. That is how a man reaches the ultimate truth; by working without anxiety about results…Your motive in working should be to set others, by your example, on the path of duty. Whatever a great man does, ordinary people will imitate; they follow his example. Consider me: I am not bound by any sort of duty. There is nothing, in all the three worlds, which I do not already possess; nothing I have yet to acquire. But I go on working nevertheless…It is better to do your own duty, however imperfectly, than to assume the duties of another person (Chapter III).

A high calling indeed, though one that runs directly counter to our modern culture of personal fulfillment and self-actualization. Duty-dharma in its full Stoic-Hindu sense means that one must detach his desires from what he has been assigned to do. He must not yearn after someone else's duty, nor feel undue anxiety about his own.

I just said that this idea runs contrary to our modern ethos of individualism, and yet there is one way in which it does not. As our age continues to throw off all absolute moral-ethical standards and to embrace pure relativism, I hear more and more young people express a desire to lose themselves in some greater cause. While such a desire can be both healthy and noble, it can also act as a cover for an unhealthy and ignoble desire to have one's individuality swallowed up: to join Rousseau's general will or the one soul of Eastern mysticism.

Only incarnational Christianity, I would argue, can hold in balance that great paradox taught by Jesus: that the only way to gain our life is to lose it (Matthew 11:39; Mark 8:35; Luke 9:24). We surrender our selfish, sinful, disobedient will so that God can take our broken, fragmented personhood and make it truly whole and truly ours. In fact, only by making ourselves his can we hope to become who we were created to be. Too often, the Stoic way of doing one's duty leads to a loss of hope: It may bring contentment, but it does not bring joy; it may bring calm and equanimity, but it does not bring that full, abundant life that Christ promises (John 10:10). There is a deep sadness at the heart of Stoicism, a resignation that, while noble in itself, is cut off from that wonderful fruit of the Spirit (Galatians 5:22-23) that transforms us into the triumphant creatures we were meant to be.

As part of his Stoic duty, Aurelius waits "for death with a cheerful mind," but his vision of death is hardly one to inspire hope or cheer: "a dissolution of the elements of which every living being is compounded" (II.17). True, there are several places in the *Meditations* where Aurelius gravitates away from this more Epicurean view of death and toward the more classically Stoic vision of one soul, but he inevitably comes back to dissolution. Still, whether the soul dissolves or joins one soul, the upshot is the same: the devouring of identity and the loss of selfhood. Duty apart from a loving, active God who made us in his own image and gave us each a calling (*vocation* in Latin) so that we might become more—not less—ourselves ever risks becoming a dry, passionless affair that saps our humanity rather than transfiguring it into something finer.

> At the heart of Stoicism and Hinduism lies the central
> tenet of duty-dharma; the initiate must detach
> himself from personal desire and resign himself to his
> assigned post.

Detachment, Resignation, and Acceptance

And that takes us to that aspect of Stoicism and the *Meditations* that is at once the most glorious and the most sad. When the modern man on the streets hears the word *Stoic*, his first thought is likely to be of a person who does not complain, who keeps a stiff upper lip no matter what the situation. Though a simplification of the philosophy of Stoicism, this gut reaction to the word is quite accurate and reveals that which is most praiseworthy in the disciple of Stoicism.

How can one not respect someone who lives by a code such as this:

Suppose any man shall despise me. Let him look to that himself. But I will look to this, that I be not discovered doing or saying anything deserving of contempt. Shall any man hate me? Let him look to it. But I will be mild and benevolent towards every man, and ready to show even him his mistake, not reproachfully, nor yet as making a display of my endurance, but nobly and honestly...For the interior parts ought to be such, and a man ought to be seen by the gods neither dissatisfied with anything nor complaining. For what evil is it to thee, if thou art now doing what is agreeable to thy own nature, and art satisfied with that which at this moment is suitable to the nature of the universe, since thou art a human being placed at thy post in order that what is for the common advantage may be done in some way? (XI.13).

This very high calling comes remarkably close to Paul's admonition that we not be overcome by evil but that we overcome evil with good (Romans 12:21). It reveals a man at peace with himself, his world, his fellow man, and his calling.

As I read this noble passage from the *Meditations*, I am reminded of the best aspects of what at first might seem a very different worldview that is as prevalent in the East as Stoicism is in the West: Buddhism. Indeed, I do not think it a stretch to say that Buddhism is in great part an Eastern version of Stoicism, even as Stoicism is in great part a Western version of Buddhism. In both worldviews—which are properly categorized as philosophies rather than religions—the would-be initiate is called to detach himself from the world not so that he might attain salvation and heaven, but so that he might free himself from the madness of passion and desire and rise above both pleasure and pain. In a fickle world, only the pure pursuit of philosophy, whether Stoic or Buddhist, can bring that sought-after stability and equanimity, that undisturbed peace of mind and tranquility that the Hellenistic Greeks referred to as *ataraxia*.

Although in chapter 8 I presented the West as being more deistic, focusing on God's transcendence, and the East as more pantheistic, focusing on God's immanence, both Stoicism and Buddhism lead in the end to a vision that is radically monistic. As the disciple resigns and removes himself more and more, distinctions begin to collapse between God and nature, God and man, soul and body, the individual (Atman) and the world (Brahman). All becomes one.

In chapter 8 of *Orthodoxy*, Chesterton makes a powerful distinction between Buddhism and Christianity that I would argue applies equally well to Stoicism and Christianity:

> By insisting specially on the immanence of God, we get introspection, self-isolation, quietism, social indifference—Tibet. By insisting specially on the transcendence of God we get wonder, curiosity, moral and political adventure, righteous indignation—Christendom. Insisting that God is inside man, man is always inside himself. By insisting that God transcends man, man has transcended himself.

As always, Chesterton is right, but his last statement could use a mild tweak. Both the Christian and the Stoic-Buddhist transcends himself; however, whereas the latter loses himself in that transcendence, the former becomes more fully and eternally himself.

I have the utmost respect for Marcus Aurelius, and in some ways, I try to model myself after him. But there is a deep sadness that falls on me when I read his *Meditations*. It is the same sadness I feel when I visit the first circle of Dante's *Inferno* (Canto IV), where dwell the virtuous pagans, many of them philosophers of a Stoic or Epicurean bent. Though none of the souls in this first circle suffer active punishment, they utterly lack hope. In fact, when Dante first arrives, he does not hear the sounds of weeping and wailing, "but sounds of sighing…a grief breathed out of untormented sadness, / the passive state of those who dwelled apart" (lines 26, 28-29).

For Aurelius and his fellow Stoics, there can be no final hope, no redemption of the body or of the world. That is why detachment, resignation, and acceptance—rather than faith, hope, and love—are the three central virtues of Stoicism. Joy, true joy, must ever elude the one who is afraid to engage life fully, who protects himself from its passions and its risks, who seeks ultimately his own annihilation.

But what of duty and fame and one's legacy to the next generation? Alas, I fear that Aurelius's Stoicism, though it made him noble and even praiseworthy, made him too removed. Whereas all emperors since Nerva had adopted a handpicked successor, thus ensuring that Rome would have the best possible ruler, Aurelius allowed his mad and brutal son Commodus to succeed him. Though it pains me to say it, Rome's one true philosopher-king was succeeded by a son who began its slow decline and fall.

Postscript

If the names Marcus Aurelius and Commodus sound familiar to you, it may be because you saw Ridley Scott's excellent epic film *Gladiator* (2000), in which Aurelius is played brilliantly by Richard Harris and his evil son by a creepy Joaquin Phoenix. But *Gladiator* marks the second time that Aurelius was brought in all his majesty to the big screen. Though few critics mentioned it, *Gladiator* is in part an unofficial remake of an older film directed by Anthony Mann: *The Fall of the Roman Empire* (1964).

In that grand old film, Aurelius is played even more brilliantly by one of the greatest actors of all time: Alec Guinness. The mad and bad Commodus is played by a young Christopher Plummer (just one year before he appeared in *The Sound of Music*). In addition to mounting a grand opening scene in which Aurelius addresses his multinational army on his one-world vision for an eternal *pax romana*, the film invites us to eavesdrop as the sick and weary emperor meditates in his chambers on his mortality.

The screenwriters of this memorable and highly literate scene (Ben Barzman, Basilio Franchina, and Philip Yordan) lift much of the dialogue directly out of the *Meditations*. But they end the scene by giving Aurelius some lines that do not appear in the *Meditations*, lines that suggest, perhaps, that the estimable Stoic yet yearned for the fuller revelation of that Christianity that he sadly persecuted rather than embraced:

> Forgive me, Boatman [Charon, who ferried the dead across the river Acheron into the underworld]. I did not realize you were blind and deaf. Come for me when you will. My hand shall lead us. But I tell you this: There is a great truth we have not yet divined.

CONCLUSION:

What If It's True?

Most of this book has been written from the defensive point of view, a natural result of my goal of fielding and cross-examining the critiques raised against God and Christianity by 2,600 years of secular, deistic, and atheistic critics. Now, in this brief conclusion, I would like to ask you, the reader, to consider what it would mean if Christianity were true—if the Trinity, incarnation, atonement, and resurrection were not just dusty old doctrines but descriptions of reality. Here is what it might mean in terms of the ten chapters that make up this book:

1. Our universe did not simply come into being by accident, but was shaped and formed by the loving hands of a creator.

2. The order and beauty we see in the heavens is not random but purposeful. It sings of God's glory and serves the purposes of our tiny planet Earth.

3. Miracles *do* happen—not because God is a bad designer who has to constantly fix things, but because his love and bounty transcend the mechanical laws of nature.

4. There are truths that transcend what we can perceive with our senses. Revelation, intuition, imagination, and wonder are all windows on to a richer reality.

5. Real standards of goodness, truth, and beauty exist and can be striven for; we are not trapped in a relativistic world with no signposts.

6. Because justice is as much a quality of God as mercy, we can be assured that the mercy and justice that we yearn for will be realized in the end.

7. The pain and suffering that we experience in our lives has meaning and purpose, even if we cannot always discern that meaning or purpose.

8. God is almighty and all-knowing and is in control of history and our lives, but he is also as near to us as the ground we tread on or the light that illumines us.

9. Our lives have intrinsic value and worth, and the choices we make *do* matter. We are not adrift in an empty, uncaring world.

10. We can work and strive for goodness and perform our assigned duties without sacrificing our uniqueness, our hope, or our joy.

That is what a God-filled world and life look like. Yes, with it come accountability, obedience, gratitude, and worship, but if Christ really was who he claimed to be, if he really rose from the dead, then those things should come to us as naturally as breathing.

Annotated Bibliography

Chapter One

In this chapter, and in several others, I highlight the work of the Pre-Socratic philosophers, a group of Greek thinkers from around the Mediterranean world who flourished from 600 to 400 BC. The main figures in the group are Thales, Anaximander, Anaximenes, Xenophanes, Heraclitus, Parmenides, Zeno, Pythagoras, Empedocles, Anaxagoras, Leucippus, and Democritus. Although Pythagoras and Parmenides remained open to the supernatural and the metaphysical, the others held an essentially materialist view of the world.

No books or manuscripts by these thinkers have come down to us. Rather, as is the case with the poet Sappho, scholars have been able to piece together their work and thought by collecting fragmentary sayings and verses as they are quoted in the works of such extant writers as Plato, Aristotle, and Cicero. My preferred edition of these fragments is Philip Wheelwright's *The Presocratics* (Odyssey Press, 1966). I find it to be the most accessible for the lay reader with good, helpful introductions and commentaries.

For a more scholarly textbook edition that presents the fragments in both Greek and English, consult G.S. Kirk and J.E. Raven's *The Presocratic Philosophers: A Critical History with a Selection of Texts*, 2d ed. (Cambridge, 1984). Another reliable edition is John Manley Robinson's *An Introduction to Early Greek Philosophy* (Houghton Mifflin, 1972).

I should mention here that the German philosopher Martin Heidegger (1889–1976) was highly influenced by the Pre-Socratics and helped bring them back in vogue in the academy. For his views on the Pre-Socratics, see *Early Greek Thinking: The Dawn of Western Philosophy*, translated by David Farrell Krell and Frank A. Capuzzi (Harper & Row, 1985). For myself, I have been guided on the subject by the opening chapters of the following three books: Reginald E. Allen's *Greek Philosophy: Thales to Aristotle*, 3d ed. (Free Press, 1991); F.M. Cornford's *Before and After Socrates* (Cambridge, 1932); and Rex Warner's *The Greek Philosophers* (New American Library, 1958).

The works of Hesiod are available in Hesiod's *Theogeny and Works and Days*, with Theognis's *Elegies*, translated and introduced by Dorothea Wender (Penguin, 1986).

For an excellent edition of the writings of Epicurus prefaced by a lengthy introduction that includes a helpful survey of the theories of the Pre-Socratics, see Epicurus's *Letters, Principal Doctrines, and Vatican Sayings*, translated and introduced by Russel M. Geer (Library of Liberal Arts, 1964).

Many editions of Lucretius's epic poem *De Rerum Natura* (*On the Nature of Things*) are available, including ones from Penguin, Oxford, and the Loeb Library. My preferred copy, and the one I quote from in this book, is Frank O. Copley's translation of *The Nature of Things* (Norton, 1977). The passage I quote is taken from page 4 (Book I, lines 146-148), though it appears three more times on pages 30, 59, and 147.

The iconoclastic literary theorist Stephen Greenblatt presents Lucretius and his Epicurean ideals in a very positive light as energizing the Renaissance in his *The Swerve: How the World Became Modern* (Norton, 2012). His enthusiasm for Lucretius as a founding father of the modern world segues nicely with the thesis of my chapter (and book), though, as a secular humanist, he thinks the legacy a good and positive one! Another book that traces the influence of Lucretius on modernity in a very positive way is Catherine Wilson's *Epicureanism at the Origins of Modernity* (Oxford, 2008).

For Aristotle's cosmological arguments see *Physics* VIII and *Metaphysics* XII; for Aquinas's, see *Summa Theologica* I.2. More generally, consult William Lane Craig's *The Cosmological Argument from Plato to Leibniz* (Wipf & Stock, 2001).

Other books I highlight in this chapter are Stephen Hawking and Leonard Mlodinow's *The Grand Design* (Bantam, 2010) and John Lennox's *God and Stephen Hawking: Whose Design Is It Anyway?* (UK: Lion, 2011). Also see the book that made Hawking famous, *A Brief History of Time: From the Big Bang to Black Holes* (available in numerous editions), and the successful, fictionalized-but-faithful film about his life, *The Theory of Everything* (2014; directed by James Marsh and starring Eddie Redmayne). Finally, you might rent Carl Sagan's secular-humanist 13-part documentary, *Cosmos* (1980), or its equally secular-humanist rebooting, *Cosmos: A Spacetime Odyssey* (2014), hosted by Neil deGrasse Tyson.

Though the author is quirky, to say the least, Fred Heeren's *Show Me God: What the Message from Space Is Telling Us About God* (Searchlight Publications, 1995) offers a well-researched, accessible, and entertaining overview of the scientific discoveries that led up to the almost universally accepted theory of the Big Bang. Two other excellent books that helped me prepare this chapter and the two that follow are Hugh Ross's *The Creator and the Cosmos: How the Latest Scientific Discoveries of the Century Reveal God* (NavPress, 1993) and Lee Strobel's *The Case for a Creator* (Zondervan, 2004). The latter book surveys the main arguments for the existence of an eternal, personal Creator that have come out of physics, cosmology, and astronomy, not to mention biology, biochemistry, and other sciences.

Chapter Two

I start this chapter by referring to C.S. Lewis's seminal academic work *The Discarded Image: An Introduction to Medieval and Renaissance Literature* (Cambridge, 1964). Those interested in the point of view expressed in the first two paragraphs of the chapter should read carefully the epilogue to Lewis's book.

The quote from Lucretius can be found on page 36 of the Copley translation (Book II, lines 302-306). The quote from Epicurus can be found on page 10 of Geer's translation of "The Letter to Herodotus" (39a) in *Letters, Principal Doctrines, and Vatican Sayings*.

My text for Spinoza is Baruch Spinoza's *The Ethics and Selected Letters*, translated by Samuel Shirley and edited with an introduction by Seymour Feldman (Hackett, 1982). Feldman's lengthy introduction sets Spinoza in his historical and religious milieu and helps unpack some of the difficult terminology. My quotes from Spinoza's *Ethics* can be found, respectively, on pages 31, 34, 45, 46, 54, and 54. Hackett has also published *The Essential Spinoza* (2006) for those wanting to sample more of Spinoza's writing.

Those who would like fuller background on Spinoza as a man and as a profound influence on later thought should consult Antonio Damasio's *Looking for Spinoza: Joy, Sorrow, and the Feeling Brain* (Harvest, 2003). Though Damasio's focus is neuroscience and cognition, he offers a rounded view of Spinoza's influence. As with Greenblatt's assessment of Lucretius (see above), Damasio regards that influence as strongly positive. If you would like the rare opportunity to get into the mind and soul of Spinoza, then I would encourage you to read Irving D. Yalom's haunting novel *The Spinoza Problem* (Basic Books, 2012). Though fictionalized, it helps modern readers to get to the core of Spinoza as a thinker who broke from both Jewish and Christian thought and belief.

For a positive assessment of Spinoza's legacy, see Steven Nadler's *A Book Forged in Hell: Spinoza's Scandalous Treatise and the Birth of the Secular Age* (Princeton, 2013); for a more critical assessment, see Roger Scruton's *Spinoza: A Very Short Introduction* (Oxford, 2002).

To read some of the sermons and other writings of Meister Eckhart, see *Selected Writings*, translated by Oliver Davies (Penguin, 1995). Chapter 8 of Umberto Eco's brief but illuminating *Art and Beauty in the Middle Ages* (Yale, 1996) explains well the dangers of radical mysticism.

My edition for Cicero's *The Nature of the Gods* is the Penguin edition (1972), translated by Horace C.P. McGregor and prefaced by a very thorough introduction by J.M. Ross. The passages I quote from Book II can be found on pages 163 and 161-162.

For Anaxagoras, see the section on him in Philip Wheelwright's *The Presocratics* (Odyssey Press, 1966). For Aristotle's four causes, see *Physics* II and *Metaphysics* V. William Paley's design arguments can be found in his *Natural Theology* (Oxford, 2008).

For William Dembski's concept of specified complexity, see *The Design Inference: Eliminating Chance through Small Probabilities* (Cambridge, 1998). For Michael Behe's concept of irreducible complexity, see *Darwin's Black Box: The Biochemical Challenge to Evolution* (The Free Press, 1996). For Stephen C. Meyer's research on the complexity of DNA, see *The Signature in the Cell: DNA and the Evidence for Intelligent Design* (HarperCollins, 2010). Also see Guillermo Gonzalez and Jay Richards's *The Privileged Planet: How Our Place in the Cosmos Is Designed for Discovery* (Regnery, 2004). This fascinating book not only shows that our earth is fine-tuned for life, but argues that we were placed in just the right part of the cosmos to allow us to study the universe and thus determine its laws. I discuss the bearing of modern scientific discoveries on Christian apologetics at greater length in chapters 14 and 22 of my *Apologetics for the 21st Century* (Crossway, 2010).

For Einstein's personal philosophy, see his *The World as I See It* (Citadel, 2006) and *Ideas and Opinions* (Broadway Books, 1995). The two passages from Einstein that I quote can be found on Stephen Jay Gould's secular humanist website, *Critical Thought and Religious Liberty* (CTRL), under the subheading, "Albert Einstein: Thoughts of a Freethinker" at http://www.stephenjaygould.org/ctrl/quotes_einstein.html.

Fred Heeren's *Show Me God* (Searchlight Publications, 1995) carefully traces Einstein's attempts to evade the mounting evidence for the Big Bang. See also Donald Goldsmith's *Einstein's Greatest Blunder?: The Cosmological Constant and Other Fudge Factors in the Physics of the Universe* (Harvard, 1995).

Chapter Three

The passage I quote from *The New Oxford Annotated Bible with the Apocrypha*, exp. ed. (Oxford, 1977) is taken from a note to Exodus 16:14 and refers to the manna that God sent to sustain the Israelites in the wilderness; it appears on page 88.

Penguin offers both a prose and verse translation of Ovid's *Metamorphoses*. I prefer reading the prose one (translated by Mary Innes, 1955) to the verse one (translated by David Raeburn, 2004). Read Book I for Ovid's retelling of the myth of the Four Ages of Man (gold, silver, bronze, and iron); this myth is also told in the opening section of Hesiod's *Works and Days*.

My three quotes from Epicurus can be found on pages 41-42 of Geer's translation of "Letter to Pythocles" (97), page 61 of "Principal Doctrines" (XII.143), and page 54 of "Letter to Menoeceus" (12a) in *Letters, Principal Doctrines, and Vatican Sayings*.

My quotes from Samuel Shirley's translation of Spinoza's *Ethics* can be found on pages 154 and 103.

My quote from Huxley is taken from page 281 of his 1868 lecture "On the Physical Basis of Life" as it appears in *Victorian Poetry and Prose*, edited by Lionel Trilling and Harold Bloom (Oxford, 1973).

To read Thomas Jefferson's miracle-free version of the Gospels, see *The Jefferson Bible: The Life and Morals of Jesus of Nazareth* (Wilder Publications, 2007).

My text for Hume's *Enquiry* is taken from David Hume's *An Enquiry Concerning Human Understanding with a Letter from a Gentleman to His Friend in Edinburgh and Hume's Abstract of a Treatise of Human Nature*, 2d ed., edited, with an introduction, by Eric Steinburg (Hackett, 1993). My quotes, all taken from Section X ("Of Miracles") of the *Enquiry*, can be found, respectively, on pages 73, 77, 78, and 90.

Parts of my argument rely heavily on C.S. Lewis's *Miracles: A Preliminary Study* (HarperCollins, 2001). See in particular chapter 8 and chapters 12-16.

Craig Keener's ambitious, exhaustively researched two-volume *Miracles: The Credibility of the New Testament Accounts* (Baker, 2011) is a must-read for anyone seeking rational arguments for the existence of miracles. Keener not only directly addresses each and every one of Hume's arguments against miracles; he boldly exposes the ethnocentrism of Humeans who think we can dismiss miracles because so many of them take place in "backward" countries.

My overview of the resurrection, particularly my list of possible but untenable natural explanations for the empty tomb, is adapted from chapter 18 of my *Apologetics for the 21st Century* (Crossway, 2010). In chapter 5 of that book, I offer a much fuller overview and assessment of the main arguments of Lewis's *Miracles*; in chapters 16-17, I argue for the authority and reliability of Scripture in general and the Gospels in particular.

For a thorough, carefully argued, rhetorically effective defense of the resurrection, see Gary Habermas and Michael Licona's *The Case for the Resurrection of Jesus* (Kregel, 2004). For an older, classic defense of the resurrection, first published in 1930 by a skeptic who set out, Hume style, to disprove it, see Frank Morrison's *Who Moved the Stone?* (Zondervan, 1958). For one of the most original and thoughtful academic defenses of Easter, see N.T. Wright's *The Resurrection of the Son of God* (Augsburg, 2003). Lee Strobel's *The Case for Christ* (Zondervan, 1998) includes a fine section on the resurrection. W. Mark Lanier's *Christianity on Trial: A Lawyer Examines the Christian Faith* (InterVarsity, 2014) concludes with a knockout chapter on the resurrection, specifically showing how an impartial judge would rule in favor of its authenticity.

Finally, for two scholarly but accessible studies of the reliability of the eyewitness testimony on which the four Gospels are based, see Richard Bauckham's *Jesus and the Eyewitnesses: The Gospels as Eyewitness Testimony* (Eerdmans, 2008) and Craig Bloomberg's *The Historical Reliability of the Gospels* (InterVarsity, 1987).

Chapter Four

I begin the chapter with three quotes from pages 89, 89, and 90 of Section X ("Of Miracles") of Eric Steinburg's edition of Hume's *Enquiry*. I then move on to David Hume's *Dialogues Concerning Natural Religion*, edited and with a very helpful introduction by Martin Bell (Penguin, 1990). My quote from this book is taken from pages 138-139. I then return to quote the final page of Hume's *Enquiry* (page 114) and reference William James's *The Varieties of Religious Experience* (CreateSpace, 2013).

For Stephen Jay Gould's concept of "non-overlapping magisteria" (NOMA) see his book *Rocks of Ages: Science and Religion in the Fullness of Life* (Ballantine, 2002).

Much has been written, and continues to be written, on the faith/values split that came out of the Enlightenment. The books that have most influenced me in this area, and that first helped me to see the split and its consequences, are Alisdair MacIntyre's *After Virtue*, 2d ed. (Notre Dame, 1984), Mark Noll's *The Scandal of the Evangelical Mind* (Eerdmans, 1994), Lesslie Newbigin's *Foolishness to the Greeks: The Gospel and Western Culture* (Eerdmans, 1986), and the apologetics trilogy of Francis Schaeffer: *The God Who Is There* (InterVarsity, 1968), *Escape from Reason* (InterVarsity, 1968), and *He Is There and He Is Not Silent* (Tyndale, 1985).

For Parmenides, see the section on him in Philip Wheelwright's *The Presocratics* (Odyssey Press, 1966). Plato most clearly distinguishes between the World of Being and the World of Becoming in the Divided Line and Allegory of the Cave sections (Book VII) of *The Republic*, translated by Richard W. Sterling and William C. Scott (Norton, 1996). For Francis Bacon's ant-spider-bee metaphor, see aphorism XCV in the first book of aphorisms of his *The New Organon*, edited by Lisa Jardine and Michael Silverthorne (Cambridge, 2000), page 79. My quote from Hobbes is taken from *Leviathan*, edited by Edwin Curley (Hackett, 1994), page 6 (Part I, Chapter 1). On Hobbes's attempt to purge and purify language, see especially Part I, Chapter 5, pages 22-27.

My text for John Locke's *An Essay Concerning Human Understanding* is the Penguin Classics edition (2004), edited with a helpful introduction by Roger Woolhouse. My quotes can be found, respectively, on pages 109 and 202. My two quotes from Descartes can both be found on page 31 of Descartes's *Meditations on First Philosophy, with Selections from the Objections and Replies*, rev. ed., translated and edited by John Cottingham (Cambridge, 1996).

For an excellent edition of Wordsworth's *Prelude* that presents the poem in its three stages of composition along with much helpful history and criticism, see *The Prelude: 1799, 1805, 1850*, edited by Jonathan Wordsworth, M.H. Abrams, and Stephen Gill (Norton, 1979). My text for "Ode: Intimations of Immortality from Recollections of Early Childhood" is taken from *English Romantic Poetry and Prose*, edited by Russell Noyes (Oxford, 1956), pages 327-329. I offer a full analysis of this poem in chapter 9 of my *The Eye of the Beholder: How to See the World like a Romantic Poet* (Winged Lion Press, 2011).

The quotes from G.K. Chesterton are taken from his *The Everlasting Man* (Image Books, 1955), pages 44 and 47-48. C.S. Lewis's *Mere Christianity* (HarperCollins, 2001) argument that we all possess an inbuilt sense of morality can be found in book 1 of *Mere Christianity* (HarperCollins, 2001). My quote from Lewis's *The Problem of Pain* (HarperCollins, 2001) can be found on pages 5-6. For Lewis's argument by joy/desire, see chapter 1 of his spiritual autobiography, *Surprised by Joy* (HBJ, 1966), the "Afterword to the Third Edition" of his allegorical autobiography, *The Pilgrim's Regress* (Eerdmans, 1992), book 3, chapter 10 of *Mere Christianity*, chapter 10 of *The Problem of Pain*, and his sermon, "The Weight of Glory," in *The Weight of Glory and Other Addresses* (Collier, 1980). For his discussion of fish and the wetness of water, see chapter 12 of *Reflections on the Psalms* (Harvest, 1964).

In chapter 2 of my *Apologetics for the 21st Century* (Crossway, 2010) I deal at greater length with Lewis's argument by joy; in chapter 9, I offer a full overview of Chesterton's *The Everlasting Man*. In chapter 2 of my *Lewis Agonistes: How C.S. Lewis Can Train Us to Wrestle with the*

Modern and Postmodern World (Broadman & Holman, 2003), I trace in detail the many things that Lewis believed could not have evolved.

The quote from Augustine appears on page 3 of the *Confessions*, translated by Henry Chadwick (Oxford, 2009). The quote from Pascal appears on page 45 of *Pensées*, translated by A.J. Krailsheimer (Penguin, 1995).

Chapter Five

For an excellent edition of Fyodor Dostoevsky's *The Brothers Karamazov*, see the translation by Richard Pevear and Larissa Volokhonsky (Farrar, Straus and Giroux, 2002). For a quick overview of the sophists that includes the mottos of Protagoras and Gorgias, see *Greek Philosophy: Thales to Aristotle*, edited with a good introduction by Reginald E. Allen (Free Press, 1966), pages 17-19. For a handy collection of all of Gorgias's extant writing, see *Language Is a Mighty Lord: A Gorgias Reader*, edited by Andrew J. Patrick (Riposte, 2012). For more on the sophists and their links to the Pre-Socratics, see Robin Waterfield's *The First Philosophers: The Presocratics and Sophists* (Oxford, 2009). See also the opening chapters of F.M. Cornford's *Before and After Socrates* (Cambridge, 1932) and Rex Warner's *The Greek Philosophers* (New American Library, 1958).

For Francis Bacon's discussion of the idols of the marketplace (as well as of the tribe, the cave, and the theater), see aphorisms XXXIX-XLIV in the first book of aphorisms of his *The New Organon*, edited by Lisa Jardine and Michael Silverthorne (Cambridge, 2000), pages 40-42.

My quotes from Plato's *Republic*, translated by Richard W. Sterling and William C. Scott (Norton, 1996) can be found, respectively, on pages 57, 280, 281, 212, 215, and 214. To study the early dialogues of Plato, those which seem most true to the historical Socrates and thus end with an impasse rather than a clear definition, see *Early Socratic Dialogues*, edited with a general introduction by Trevor J. Saunders (Penguin, 1987). This excellent, heavily annotated edition includes

Ion, Laches, Lysis, Charmides, Hippias Major, Hippias Minor, and *Euthydemus.*

My quote on nominalism is taken from chapter 8 of Umberto Eco's *Art and Beauty in the Middle Ages* (Yale, 1996), pages 88-89. Lewis's discussion of the Tao can be found in book 1 of *Mere Christianity* (HarperCollins, 2001) and in *The Abolition of Man* (Macmillan, 1947). For a recent apologetics book that reveals how atheists are forced to borrow their morality from Christianity, see Nancy Pearcey's *Finding Truth: 5 Principles for Unmasking Atheism, Secularism, and Other God Substitutes* (David C. Cook, 2015). For Margaret Mead's long-since discredited study of cultural relativism, see her *Coming of Age in Samoa* (Perennial Classics, 2001).

For Alvin Plantinga's discussion of our *sensus divinitatis,* see his *Knowledge and Christian Belief* (Eerdmans, 2015). This difficult but accessible book offers a condensed and simplified version of his earlier magnum opus, *Warranted Christian Belief* (2000). Plantinga's philosophical insight and clarity have gained him the respect of most of his secular colleagues and helped raise the reputation of theism in general and Christianity in particular in the academy.

For Lewis's reworking of Plato's Allegory of the Cave, see chapter 12 of *The Silver Chair* (Collier, 1970). I discuss this scene further in chapter 2 of my *Lewis Agonistes* (B&H, 2003), and chapter 7 of my *Apologetics for the 21st Century* (Crossway, 2010). For Freud's argument that divine fatherhood is a projection of earthly fatherhood, see *Totem and Taboo* (Freud Press, 2013) and *Moses and Monotheism* (Vintage, 1955).

Chapter Six

Dan Brown's bestselling *The Da Vinci Code* (Doubleday, 2003) helped popularize the false belief that Nicene orthodoxy was an invention of Constantine and his crony bishops. Refutations of Brown's book include Darrell Bock's *Breaking the Da Vinci Code* (Thomas Nelson, 2004), Josh McDowell's *The Da Vinci Code: A Quest for Answers* (Green Key Books, 2006), and Lee Strobel and Garry Poole's *Exploring the Da Vinci Code* (Zondervan, 2006). I devote chapter 20 of my *Apologetics for the 21st Century* to a discussion of *The Da Vinci Code*.

To find out what the early Christians really believed, please read carefully through *Early Christian Writings: The Apostolic Fathers*, translated by Maxwell Staniforth and revised by Andrew Louth (Penguin, 1987). Also see Eusebius's *The Church History*, translated by Paul Maier (Kregel Academic, 2007). For an accessible overview of the authority of the Scriptures, see F.F. Bruce's *The New Testament Documents: Are They Reliable?* (InterVarsity, 1973) and *The Defense of the Gospel in the New Testament* (Eerdmans, 1977). Philip Schaff's classic *The Creeds of Christendom: Volume 1* (Baker, 1998) gives background to the formation of the early creeds. Dorothy Sayers's "Creed or Chaos?" in *The Whimsical Christian* (Macmillan, 1978) offers a breezy but solid defense of the creeds of the church.

My text for *Against Marcion* is taken from volume 3 of *Ante-Nicene Fathers*, translated by Peter Holmes and edited by Roberts, Donaldson, and Coxe (Christian Literature Publishing, 1885), as it appears online at newadvent.org. My quotes are referenced in the text by book and chapter number. For an inexpensive edition, see Tertullian's *Against Marcion* (Beloved Publishing, 2014).

The infamous quote from Richard Dawkins can be found on page 51 of *The God Delusion* (Houghton Mifflin, 2008). C.S. Lewis's quote on our desire for a grandfather in heaven can be found on page 31 of *The Problem of Pain* (HarperCollins, 2001). For Moralistic Therapeutic Deism, see Christian Smith and Melinda Lundquist Denton's *Soul Searching: The Religious and Spiritual Lives of American Teenagers* (Oxford, 2005).

My quotes from John Milton are taken from *Paradise Lost*, 2d ed., edited by Scott Elledge (Norton, 1993), pages 65-66, and "Areopagitica," in *Seventeenth-Century Prose and Poetry*, 2d ed., edited by Alexander M. Witherspoon and Frank J. Warnke (HBJ, 1982), page 402.

Chapter Seven

Aquinas's *Summa* is available in various editions. For the reader new to Aquinas, or even for one who has read some of his work, I would highly recommend Peter Kreeft's skillfully edited, heavily annotated, compulsively readable *A Summa of the Summa: The Essential Philosophical Passages of St. Thomas Aquinas' Summa Theologica* (Ignatius, 1990). My quote from Hume can be found on pages 108-109 of his *Dialogues Concerning Natural Religion* (Penguin, 1990).

Voltaire's *Candide: or, Optimism* is available in many editions; however, the Penguin Classics Deluxe Edition (2005), translated by Theo Cuffe, is best, for it includes the 180-line poem that Voltaire wrote shortly after the Lisbon earthquake and in which he savagely attacks Leibniz's optimism, thus laying the groundwork for the somewhat less savage *Candide* to follow. For those interested in reading some Leibniz, a good place to start is G.W. Leibniz's *Philosophical Essays*, edited and translated by Roger Ariew and Daniel Garber (Hackett, 1989). For Leibniz's central work on the origin of evil and the problem of pain see his *Theodicy* (CreateSpace, 2014); Leibniz, in fact, coined the word *theodicy* to mean a meditation on God's justice.

My quotes from Lewis are taken from *The Problem of Pain* (Harper-Collins, 2001), pages 26, 32-33, 76, and 79. Readers interested in Lewis's fuller thoughts on the problem of pain should also read his *A Grief Observed* (Bantam, 1976), a more personal, anecdotal book that documents the grieving process Lewis went through after the death of his wife Joy in 1960. The quote from Augustine is from page 254 of the *Confessions*, translated by Henry Chadwick (Oxford, 2009).

Although I don't mention it in the text, my thoughts on the way that pain protects us comes in part from the work of the great missionary doctor Paul Brand, who discovered that leprosy (or at least certain forms of it) causes people to "fall apart" because it attacks the central nervous system and thus deadens their pain sensors. Brand discusses the deeper spiritual dimensions of his discovery and how pain is in many ways a blessing in two books he cowrote with Philip Yancey,

Fearfully & Wonderfully Made (Zondervan, 1980) and *In His Image* (Zondervan, 1984).

Yancey later wrote his own book on pain that has influenced me: *Where Is God When It Hurts?* (Zondervan, 1990). In it, he takes a more pastoral approach, introducing us to real Christians who have suffered greatly and discussing how they have wrestled with God through their pain. Midway between Yancey's pastoral approach and Lewis's more philosophical approach comes another book that has guided my thoughts on these matters: Peter Kreeft's *Making Sense Out of Suffering* (Servant, 1986).

Lee Strobel also devotes several incisive chapters of *The Case for Faith* (Zondervan, 2000) to the problem of pain that I have found helpful. Joni Eareckson Tada, who was paralyzed from the neck down at an early age, offers a very personal look at pain in *When God Weeps*, cowritten with Steven Estes (Zondervan, 2000). Finally, deep insight is to be found in Randy Alcorn's *If God Is Good: Faith in the Midst of Suffering and Evil* (Multnomah, 2014). I discuss the problem of pain in detail and from numerous angles in chapters 4 and 15 of my *Apologetics for the 21st Century* (Crossway, 2010). I also devote chapter 4 of my *Lewis Agonistes* (B&H, 2003) to this topic.

For Alvin Plantinga's philosophical refutation of the problem of pain, see *God, Freedom, and Evil* (Harper & Row, 1974).

Chapter Eight

My quote from the Pope is taken from His Holiness John Paul II's *Crossing the Threshold of Hope*, edited by Vittorio Messori and translated by Jenny McPhee and Martha McPhee (Knopf, 1994), pages 40-41 (the ellipsis and italics are in the original).

If you would like to dive into the Arian controversy and the Council of Nicea, there are two books by J. Stevenson and W.H.C. Frend that offer up both primary texts and analysis: *A New Eusebius: Documents Illustrating the History of the Church to AD 337* (Baker, 2013) and *Creeds, Councils, and Controversies: Documents Illustrating the History of the Church, AD 337–461* (Baker, 2012). To read the collected writings of the various Gnostic sects, see *The Nag Hammadi Library*, edited by James M. Robinson (HarperCollins, 1990). This volume includes the Gospel of Thomas, which ends with those two infamous sentences in which Jesus makes the following promise to Mary Magdalene: "I myself shall lead her in order to make her male, so that she too may become a living spirit resembling you males. For every woman who will make herself male will enter the kingdom of heaven" (page 138). For an excellent overview of the early church and its struggle to preserve orthodoxy against heresy, see J.N.D. Kelly's *Early Christian Creeds*, rev. ed. (HarperCollins, 1978).

For a quick but incisive overview of the Orthodox theology of icons and the iconoclastic controversy, see pages 38-43 of Timothy Ware's *The Orthodox Church* (Penguin, 1984). To read the writings of the greatest defender of icons, see John of Damascus's *Three Treatises on the Divine Images*, translated by Andrew Louth (St. Vladimir's Seminary Press, 2003). John's treatises were written from 726 to 743.

My quotes from Athanasius are taken from his *On the Incarnation of the Word*, translated by Archibald Robertson, in *Christology of the Late Fathers*, edited by Edward R. Hardy (Westminster John Knox Press, 1954), pages 107-108, 95-96, 97, 62, and 71. This same fine edition includes *The Theological Orations* and the "Letters on the Apollonarian Controversy" of Gregory of Nazianzus (both are translated by Charles Gordon Browne and James Edward Swallow). The passage I quote from the first letter can be found on page 216. The section I allude to from Augustine at the end of the chapter can be found on page 121 of his *Confessions* (Oxford, 2009).

My text for the *Gita*, one which captures nicely the poetry of the original, is *Bhagavad-Gita: The Song of God*, translated by Swami Prabhavananda and Christopher Isherwood (Marcel Rodd Co., 1944); it features a good introduction by Aldous Huxley, the author of *Brave New World*. For Parmenides and Heraclitus, see the sections on them in Philip Wheelwright's *The Presocratics* (Odyssey Press, 1966). My quotes from Spinoza are taken from his *The Ethics and Selected Letters*, translated by Samuel Shirley (Hackett, 1982) and can be found on pages 42 and 81.

For two excellent books that defend the clear biblical teaching of the resurrection of the body, see N T. Wright's *Surprised by Hope: Rethinking Heaven, the Resurrection, and the Mission of the Church* (HarperCollins, 2008) and Randy Alcorn's *Heaven* (Tyndale, 2004).

For books by the cognitive scientists I mention at the end of the chapter, see Antonio Damasio's *Looking for Spinoza: Joy, Sorrow, and the Feeling Brain* (Harvest, 2003), Oliver Sacks's *The Man Who Mistook His Wife for a Hat: And Other Clinical Tales* (Touchstone, 1998), and Steven Pinker's *How the Mind Works* (Norton, 2009). But there are many more books of this sort—some written by new atheist big shots Richard Dawkins and Daniel Dennett—that try to offer a Darwinian answer to the origin of consciousness. Interestingly, one brave atheist writer, Thomas Nagel, has had the courage to push back against those who think they can explain away consciousness on purely material grounds (as an epiphenomenon that just happens when the brain gets big enough): *Mind & Cosmos: Why the Materialist Neo-Darwinian Conception of Nature Is Almost Certainly False* (Oxford, 2012). Needless to say, he has taken a lot of flack!

Chapter Nine

My quote from Marx is taken from his *A Contribution to the Critique of Political Economy*, edited and translated by N.I. Stone (Charles H. Kerr & Company, 1904), pages 11-12. My quote from Epicurus can be found on page 58 of Epicurus's *Letters, Principal Doctrines, and Vatican Sayings*, translated and introduced by Russel M. Geer (Library of Liberal Arts, 1964). My quote from Lucretius can be found on pages 34-35 of Frank O. Copley's translation of *The Nature of Things* (Norton, 1977).

My quotes from Huxley are taken from pages 285, 286, 286, 287, 286-287, and 287 (note 34) of his "On the Physical Basis of Life," as it appears in *Victorian Poetry and Prose*, edited by Lionel Trilling and Harold Bloom (Oxford, 1973).

The passages I quote from Nancy Pearcey can be found on pages 149, 154, 158, and 162 of her *Finding Truth: 5 Principles for Unmasking Atheism, Secularism, and Other God Substitutes* (David C. Cook, 2015). In my quotes of Pearcey's quotes I have preserved her italics, ellipses, and bracketed insertions. Though a bit academic, J.P. Moreland's *Consciousness and the Existence of God: A Theistic Argument* (Routledge, 2008) and *The Soul: How We Know It's Real and Why It Matters* (Moody, 2014) argue that human consciousness (and, with it, free will) cannot arise apart from God. For a more accessible look at the way atheists lift ideas from Christianity, see Frank Turek's *Stealing from God: Why Atheists Need God to Make Their Case* (NavPress, 2015).

My quote from Timothy Keller can be found on page 164 of his *The Reason for God: Belief in an Age of Skepticism* (Dutton, 2008); Keller discusses the issue of slavery in chapter 4. This book, which carries on an irenic dialogue with the new atheists, is well worth reading in full.

Chapter Ten

For Walker Percy's comments on Stoicism, see his essay "Stoicism in the South," anthologized in *Signposts in a Strange Land*, edited by Patrick Samway (Picador, 2000). My quotes from G.K. Chesterton are taken from *Orthodoxy: The Romance of Faith* (Image Books, 1990), pages 15, 76, and 134. The quote from Aleksandr Solzhenitsyn appears on page 312 of *The Gulag Archipelago: 1918–1956* (Harper, 2002).

My two quotes from John Stuart Mill can be found on pages 27 and 26-27 of *On Liberty*, edited by David Spitz (Norton, 1975). My two quotes from Rousseau can both be found on page 20 of *The Social Contract*, in *The Essential Rousseau*, translated by Lowell Bair (New American Library, 1974).

My text for Marcus Aurelius's *Meditations* appears in *Marcus Aurelius and His Times* (Walter J. Black, 1945); the translation is by George Long. My quotes appear on pages 115, 116, 85, 53, 28-29, 25, and 118.

For Socrates's daemon, see pages 64 (31d) and 74 (40a-c) of Plato's *Apology*, in *The Last Days of Socrates*, translated by Hugh Tredennick (Penguin, 1969); in that same work, on page 60 (28d-e), Socrates compares himself and his duty to that of a soldier who must remain at his post. Cicero uses this metaphor to explain why suicide is wrong on page 299 of "The Dream of Scipio" (Book VI, Chapter 15 of *On the Republic*), in *Nine Orations and The Dream of Scipio*, translated by Palmer Bovie (Mentor, 1967). My quote from the *Gita* can be found on pages 55-58 of *Bhagavad-Gita: The Song of God* (Marcel Rodd Co., 1944). My quote from Dante appears on page 27 of his *Inferno*, translated by John Ciardi (Signet, 2009).

If you enjoy the *Meditations*, I would highly encourage you to read two other accessible works by Stoic writers: *Epictetus: The Handbook (the Encheiridion)*, translated by Nicholas White (Hackett, 1983) and Seneca's *Letters from a Stoic (Epistulae Morales ad Lucilium)*, translated by Robin Campbell (Penguin, 1969). Epictetus (AD 50–130) spent at least part of his life as a slave; Seneca (c. AD 4–65) was an advisor to Nero who courageously (but fatally) participated in a failed plot to end the tyrant's life. To read them alongside Marcus Aurelius is to grasp how the teachings of Stoicism could appeal to, and be practiced by, people of all classes and positions. For Spinoza's Stoic-like musings on how to find happiness and equanimity in life—in a nutshell, we gain control over negative emotions by tracing and understanding their true causes (sometimes a traumatic experience) and associations and then retraining the mind—see *Ethics*, Part V.

Name Index